1-23-90

JACK FLYNN, INST.
R-104
OFFICE
(818) 287-9894

Real Estate Investment

FOURTH EDITION

John P. Wiedemer

University of Houston

PRENTICE HALL
Englewood Cliffs, New Jersey 07632

Library of Congress Cataloging-in-Publication Data

Wiedemer, John P.
    Real estate investment / John P. Wiedemer. —4th ed.
    p. cm.
    Bibliography: p.
    Includes index.
    ISBN 0-13-763236-3
    1. Real estate investment. I. Title.
HD1382.5.W53 1988   88-28853
332.63′24—dc19   CIP

Editorial/production supervision and
   interior design: Laura L. Cleveland
Cover design: Baldino Design
Manufacturing buyer: Margaret Rizzi

 © 1989, 1985, 1982, 1979 by Prentice-Hall, Inc.
A Division of Simon & Schuster
Englewood Cliffs, New Jersey 07632

Printed in the United States of America

10 9 8 7 6 5 4 3 2 1

ISBN 0-13-763236-3

Prentice-Hall International (UK) Limited, *London*
Prentice-Hall of Australia Pty. Limited, *Sydney*
Prentice-Hall Canada Inc., *Toronto*
Prentice-Hall Hispanoamericana, S.A., *Mexico*
Prentice-Hall of India Private Limited, *New Delhi*
Prentice-Hall of Japan, Inc., *Tokyo*
Simon & Schuster Asia Pte. Ltd., *Singapore*
Editora Prentice-Hall do Brasil, Ltda., *Rio de Janeiro*

Contents

4   *Financing Real Estate*   42

5   *Property Taxes and Income Taxes*   67

6 Depreciation Deductions 86

7 Special Income Tax Rules 103

8 Single Family Dwellings and Condominiums 121

9 Business Organizations 145

10   *Forms of Ownership*   165

11   *Tools of Analysis*   181

12   *Comparison Screening*   198

13 *Discount Analysis*   **214**

14 *Cash Flow Projections*   **232**

15 *Examining Real Property Risk*   **247**

16 *Marketing Investment Property*   **269**

Preface

Investment is defined in the dictionary as "the act of investing capital productively." The purpose of this book is to examine and explain real estate investment in a concise and practical way, to make the information truly productive for the reader.

Investing wisely, of course, requires knowledge. For many kinds of business investments, the knowledge required may be rather narrow, limited by the nature of the asset and its market. The knowledge requirement for real estate, however, is very broad as there are many factors that can help create a safe and productive investment. Not all of them are apparent in an examination of the property itself. For example, land ownership is governed by state laws that differ from one state to another. Also, real property is one of the few investments whose value can be substantially changed by land use and environmental control laws. Further, sound investment in real property involves a practical knowledge of the specialized field of real estate law in order to understand and act upon the advice of a qualified attorney. Often, a real estate investment involves setting up a business organization which requires knowledge of the available alternatives.

The financial analysis of a real property investment is crucial in making a prudent decision. Yet there are few standards and no public markets to guide a novice in this area. There are no national exchanges, as in the commodity and financial markets, giving daily quotations and a ready market. There are no publications for real estate offering risk ratings such as those found in Standard & Poor's or Moody's guides for listed securities. Good real estate analysis is accomplished by gathering information from many diverse sources, sorting out the relevant data, and recasting the figures to provide greater accuracy and consistency for factual comparisons.

Income tax laws affect all investments, and have a special impact on real estate. For instance, the Tax Reform Act of 1986 directed substantial changes in how real estate investment is treated. Key provisions diminished the value of losses by prohibiting offsets against certain other income. The effect on real estate is that a property investment should be expected to produce a profit on its operations, rather than a loss. This alters the market for such property. Because these laws continue to change, an investor should understand tax terminology and such basics as how the Tax Code treats different kinds of income, the methods by which "capital gain" is calculated, and how the Internal Revenue Service defines and treats depreciable property. It then becomes easier to understand how tax changes affect an investment.

The English language offers many words with a number of different meanings, and *investor* is one of them. In another text by this author*, the term *investor* refers to the lender of investment funds—a source of mortgage money. In this book, *investor* refers to the person or company acquiring property for productive purposes. Other words used to identify such an owner are equity holder, buyer, landlord, developer, builder, sponsor, or partner. For consistency in terminology, the source of mortgage money will be identified as the lender.

While the subject of financing real estate investment is considered in only one chapter of this book, this is not to diminish its importance. The reason for not including in-depth discussion of financing is that it is quite a different subject from investment. The distinction made here is that financing involves the sources of mortgage money, the constraints within which the sources function, the qualifications necessary to obtain a mortgage loan, and the growing importance of the federal government agencies involved with the residential loan market. Contrasted to this, investment focuses on a property's productivity—the return, or yield, to the owner, who is the primary risk taker. Nevertheless, how and when financing is used has an immediate impact on the return realized from an investment. So financing is considered here from the standpoint of cost effectiveness.

While adequate knowledge may be the key to wise investment, it is actually the investor's judgment that unlocks the door to a successful project. And even the most experienced investor would probably admit in all candor that a little bit of luck can make all the difference in a marginal decision. But one might keep in mind that luck tends to favor those who prepare!

John P. Wiedemer

---

*John P. Wiedemer, *Real Estate Finance*, 5th Ed., Prentice-Hall, Inc. Englewood Cliffs, N.J., 1987.

1

Real Estate as an Investment

There are many ways for individuals, groups, and companies to invest time and money in pursuit of a profitable return. No single type of investment is "best" for everyone: the needs of each investor vary with individual requirements for safety of the principal, probability of a return, the term of the investment, and personal satisfaction.

Since the purpose of any investment is to achieve some kind of return, investments can best be compared by first defining the measurable returns that are available in our economic system. These returns are (1) income, (2) appreciation, and (3) value gain.

1. *Income.* The dollar return on an investment (gain or loss) is its income. Many investments are made strictly for the income they produce. Savings accounts, corporate and municipal bonds, government bonds, and treasury bills all fall into this category. For the holder, these investments generally represent good security for the principal, plus a fixed income. These investments are easily converted into cash (i.e., they are highly "liquid") and provide a cushion against emergency needs. The disadvantage of fixed-income investments lies in the fact that (persistent) inflation reduces the value of the dollar and, thus, the value of any fixed income. Based on a 5% annual rate of inflation, $1,000 invested in a savings account will produce a steady income of interest and have a purchasing power of only $783.52 (in constant dollars) at the end of five years.

2. *Appreciation.* Appreciation is a "passive" increase in investment value resulting from scarcity and price inflation. Certain investments are made specifically to profit from an anticipated increase in value caused by appreciation alone. Investments of this type include gold, jewelry, fine rugs,

furniture, paintings and other art objects, stamps, rare coins, antiques, and other collectors' items. While investments of this type can provide an intangible return through "pride of ownership," an increase in monetary value is not assured. Therefore these investments are speculative. An investment in tangible goods requires some method for safekeeping, the cost of which can easily outweigh any increase in value. And, except for gold, there are no organized trading markets for these goods—making a conversion to cash at true value a potentially slow and difficult task.

3. *Value gain.* Value gain is the active side of increase in value, as distinguished from the passive type identified as "appreciation." Value gain results from the input of expertise by an owner or manager. Examples of investments seeking value gain include such enterprises as building a business operation, planning the development of a tract of land, or purchasing selected common stocks. This type of investment seeks a profit from growth in "real" value, in addition to any increase in monetary value resulting from inflation.

Some investments mix all three types of measurable return. A dividend-paying common stock, for example, could provide a steady dollar income, some degree of appreciation from inflation, and a possible value gain from the profitable growth of the company.

Real estate as an investment covers such a diverse range of properties that the three types of return can be found both separately and in combination:

- *For income only*—mortgage loans.
- *For appreciation only*—holding undeveloped land.
- *For value gain only*—development of building lots.
- *For all three*—income property, such as an apartment building.

Because of this diversity, a blanket comparison of real estate investment with other available forms of investment is ruled out. Any meaningful comparison must consider how a *specific property* relates to alternative investment opportunities. Each investor must balance needs and goals, security, and income. And tax requirements affect each taxpayer differently. The selection of an investment is thus a personal matter, requiring the investor to carefully weigh the advantages and disadvantages.

Advantages of Real Estate as an Investment

Itemized below are a number of the advantages of real estate investment, along with some comparisons with other forms of investment.

Return on Investment

All investors seek a fair return, plus safety for their invested assets. Real estate can provide both, in varying amounts. The three basic types of return are listed below, with some tables for comparison.

Income. Because of the higher risk involved, real estate is expected to produce a better return compared to most other investment possibilities. The following table compares yields from other investments over a 20-year period with yields from several types of real estate property.

This comparison of yields is distorted by the inclusion of real properties of all ages. The dollar return on a property built five years ago, for example, would show the effects of inflation on income and operating expenses, but not on invested capital. Further distortion may result from the fact that only a small fraction of property owners release income figures.

Appreciation. On the average, few forms of investment have weathered the inflation-caused loss in purchasing power better than has real property. Savings accounts and other cash investments have lost value as the purchasing power of the dollar diminished. Collectibles, such as paintings, stamp collections, art objects, antiques, and jewelry have all appreciated in value although precise measurement of the increase is difficult. Appreciation varies with the kind of investment as well as with each individual investment. The change is not uniform. In regard to inflation, which is one component of increased value resulting directly from the debasement of currency (i.e., loss of purchasing power), economists project a long-range average increase of 6.75% annually.

TABLE 1–1
Investment Yields

Type of Investment	Annual Yield (%), End of Year			
	1987	1983	1977	1967
AA corporate bonds (S&P)	10.75	11.29	7.93	5.66
AAA utility bonds (Salomon)	10.50	11.13	8.15	
Savings passbook account	N/A	5.50	5.25	4.50
U.S. Govt. bonds (long-term)	9.81	10.48	7.68	4.74
90-day Treasury bills	6.75	8.14	5.42	3.46
Avg. dividend yield (1,500)	2.78	4.29	4.20	5.12
Consolidated Yields for Real Property				
Apartments (over 100 units)	4.35	7.46	9.21	6.35
Office buildings	6.14	9.16	9.85	7.68
Shopping centers	8.60	10.05	9.78	7.01

Value Gain. While figures are not available to lend statistical support, it is a reasonable assumption that few other investments can benefit as much as real property can from the input of management expertise. A perceptive owner *can* increase the value of collectors' items, but imaginative management has little effect on most other forms of investment. (The management of one's overall portfolio of investments [stocks] is, of course, crucial. But the stock market investor can have little effect on the *individual* holding, once it has been acquired.) Sound management *can* add considerable value to an investment in real property; the lack of it invites disaster.

Tax Advantages

Real estate has always offered certain tax advantages that reached their peak in the Tax Reform Act of 1981 when depreciation deductions could be taken over a 15-year period. In successive years, Congress reduced deductible amounts, and the Tax Reform Act of 1986 increased the cost recovery period for nonresidential property to 31.5 years. In addition, the accounting transfer of tax losses was limited solely to off-setting "passive income." Nevertheless, a basic advantage remains for those holding income-producing properties, in that the total basis-value of the building qualifies for cost recovery deductions, rather than just the equity interest. Since the depreciation deduction represents a non-cash item, it does afford a tax savings. Additionally, certain property improvements such as sidewalks and parking lots may qualify for shorter-life personal property deductions. While the tax advantages have been diminished, perhaps the most significant decrease has been in the restrictions placed on offsetting tax losses.

Other Advantages

Use as Collateral. Almost all forms of investment can serve as collateral for a loan. Mortgage loans are normally available for both residential and commercial properties at 80% to 90% of their value.

If the property has a proven income from long-term leases, a loan based on that assured income may exceed the amount that it cost to develop the property, thereby permitting the owner to borrow up to 100% of the money needed.

Pride of Ownership. The personal satisfaction of any investment is especially important in real property. For many Americans, land ownership retains a mystical quality, with a value that defies measurement.

Land is Tangible. Land can be seen, and it can be touched. It has a specific form and a specific size, and it cannot be lost or misplaced. It gives its owner a sense of security and emotional support.

Disadvantages of Real Estate as an Investment

Lack of Liquidity

It is often difficult to convert a real estate asset into cash. Since the market for a particular piece of property is limited to those people who both desire it and can afford it, an immediate need for cash can't always be satisfied through the sale of real property. The record of forced sales is not encouraging—fair value can seldom be obtained. Even if an interested buyer *does* appear, financing can be time-consuming. Property is often encumbered with existing financing; usually the buyer must either refinance the property or obtain a second mortgage loan. Both procedures, however, require considerable time and effort.

Long-Term Investment

A corollary to the lack of liquidity is that one must usually hold onto real estate for a number of years in order to realize the best possible return. It generally takes from three to five years to verify increases in value resulting from inflation and good management. There are, of course, examples of short-term gains in real property, but more often than not, they are speculative investments to begin with.

Management Requirements

Capable business management is fundamental to the success of many real estate investments. This necessarily takes the owner's personal time and attention, or else requires the hiring of a professional property manager. The real estate investor may face all of the problems associated with any business operation—sales, customer relations, employee relations, property maintenance and operation, tax and reporting requirements, and many more. Income properties especially benefit from good management, or suffer from the lack of it.

Property Hazards

Any piece of real estate—and particularly the improvements made to it—can be damaged by the elements or by people. Losses from fire, flood, vandalism, or other disaster can usually be recovered through insurance. But such a recovery is rarely a profitable procedure.

Legislation

Unlike many other kinds of investment, real estate is faced with an additional concern. While private property rights have long been subject to state police powers protecting safety and health, there is growing social concern over abuse of the environment. Land-use laws and environmental controls can affect property value by creating certain restrictions on its development. Other laws, such as rent controls and development set-asides, also affect where additional investment will be made and the ultimate cost of its use by consumers.

Ownership Recorded

Opinion is sharply divided on whether or not the need to record land ownership is an advantage or disadvantage to the investor. Recording, being a form of public notice, helps to protect an owner's rights against possible third party claimants. On the other hand, recording also publicizes an asset that may be subject to attachment by the creditor of an owner. Some people protest that the public record discloses personal assets that they would prefer to keep private.

The Value of Land

There is strong support for the thesis that land is the basis of all wealth. Historically, landownership distinguished the aristocracy from the rest of the people of a country or state. In early societies, the productivity of land was virtually the only source of wealth. New ways to produce wealth emerged as economic systems and trade grew, but few of these were completely divorced from land. Today, landownership is a distinction enjoyed by many. While it can prove to be a burden as well as a blessing, landownership is still commonly associated with power.

The potential productivity of land determines its value. Land's productivity is, in turn, dependent on the addition of labor and capital. Following are the basic combinations of land, labor, and capital that can produce valuable goods for society—plus wealth for the real estate's owner:

- *Cultivation*—produces grains, vegetables, fruits, timber, and pasture lands.
- *Mining*—produces coal, fertilizers, clays, oil shale, and metallic ores.
- *Drilling*—produces oil, gas, steam, and water.
- *Development*—produces houses, stores, factories, transportation systems, utility systems, and recreational facilities.

Each type of productivity listed above could be called a form of real estate investment. However, this book confines itself to the development of the land surface with buildings and other facilities used by people. For this purpose, land can be categorized and evaluated as it passes through the following stages of usage from raw land to land development.

Raw Land

Raw land is any land lacking the facilities needed to support building construction. It is unproductive land and, if left undeveloped, can create a tax burden for its owner. The value of raw land first depends on its proximity to such features as transportation systems, mineral resources, water, and recreational facilities—all of which can attract people. In the final analysis, the value of land for surface development depends on its ability to attract people.

People may be attracted to an area for a variety of reasons. It might be a beautiful recreation area, or it could be to support a large development project. While even tourist traffic can increase land value, it is the availability of jobs that causes people to settle in an area. An exception to this rule is the growing segment of the population now retired and living on incomes independent of current employment.

Where people are present, the major determinant of land value is the land's ultimate potential for use. Land speculators in outlying suburban areas often ignore these basic needs for population and for potential use. As a result, they buy land at a price well above its ultimate usage value. These owners are thus forced to leave their land unused or, eventually, to sell it at a loss for a price compatible with its ultimate potential use.

There are no simple formulas—or even complex ones—to guide the land investor. The direction of population growth is the basic clue to rising or falling land values. Population growth follows three main patterns: working patterns, traffic patterns, and living patterns.

Working Patterns. Where there are jobs, people will follow. It's that simple. The establishment or growth of any job-producing activity will create demands in the area for supporting services (schools, shops, recreation, etc.), housing, and land that's suitable for development. New jobs provide the primary pressure for land development.

Traffic Patterns. The second influence on growth patterns comes from traffic patterns and the availability of transportation. The growth of large metropolitan areas in the eastern United States was dictated by the rail lines radiating from urban centers. Later growth in the West followed rail lines for a time, but rapidly shifted to freeway patterns. So far, efforts to integrate automobile transportation with modern rapid transit facilities have not attracted enough people to create a new pattern.

Living Patterns. The third (and probably the least important) influence on growth patterns is the people's style of living. Most people, especially families, want better housing. But few people are willing or financially able to separate themselves from working and transportation patterns in order to relocate in an improved but remote area. This universal aspiration for better living conditions inspired the Great Society programs of the 1960s, with the Model Cities program designed to lead the way. Total communities were planned for large tracts of land outlying major urban areas. The federal government provided substantial financial support to private developers. Many innovative ideas were implemented, and attractive living patterns were established. Lacking good jobs, however, these well-planned communities could attract few residents. As a result, most of these projects failed. A few well-planned communities such as Columbia, Maryland and Reston, Virginia have been built by private developers. But they developed slowly and offered jobs as part of the growth. Communities that have prospered primarily from good living patterns are those oriented to retirees. In this category, the resident's income derives from sources outside the local community.

Land Development

As people are attracted to an area, the land becomes more useful and, thus, more valuable. An influx of people may result from manufacturing growth, extraction of natural resources, or a favorable location for commerce. Whatever the cause, the direct result of more people is a demand for more buildings—to live in, to play in, to work in, to store goods in. Land in a growing area increases in value because of its location, which in turn dictates its use. Land use may be broadly categorized as (1) single-family residential, (2) multi-family residential, (3) commercial, and (4) industrial. Each category is discussed below.

Single-Family Residential. The largest portion of developed land is used to build single-family houses. When land surrounding major growth areas is priced above the use value of single-family housing, it becomes very speculative. But what is the limit of value for land that can be used most profitably for single-family housing? The answer, of course, depends on the local area and the local housing market. Here are some guidelines.

First, a modern subdivision meeting local standards (and, usually Federal Housing Administration requirements under the ASP-9 form) will have housing density of approximately 3.5 to 4.3 building lots per acre of land. This density allows for curbs and gutters, streets, and utility easements. A small lot in this category would be 60′ × 100′; a large one, 80′ × 120′.

Second, the value of a building lot in relation to the value of the building may be expressed as the ratio of the land cost to the total property value. Where land is reasonably plentiful, the value of the land may represent as little as 15% of the total value—a $75,000 house, for example, might represent $63,750 in building cost and $11,250 in land cost. Where growth is restricted by natural barriers, the portion attributable to land value increases substantially. In many urban areas, the lot may represent as much as 75% or more of the total property value.

Third, the cost of land development has skyrocketed since the late 1960s. Material and labor costs have escalated, as have the requirements of various governmental authorities. The time lag in complying with new water standards and new sewage disposal requirements has also inflated development costs. At one time, a building lot developer could estimate the development cost at roughly 25% of the lot's eventual sale price. Now that estimate has risen to nearly 50%, leaving the other 50% to cover land costs and the substantial risk factor.

Let's return to our earlier question: What is the limit of value for land that's destined for single-family housing lots? Basic percentages don't change as rapidly as costs, which means that the traditional guideline still has some validity: the value of an average-sized finished lot is about equal to the value of an undeveloped acre of land. This guideline *is* changing, however. As development costs rise, the value of undeveloped land accounts for a diminishing percentage of the finished lot's cost structure.

Increases in the cost of developed lots have encouraged higher-density, single-family housing such as "townhouses" and "patio homes." These terms are not clearly defined, and vary somewhat across the country. But both concepts use the "zero lot line" design. Zero lot line means one or more exterior walls abut the property line or are common walls. The townhouse design basically follows the pattern of the historical "row house" but includes modern variations in exterior design and materials to avoid a monotonous appearance. Patio homes are a "cluster" type of housing, where three or four units use common or closely spaced back walls; patio, or courtyard-style frontal areas; and country lane streets. Density of both types of housing can be increased to six or seven units per acre, thereby lowering the "per unit" land cost.

Multi-Family Residential (Apartment). Land suitable for an apartment commands a higher price per acre than land suitable only for single-family housing. The density of living units per acre for an apartment varies greatly, starting at approximately 18 to 20 units for a one- or two-story garden apartment. A modern three-story apartment checks in at around 30 to 38 units per acre. High-rise apartment units can have still higher densities. (The FHA prefers to insure "multi-family housing" [its term] with densities of approximately 26 to 28 units per acre.) The apartment builder obviously can offset rising land costs by spreading them over a larger number of housing units.

It would be no more than wild conjecture to set down strict value guidelines for apartment sites. But there *are* a few clues. One is the relation of housing unit densities. The one-acre ratio of 28 apartment units to four single-family units is 7 to 1. Thus, land suitable for apartment development can be worth about seven times as much as land suitable only for single-family housing. Another clue to land value is the apartment builder's own goal for land-to-building cost ratio. Again the variation is considerable, but the average builder tries to hold land costs per unit to 20% of the cost of each completed unit. At $40,000 per apartment unit, therefore, the land cost per unit should not exceed $8,000. Assuming a density of 25 units per acre, the land cost should not exceed $200,000 per acre.

Commercial Land.　Commercial land is that which is suitable for stores, service facilities, and office buildings. The need for accessibility to the general public places a premium on frontages along major thoroughfares and freeways. In fact, commercial land is often valued by the "front foot," i.e., a value per lineal foot along the frontage line.

There are few, if any, guidelines for estimating the value of commercial land. One common measure is the traffic count, i.e., how many cars per hour pass a given point. This is an essential measurement for the location of a gasoline service station, and it also carries considerable weight with shopping center developers. In downtown areas, a "people count" can serve a similar purpose.

Industrial Land.　Land used for manufacturing, refining, or any other process industry must usually satisfy more specialized needs than the people-oriented residential and commercial categories. Good industrial land must provide access to extensive support facilities, including adequate transportation, power, materials, manpower, service facilities, and suppliers. Of increasing importance is the criterion that industrial land must be so located that industrial operation will not violate the area's environmental standards.

The value of land for industrial use follows no pattern. It depends on how well a particular tract of land fits the purchaser's requirements. And more significantly than with other categories of land use, the value of industrial land reflects the financial strength of the purchaser.

2

Investment Cost Components

Even the simple acts of buying and selling can become complicated if the trade involves real property. Unlike many other kinds of investment, the price of real property is often negotiable. The real cost can vary enormously with the manner of payment. Some costs of real estate transactions are obvious; others can be buried in the procedures. Neither a standard procedure nor a common form exists to document all the information essential to proper analysis of real estate investment. (The Real Estate Settlement Procedures Act [RESPA], passed by Congress in 1974 and later amended, establishes certain standards for information applicable to residential property only.) The real estate market is too varied to provide the kinds of reference guides and statistical histories that are standard fare for securities investment. To make a serious analysis of a real estate investment, the investor must know what information is needed and be able to assess the accuracy of that information. This chapter focuses on the various costs that can be involved in a real estate transaction.

The Purchase Price

The sum total of a real estate investment includes the purchase price, the cost of acquisition, and all applicable carrying charges. Some acquisition costs may be tax-deductible, and some may be capitalized as a part of the investment. First though, let's look at the purchase price, where it soon becomes apparent that the real cost of a property is not simply the acquisition price.

Cost of Search

The idea that there are always good property investments seeking buyers may be true, but finding the right one is not so easy. An experienced investor once expressed the opinion that "buying right is just as hard as selling, even harder." It takes screening and analysis to make a prudent decision and that takes time and money. So the search for a good investment becomes a cost of the acquisition, albeit a difficult one to count in dollars expended.

Cash Price

Like most investments in tangible commodities—and *unlike* security-type investments—the price of real property is usually negotiable. Cash is almost always the strongest inducement for a seller to accept a lower price than originally asked. Financing arranged in advance of a bid for property provides the buyer with a stronger offer than does a proposal to buy, subject to obtaining financing later. An exception to the cash rule would be a high-income seller who prefers extended payments as a method of deferring the tax liability.

Extended Payment Terms

Often a seller of real property is willing to assist in the financing of the sale. In these situations the price is usually somewhat higher than for a cash sale, but the interest rate for future payments may be lower than prevailing market levels. If no other financing is involved, borrowing costs can thus be substantially lower than with a new loan.

Under an extended payment purchase agreement, the seller normally holds a lien on the property as security for future payments. If the buyer anticipates a partial sale or a building expansion during the term of payments, the sale agreement should provide for it. Most sellers are reluctant to release any portion of their lien rights until full payment has been made.

Carrying Charges

Often overlooked amidst other costs of buying real property are the carrying charges. If the acquisition is an income property, carrying charges become a part of the operating expenses. But if the property is being purchased for resale, or for development and resale, the carrying charges become an important addition to the cost. Carrying charges include:

- *Taxes.* No private investment land is exempt from taxes. When property taxes are assessed, they become a prior lien on the land and must be paid. Otherwise the owner may forfeit ownership. On unimproved land, property taxes can become a real burden because of the lack of income.

- *Interest.* Property purchased with any form of financing requires the payment of interest.

- *Maintenance charges.* If land is in an improvement district, charges may be assessed for maintenance of public areas.

- *Utility standby charges.* In some cases, utilities may already be installed, but not yet in use. Utility companies may assess a standby fee to cover their investments until they can be put to use.

- *Insurance.* Landowners usually want to be insured against general liabilities and hazards if the property includes buildings.

Preliminary Evaluation Costs

One must usually spend some money to determine if a particular property is a suitable investment. Time and professional advice may be needed to reach a sound decision. The following are costs that may be incurred *before* deciding to buy.

Option Costs

Real property is always a "one of a kind" investment. No two properties are exactly comparable. Therefore, well-reasoned "snap judgments"—to buy, or not to buy—are rare, if not impossible. Property owners, on the other hand, aren't always willing to hold property off the market while a prospective buyer studies the property and decides whether or not to buy it. In a situation of this kind, the prospective buyer may purchase an *option* from the seller. An option agreement assures the prospective buyer that the property will not be sold for a specified period of time. Thus the buyer can spend time and money evaluating the property, secure in the knowledge that it won't be sold to another buyer in the meantime. The prospective buyer pays the owner for temporarily waiving the right to sell. The price of an option is negotiable, depending on the market at the time and the parties involved. The price may range from a token payment of a few dollars to as much as 5% of the purchase price.

Option agreements can be structured so that the price of the option counts as part of the purchase price if the sale is consummated. Or the option price can be considered an additional charge to the purchase price stated in the option agreement. If the option to buy is not exercised, the option price is normally forfeited to the property owner with no further obligation imposed on either party.

Earnest Money Contract

An earnest money contract is a commitment to buy and a commitment to sell —*provided that certain conditions are met*. If the conditions are not met, the earnest money contract may become void. The conditions can be worded in such a manner that they provide an escape clause for the potential buyer. In contracts for homes, it is fairly common to allow a condition that makes fulfillment of the contract subject to the buyer being able to qualify for financing. In contracts for commercial property, the buyer may ask for a clause that permits withdrawal if "suitable" financing is not available. The suitable financing clause allows the prospective buyer time to make an evaluation of the property in a deliberate manner much the same as if it were under option. If the property proves to be impractical for the anticipated use, suitable financing would become most unlikely. For a seller's protection, the terms should be more precise.

An earnest money contract normally requires that a specified sum of money be placed in escrow to show good faith on the part of the buyer. If the buyer fails to consummate the deal without good cause, the earnest money forfeits to the seller, with a portion usually paid to the sales broker. But if the contract is voided for a just cause, such as inability to find suitable financing (if that is one of the conditions), then the earnest money is returned to the buyer posting it. An earnest money contract may be prepared by an attorney, or, as is the case in many states, real estate brokers may complete standard form contracts.

Feasibility Report

A feasibility report is a formal study designed to determine the odds for success or failure of an income property. This report contains property evaluation information similar to that found in property appraisals. But it also examines the *market* in detail. It analyzes the rental structures, rates of occupancy, and expected profitability of competing properties in the same market area. A feasibility report is generally prepared by a qualified appraiser or professional property manager, but *can* be prepared by the prospective buyer. There are no professional "designations" in this specialized field. Cost for such a study is comparable to that for a professional appraisal but may be greater because of the in-depth market study.

Property owners and selling brokers commonly present completed feasibility reports to prospective buyers. Sometimes a buyer can trust such a report, but at other times, it should be ignored. The key question is: "Who prepared the report?" If it was prepared by qualified professionals known to the buyer, then no further studies may be necessary. A report prepared by the owner or owner's agents is always suspect, however, since it is difficult to be objective when one's own interests are at stake. In short, owner-sponsored studies are likely to exaggerate a property's potential.

Property management firms are well equipped to evaluate an income property if they have experience with similar property. The reports of management firms are sometimes suspect, however, because a firm may have a vested interest in expediting a sale. For example, it may hope to be hired as the buyer's property manager. To reduce this temptation to inflate the property's potential, some firms project a return on the investment and then base their management fees on their ability to prove the accuracy of their projection.

Planning Fees

Before an investor can make a sound decision on whether or not to buy a specific piece of real property, it may be necessary to assemble a variety of technical information. This technical information is particularly important if the land in question will be used for development. Architects must be consulted at a very early stage of a project to coordinate all necessary information and determine how that information will affect the cost of the proposed investment. Engineers may be asked to study the property's drainage requirements, including the cost of providing proper drainage. Utility specialists and engineers may be called upon to examine the requirements for, and availability of, service facilities. A new and growing breed of specialists can analyze the environmental impact of a proposed project. The charges for technical planning information are usually based on a professional hourly rate, but may be quoted on a "per job" basis.

Appraisal Costs

A property owner who decides to sell is wise to seek advice from a professional appraiser. The appraiser's objective approach to evaluation can:

1. Provide guidelines in establishing the price.
2. Be useful as a sales tool.
3. Establish the probable limits for a mortgage loan.

Since an appraisal has value for the seller, there is good reason for the seller to pay for it. But an appraisal's detailed description of the property and its condition also aids the buyer. And an appraisal must be performed before a mortgage loan can be made. In some cases, therefore, a case can be made that the buyer should pay for the appraisal. At this early stage of property examination, however, the information primarily benefits the seller.

Lenders keep lists of approved appraisers. When the buyer arranges an appraisal for a mortgage loan application, the appraiser must be one acceptable to the lender.

Organization Costs

It is difficult to draw a sharp line between preliminary evaluation costs and organization expenses. Some organization costs discussed in the following section may be an important part of a preliminary evaluation. Nevertheless, in this study the line is drawn at the point of decision to buy. Preliminary evaluation costs are incurred in order to make a sound investment decision. The organization costs are incurred after the decision to buy has been made and are necessary to properly implement that decision.

Legal Costs

Once an investor has decided to buy a specific property, attention shifts from business decisions to legal decisions. Unless the investor is an attorney (or is represented by an attorney), the investor should draw as clear a line as possible between business negotiations and legal matters. Lawyers are trained to watch for potential problems. As a result, some investors feel that in sensitive preliminary discussions, lawyers may introduce so many obstacles that negotiations can be stifled. Once a buyer and seller have worked out an acceptable deal, however, a knowledgeable attorney is invaluable for reducing the agreement to writing in a way that avoids potential legal pitfalls and provides proper protection. Also, before any sale of real property is consummated, a qualified attorney should examine the title and assure its proper transfer.

Selection of Business Organization

Real estate may be operated with any of several business organizations. Which form is used affects the initial cost of acquisition, the cost and method of operating the property, and the tax consequences. The choice of business operation is important and is discussed more fully in Chapter 9. An outline of the principal kinds follow:

Principal Business Organizations

1. Sole proprietorship
2. Partnership

3. Limited partnership

4. Trust

5. Corporation

Ownership

The ownership of land is a collection of rights including the use, enjoyment, and the right of disposition. These rights may be defined in the following categories.

Land Ownership Rights

1. *Freehold estates*

   a. Fee simple

   b. Fee simple conditional

   c. Life estate

   d. Remainder and reversion

2. *Co-ownership*

   a. Joint tenancy

   b. Tenancy in common

   c. Tenancy by entirety

3. *Leasehold estates*

   a. Tenancy for term

   b. Tenancy by period

   c. Tenancy at will

   d. Tenancy at sufferance

(Further definition can be found in Chapter 10.)

The above list should make clear the need for competent legal counsel in undertaking any real estate investment. All laws that concern ownership of real property and transfer of title are state laws, and there is considerable variation among the states in these important matters.

Accounting Fees

The need for professional accounting advice varies with the size and complexity of the investment property. If the intended acquisition is income property, an accountant may be needed to examine existing records and verify their accuracy. If financing is involved, financial statements prepared by a professional are better received by lenders than the borrower's own figures. And if a new business venture is established with the property acquisition, a competent accountant is very helpful in establishing new books and records.

Tax laws make it necessary for the taxpayer to determine the correct basis of value for the property and to select a cost recovery method in the year of acquisition. A tax-trained accountant may be needed.

Architectural and Engineering Costs

Again, the need for architectural or engineering services depends on the nature of the property being acquired. If the property is an existing building, a preliminary inspection can determine if there are any basic structural defects and if the mechanical and plumbing equipment are adequate. If the project is an apartment intended for conversion to a condominium, both an architect and an engineer may be needed to evaluate the cost of rehabilitating the units to meet local building codes and insurance requirements. If the investment is for construction of a new building, all architectural planning will be needed (at least to the point of bid drawings) before financing can be obtained.

Financing Charges

Obtaining a real estate loan can involve a number of charges and fees in addition to the basic cost of interest and discount. Following is a discussion of the additional fees that may be encountered in financing a real estate investment.

Application Charges

A nonrefundable application charge is standard practice among lenders who handle residential loans. This charge covers the cost of a credit report, a property appraisal, and the time spent reviewing the application itself. With commercial or investment-type loans, the procedure varies with the applicant, the loan, and the lender. Most commonly, the lender imposes a nominal charge to help offset the cost of reviewing an application and to discourage frivolous and repeat applications. With a commercial loan application, the applicant is expected not only to pay an application fee but also to furnish a property appraisal, pay for a credit report, and supply such additional information as the lender may request.

Commitment Fees

A commitment fee is a one-time charge made by a lender. In return, the lender promises to fund a loan at a future date. A commitment fee is most commonly assessed when a permanent loan will be funded at the completion of construction. A commitment agreement normally takes the form of a letter from the lender which, when signed by the borrower and returned with the commitment fee, becomes a binding promise for a loan at a specified future date. Commitment fees are generally from 1% to 2% of the loan amount.

The value of a permanent loan commitment to an investment builder is such that some mortgage lenders will offer "standby" commitments to assist in obtaining a construction loan. This form of commitment normally calls for a higher-than-market interest rate, a shorter-than-normal term, and two to four points in commitment fees. (A "point" is 1% of the loan amount.) It *is* a bona fide loan commitment but intended, as its name implies, to be used as a backup or standby promise, enabling a builder to first complete construction of a project and then obtain a more favorable loan commitment, if possible.

Origination Fees

An origination fee is a mortgage lender's charge for processing a mortgage loan. It may also be called a "brokerage fee" or "finance fee." This charge averages between 1% and 2% of the loan amount. Usually a portion of this fee is paid to the mortgage company's loan representative as a form of commission for the work involved in preparing the loan application and obtaining all required information.

Finance Charges

There are a number of ways for a lender to increase the yield from a loan. The nomenclature varies—some lenders are more imaginative than others! Whatever you call it, however, the bottom line is that this fee is designed not to compensate for a service, but rather to increase the yield from a loan. Following are some examples:

- *Funding fee.* At the time a loan is funded, the lender may assess a fee which is simply deducted from the loan's proceeds.

- *Renewal fee.* When a borrower asks to renew a mortgage note for an additional term, the lender may demand a renewal fee, usually one point. This kind of fee is commonly found in construction loans to smaller home builders. If the six-month term for a house construction loan is not sufficient to complete construction and sell the house, the builder-borrower may obtain an extension of time and pay a renewal fee.

- *Assumption fee.* When a new owner assumes an existing mortgage loan, the lender incurs some additional expense in reviewing and approving the assumption agreement. Hence, an additional fee is justified. Many lenders also reserve the right to increase the interest rate when a loan is assumed.

- *Warehouse fee.* Mortgage companies may utilize a line of credit extended by commercial banks to borrow money for funding loans until the loans can be sold to a secondary market purchaser. The credit line is called a "warehouse" line because the loans are held by the bank as collateral until sold to others. In normal credit markets, the long-term interest rates charged for mortgage loans are greater than the short-term rates charged for business credit lines, and no additional fee is needed. But, in *unusual* times, when the prime lending rate charged the mortgage company for its credit line *exceeds* the rate on the mortgage loan, the difference can be made up by charging a "warehouse fee" to the borrower.

Interest Costs

Interest rates are fairly simple by themselves—a fixed percentage of the loan amount becomes due on specified dates. It is the method of calculating interest rates that creates complications. Three basic kinds of interest rate calculations are used in finance:

- *Simple interest* is based on a fixed rate, or percentage, of the loan amount, calculated on an annual basis. For example, 9% per annum translates to $90 each year for each $1,000 of the loan amount. Certain types of credit, like credit card accounts, often restate the annual rate as a monthly rate, such as 1½% per month. It is still simple interest, only a different time period for calculation is used.

- *Compound interest* is a procedure whereby, at specified intervals ranging from one day to one year, the earned interest is added to, or compounded with, the principal. The added interest then earns additional interest. Compound interest is most often associated with the payment for a savings account. More recently, it has become a necessary part of the interest calculated when graduated payment, or adjustable rate mortgages, produce negative amortization. With these mortgage payment methods, the monthly payment may be insufficient to pay all of the interest due. So the unpaid interest is added to the principal balance, requiring the borrower to pay interest on the unpaid interest.

- *Add-on Calculation* is more closely associated with installment loans as found in car and furniture financing. But the method is frequently used in short-term mortgage loans, junior mortgages, and even in seller-financed transactions. Instead of a promissory note in the face amount of the loan, the add-on procedure computes the total interest for the term of the loan and adds this total to the face amount of the loan.

Example

A $5,000 loan at 8% for a term of 3 years—
Interest calculation: $5,000 × .08 = $400.00 × 3 years = $1,200

Amount of note:

Principal due	$5,000.00
Interest due	1,200.00
Face amount of note	$6,200.00

Monthly payment amount:

$$\frac{\$6,200}{36} = \$172.22$$

The Truth-in-Lending Act (implemented by Regulation Z of the Federal Reserve Bank Board) requires that lenders specify the cost of credit to the borrower. In the above example, the interest cost amounts to 14.55%.*

Rule of 78

When an installment loan is paid off *prematurely*, the calculation of "interest due" is not always based on simple interest earned as of the date of payoff. Many installment loan agreements provide that the loan may be paid off at any time during its term, with interest calculated in accordance with the "Rule of 78"— but the mathematics are not detailed in the agreement. Lenders may describe the procedures as a method of rebating unearned interest on an installment loan.

The number "78" comes from the sum of the digits of the months in a year. Under this plan, for a loan of one year, the lender considers 12/78ths of the annual interest earned in the first month, plus 11/78ths in the second month, reducing each following month.

Table 2–1 details the "Rule of 78" method of calculating the premature

Truth-in-Lending Tables, Financial Publishing Co., Boston, Mass., 1982.

TABLE 2–1
"Rule of 78" Method

Months		Interest Due for Each Month or Part Thereof	
12	1st month	12/78 × $80	$12.31
11	2nd month	11/78 × $80	$11.28
10	3rd month	10/78 × $80	$10.26
9	4th month	9/78 × $80	$ 9.23
8	5th month	8/78 × $80	$ 8.20
7	6th month	7/78 × $80	$ 7.18
6	7th month	6/78 × $80	$ 6.15
5	8th month	5/78 × $80	$ 5.13
4	9th month	4/78 × $80	$ 4.10
3	10th month	3/78 × $80	$ 3.08
2	11th month	2/78 × $80	$ 2.05
1	12th month	1/78 × $80	$ 1.03
78			$80.00

Note: Interest accrues on the first of each month, not at the end of the month. In the above example, if the loan is paid off *during* the second month, interest due would be: $12.31 + $11.28 = $23.59

payoff of a 12-month installment loan for $1,000 at 8% interest, or $80.00 interest per annum.

Application of an Interest Rate

There are no real standards as to how lenders apply an interest rate, only a variety of practices. With most commercial loans, lenders consider interest as earned each day the loan is outstanding. But even this basis has a variation: What is sometimes called the "banker's rate" considers a day as ⅟₃₆₀th of the annual rate. The method used by most federal agencies and others is an amount of ⅟₃₆₅th of the annual rate. On many mortgage loans, particularly residential loans, the interest is earned on a monthly basis, or ⅟₁₂ of the annual rate. In this way, each month that portion of the mortgage payment that applies to principal reduces the balance due for the next month's calculation. Interest may also be calculated on a quarterly, semi-annual, or even an annual basis. Once payments are established on a mortgage loan, the normal practice is to consider interest as being paid, and earned, *after* the money has been used for the prescribed time period.

Loan Discount

A loan discount is a reduction from the face amount of a note retained by the lender, usually at the time of funding the loan. It is measured in points—again, one point equals 1% of the loan amount. It is another cost of borrowed funds.

The purpose of a discount—like that of interest—is to provide a yield for the lender. But a discount is a one-time charge, and to convert this into an annual percentage amount requires a time span—a number of years—before the loan is paid off. Since most long-term mortgage loans are paid off prior to the full term, lenders generally consider 12 years as a standard to calculate the yield provided by a discount on a 30-year loan. The result is a calculated yield used for investment comparisons, but it is not necessarily the actual yield.

To clarify the yield as produced by a discount, consider a 30-year loan of $50,000 at 10% interest with a 4-point discount. The discount amounts to $2,000 (4% of the loan amount). So the lender delivers $48,000 at loan closing in exchange for a note worth $50,000 The lender has earned $2,000. But is that sum earned that day, that year, or over the life of the loan? For purposes of calculating the yield (return on investment), the lender normally spreads the return over a period of years, commonly 12 years as the normal life of a 30-year loan.

$$\frac{\$2,000}{12 \text{ yrs}} = \$166.67 \text{ earned per year}$$

$$\frac{166.67}{48,000} = .00346 \text{ annual yield produced by the discount}$$

Add interest rate of 10% plus the rate produced by the discount: .10 plus .00346 equals .10346, or 10.346% annual yield. For purposes of clarity, the above example ignores the time value of money which most lenders would consider. This means that the $2,000 picked up at closing could be put to work earning additional interest, which increases the yield even more. Further, the 10% interest rate is calculated on the $50,000 loan amount while the lender has only funded $48,000. So the return provided by the discount has some advantages over the straight interest rate for the lender.

Because it is the combination of discount and interest rate that determines the lender's yield, the borrower may elect to (1) pay more in discount points to obtain a lower interest rate, or (2) to secure a lower—or no—discount by accepting a higher interest rate.

Closing Costs

There are costs involved when a real estate transaction is closed, or "settled." While these costs are generally negotiable—some paid by the buyer, some by the seller—they are part of the cost of acquiring an investment property. These costs are listed next:

- *Legal fees*—the cost of preparing the conveyance instrument, the mortgage document, and the promissory note.
- *Mortgagor's title policy*—the assurance to the buyer that good title to the property is being conveyed.
- *Mortgagee's title policy*—the assurance to the lender that a valid title secures the mortgage loan
- *Settlement (or closing) fee*—the charge made by the agent responsible for the collection and disbursement of all required documents and considerations.
- *Copies of deed restrictions*—fees paid to the office of land records for copies of instruments needed to prepare the mortgage.
- *Lender's inspection fee*—the charge by a lender to pay for a physical inspection of the property.
- *Notary fees*—charge for providing acknowledgements of the legal documents.
- *Recording fees*—cost of recording the legal documents.

When a real estate transaction is closed, a loan is usually funded at the same time. If a loan is involved, the lender may require that the buyer-borrower pay certain costs at the time of closing. These are:

- *Insurance premiums.* The lender requires that any buildings pledged as security for the loan be insured against physical damage and that evidence of acceptable coverage be shown before the loan is funded.
- *Pro rata share of all taxes.* Taxes are adjusted to the closing date, with the buyer and seller each paying a proportionate share.
- *Prepaid interest.* If the due date for future loan payments is adjusted to a date later than the closing date, the lender asks that the interest on the loan be paid up to the adjusted date.
- *Discount.* Any discount points on the loan may be deducted by the lender before delivery of the proceeds to the settlement agent. Or the discount may be paid in cash by the borrower at or before closing the loan.

Disposition Costs

Just like birth and death, it costs money to go into real estate and it costs money to sell out. The owner of real property may have good contacts with potential buyers and sufficient knowledge to handle a sale without help—and state laws permit a property owner to sell it without a license or professional help. (Real estate licensing laws generally apply only to persons offering property belonging to someone else.) However, as this chapter clearly indicates, handling real estate can be a complex matter. Increasingly stringent educational requirements for those working in the industry have made the professional broker's help more valuable than ever.

Listing Agreements

Real estate procedures vary somewhat across the country, but three basic types of agreement to list property for sale are widely available:

1. *Open listing*—an owner's agreement with one or more brokers to offer a property for sale. An open listing agreement requires the owner to pay the sale commission to whichever broker first presents—in writing—the name of the prospect who eventually buys the property. The owner may, of course, locate a buyer on his own. But if a broker arranges the deal, the broker collects the commission. This method gives a broker little incentive to advertise or to push the sale outside a private list of potential buyers.

2. *Exclusive agency*—a listing agreement with a single broker to sell the property. But under this agreement, the owner reserves the right to sell the property also and thus avoid paying a commission.

3. *Exclusive listing*—an agreement with a single broker to handle the sale of a property on an exclusive basis for a limited period of time (usually about six months). If a sale is made *by anyone* to *anyone* during this period, the listing broker is guaranteed a commission. This arrangement provides the greatest incentive for the broker to undertake an advertising campaign for the property, thoroughly investigate all inquiries, and encourage other brokers to seek a buyer (since the commission *can* be shared).

Which is the best procedure? There's no easy answer. It depends on the people involved, the type and location of the property, and the circumstances at the time. If the owner knows of several good prospects, is knowledgeable about procedures, and has sufficient time to take care of sale details, it could be economical either to sell directly or use a limited form of listing. If the owner is seeking a broader market (and perhaps a better price), an exclusive listing with a highly qualified brokerage firm could prove to be the quickest and most economical method.

Sales Costs

To sell property and transfer title involves several costs.

Sales Commissions.   Commissions for the sale of real property range from about 3% of the sales price up to 8%, depending on the amount of service required by the owner and on the size and number of properties offered through the same broker. If substantial advertising is a part of the sales agreement, the commission is on the high side. If a tract containing several hundred homes is involved, the commission is much lower. Good real estate brokers offer the seller much more than sales prospects: they provide experienced market advice and guidance with the many problems encountered in properly handling a closing.

Sales commissions are usually negotiable between seller and broker. Flat fees for listing property are now *occasionally* used, but it is still generally true that no sales commission is paid until the property has been sold and the proceeds of the sale have been delivered to the closing agent.

Title Requirements.   A seller of real property must prove that good title to the property is being passed on to the buyer. This requirement can entail the cost of an attorney's review of the abstract of title, plus any work necessary to correct objections to the title. Or it can entail buying a title insurance policy, which insures the owner against adverse claims to the title. Such policies are generally issued in the amount of the purchase price of the property. They cover the owner's legal costs in any defense of the title or pay off the face amount of the policy in the event an adverse claim is sustained. Some states accept as proof of title the *title guarantee*, which is a certification of title as shown in county records.

Land Survey.   Local practices dictate which party pays for a survey of the land being sold. The seller has some obligation to clearly identify the land that is being sold. And the buyer must have the survey information to complete mortgage loan requirements or plan future development.

Additional Settlement Costs

- *Deed to transfer title.* The legal costs of preparing the deed and any releases needed to deliver good title are the seller's responsibility.
- *Escrow costs.* The fees charged for handling a transfer are usually divided between buyer and seller.

3

Land Use and the Environment

Of growing importance to investors is the impact of land use and environmental control laws. Such laws can enhance value, and they can also reduce value. Enhancement comes when constraints on further development create greater scarcity of the existing usable property. Conversely, if restraints are applied to the land, the owner is denied free use of it and thus suffers some diminishing of its value. What is the background of these laws that may give us insight as to the future?

There has been an interesting evolution of government land use regulations, from its beginning during the nineteenth century's westward migration of settlers, to the police powers exercised by local governments as communities developed, to the present-day concern for adequate safeguards for the living environment. The concept of private property as the basis for personal liberty continues to change as greater emphasis is placed on the needs of society as a whole.

History of the Land Use Laws

As the United States began to grow in its early years, private ownership of land represented only a small portion of available land wealth; most was held by state and federal governments. Public lands were offered free to any settler willing to work the land. The great debates of this nineteenth century expansion concerned the proper objectives for the government in the disposition of the vast land areas under its control. Should the purpose be to encourage settlement, as Thomas Jefferson so eloquently argued? Or should the objective be to generate revenue for the federal government, as Alexander Hamilton contended?

As the population moved westward, small towns grew where the need arose—where preparations had to be made to ford a river, where protection could be found from marauding tribes, where mountain passes could cause delays. The small towns grew partly by plan and partly to accommodate existing access trails. Rich farm and ranch land was purchased or homesteaded. By the middle of the nineteenth century, railroads were creating their own towns—where the tracks stopped, where junctions developed, or where difficult crossings required a support depot. Always it was individuals who found the most expeditious way to overcome the problem at hand.

By the latter part of the nineteenth century, settlers in the growing Western states and territories realized that the unstructured growth of their towns must give way to planned development. Urban planning in the large Eastern cities had focused on orderly street patterns with some landscaped park areas for beautification. Among the first of these attractive plans was William Penn's design for Philadelphia initiated in 1682, followed by Annapolis, Williamsburg, and Savannah. In 1791, Pierre L'Enfant was chosen to develop a master plan for the nation's new capital city in the District of Columbia. However, as the nation's growth accelerated, planning for beauty and open spaces within the cities became a less important goal than supporting a vibrant economic growth. The new planning centered on the more practical need for water supplies, sewage systems, and paved streets. It soon became apparent that the layout of streets and location of utility systems could be more easily accomplished if the planners also directed the usage of the land to be served. And steps were taken to include municipal zoning as an essential part of the city's planned growth.

The initial municipal effort to control the use of private land brought forth *zoning laws*. "Zoning" designates the use that may be made of each tract of land within a municipal jurisdiction and has a major impact on property values. The same police power that allows the city to zone the land provides authority to establish and enforce building codes, subdivision controls, and overall community planning. With these regulatory powers, the cities were better able to provide the individual landowner with adequate water supplies, sewage disposal systems, streets, schools, and parks.

Zoning

The police power of each state gives it the authority to protect the health, safety, and general welfare of its citizens. It is this authority that gives a state the right to restrict the use of privately owned land. Through zoning laws, a community can (1) designate which tracts of land may be used for residential, commercial, industrial, or agricultural purposes, and (2) enforce these restrictions.

The first zoning law was New York City's, passed in 1916. Then the Advisory

Committee on Zoning, set up under Secretary of Commerce Herbert Hoover, released the "Zoning Act" in 1922. And in 1926, the U.S. Department of Commerce published the Standard State Zoning Enabling Act, which set guidelines under which states were allowed to grant existing local governments the police powers needed to regulate the use of privately owned land. Implementation of the Act often resulted in disputes between the cities and the states. Urban groups had become suspicious of legislation enacted by rural-dominated legislatures. In a rather short period of time, nearly all communities adopted zoning plans that essentially confined land use to the status quo. Neighborhoods were simply zoned to their present use, with minimal allowance for any future growth.

Proponents of the zoning concept hoped that these laws could influence growth patterns. However, no method of controlling growth was incorporated in early zoning laws. No mechanisms were established to influence or control growth in the unincorporated areas surrounding the cities, even though these areas might later be annexed. And no provision was made to cover the relationship of a city to neighboring municipalities. The regional concept of growth did not evolve until later.

Nevertheless, zoning regulations found favor with municipalities. Today, over 98% of American cities with populations over 10,000 use zoning to control their development. The major exception, and only large metropolitan area without zoning, is Houston, Texas.

How Zoning Operates

A municipal zoning law is under the control of a regulatory body, usually a zoning commission. This commission develops the plans and establishes the procedures for implementing zoning legislation. A city is divided into districts, with a designation for each district indicating the type of building that may be erected (or how the land may otherwise be used). The rules and designations vary considerably. Generally, the basic designations are residential, commercial, industrial, and agricultural. Then the breakdown becomes more specific—one area may be zoned for single-family residences, with another for duplex to fourplex residences. Similar subdesignations may be made in all designated areas. The rules may even go further than listing the *general* type of building that may be constructed. They may set a minimum and/or maximum size, height, living area, setback from the property lines, and size of the lot itself. All communities with zoning laws have plans, available to the public, that identify the zones and the building requirements that apply to each tract of land.

Zoning laws may, of course, be changed. An ordinance may be amended to recognize a changing growth pattern or to accommodate a new development.

Or a property owner may seek a *variance* from a zoning requirement that causes undue hardship. Applications for variances usually require substantial evidence of the need for the variance, some proof that it won't change the basic character of the existing zone, and a public notice of the request. While the initial zoning pattern seldom creates any land value that was not already inherent in the property, variance requests are often associated with efforts to increase land value. It is in this area that political pressures can undermine the benefits attributed to zoning laws.

Under zoning laws, a landowner must obtain a building permit from the community government (township, city, or county) before commencing construction of any building. Before the permit can be issued, building plans must be submitted to show that they conform with the zoning regulations. If a building is constructed without a permit, it is subject to demolition. If a building exists before the zoning ordinance becomes effective for that tract of land, it is generally accepted under a "grandfather clause" as a nonconforming use of the land. However, a "grandfathered" building cannot be enlarged or remodeled to extend its life; when it is demolished, any new building on the site must conform to the law.

Building Codes

Both state and local governments have enacted building codes that are intended to protect the public against low-quality—and possibly dangerous—construction practices. The result has been a hodgepodge of requirements that often perpetuate outmoded and costly construction practices. In metropolitan Chicago, for example, there are between 30 and 40 separate codes (depending on what one calls a "code"). Attempts have been made to standardize requirements and encourage lower-cost "modular" housing, but these efforts have met with considerable resistance.

In spite of the problems involved, building codes serve a useful purpose in providing minimum standards for structural loads, ventilation, electrical installation, plumbing, and fire protection. Building plans must meet all code requirements before a building permit can be issued. The city building department generally inspects the building during construction to ensure compliance with the laws. Upon the building's completion, the department must issue a certificate of acceptance before the building can be occupied.

Granting a permit to build is not always based on the design of a structure and its location meeting local health and safety standards. In some communities, the authorities negotiate additional requirements, particularly for large development projects. These extras may include certain public areas within the project and even off-site construction, such as low-income housing, as a condition for granting a building permit.

Building code requirements don't end when construction is complete; they continue during its use. The methods of enforcement vary with the community, but generally the fire and health departments inspect buildings and cite any code violations.

Subdivision Requirements

In earlier times, a landowner could subdivide land into lots with little concern for government restrictions, particularly if the land lay just outside community limits. Recently, however, local governments have used their police powers to enforce subdivision requirements. Flood control districts have been created and given authority to set minimum requirements in land development. The FHA and the VA have set minimum standards for the subdivisions in which they will agree to underwrite homes. And the Office of Interstate Land Sales Registration, part of the Department of Housing and Urban Development, has certain disclosure requirements (not minimum standards) for larger land developments.

Essentially the requirements for a subdivision concern the design, location, and quality of the streets; the adequacy of water and sewage systems; the location of fire hydrants and street lighting; and the size of the lots themselves. Depending on the size of the subdivision, the developer may be required to commit a portion of the land for schools and public areas. Once all requirements have been met, the community gives its approval for construction. In general, government approval concerns only the physical aspects of the development, not its economic value for the investor.

Planning

Although the implementation of zoning laws requires a certain amount of community planning, early zoning's emphasis on the status quo gave little encouragement to the concept of urban or regional planning. As zoning laws began to create a mix of land use districts—some of which were desirable, and some of which were not—communities realized the need for better plans for growth and land use. But these efforts failed largely because communities couldn't control the land outside of their boundaries. Probably the strongest encouragement to overcome this problem came from the federal government, which has authorized planning assistance in each of the National Housing Acts passed since 1954. The program became known as the "701 program."

The 701 Program

In Section 701 of the Housing Act of 1954, Congress authorized the first program of Urban Planning Assistance. Its intent was to encourage land use planning—through surveys and land use studies—by providing federal funds to urban communities and to state, metropolitan, and regional planning agencies. As these programs multiplied, the goals were broadened to include human resources planning, fiscal planning, and the preparation of regulatory and administrative measures to implement the plans.

While the initial aim of the 701 Program has been diluted by an expansion of its goals and by increased emphasis on housing requirements, the program has been important to land use planning. One lasting contribution of the program has been its assistance in the training and development of the urban planning profession.

Restrictions by Private Agreement

As will be discussed in Chapter 10, the use of land can be restricted by the wording with which the land is conveyed. When land is conveyed with a restrictive condition (e.g., "to grantee so long as the premises are used for a public park"), the right of ownership can be forfeited through failure to comply. A more common method of limiting the right to use land is the *deed restriction*, which does not carry the potential penalty inherent in the limited conveyance of rights. A lease agreement may also contain clauses that limit the tenant's use of the land.

One purpose of a deed restriction is to protect future property value for both the grantee and the neighborhood. Building lot developers, for example, often set usage standards when a lot is sold. The deed to a lot, for instance, may contain a restrictive covenant that sets a minimum size of 1,500 square feet for the house to be built, requires that it be constructed with a brick or stone facade on the front and sides, and requires a fire resistant roof. The deed restrictions may dictate landscaping and building design, number of stories, setback, and minimum cost. As long as the requirements are reasonable and are generally for the betterment of the neighborhood, they can be enforced. (The theory is that if a buyer agrees to restrictions, he is bound by them.) Enforcement is usually accomplished by a damaged party seeking an injunction, which is a court order that forbids a certain act.

Limitations by Private Agreements

Land use cannot be unduly restricted by private agreement. It is not permissible to limit future ownership in a manner that may cause discrimination due to sex, race, national origin, color, or creed. Furthermore, no private agreement can place an unreasonable restraint upon the disposition of the property that would prohibit *any* alienation (i.e., a sale or other means of disposition) by the grantee. A reasonable restraint on disposition would be to require that the owner offer the property initially to a narrowly defined group for a limited time before offering it to persons outside the group.

Termination of Restrictions

Deed restrictions generally include a time limitation of 25 to 35 years—the character of a neighborhood usually changes during that time, leaving the original restriction irrelevant. There are other methods by which deed restrictions may be terminated. One way is by a failure to enforce the requirements. If a developer has sold all the lots, it is sometimes difficult to find a neighbor willing to sue for enforcement when damages may be ill defined. Other methods of termination include (1) by agreement among the parties involved (which may include a neighborhood association), (2) by a new zoning requirement which would take precedence, (3) by condemnation of the property for a public use, or (4) by other legislative action.

Eminent Domain

Under the state's right of eminent domain, the government can take private property for a public purpose or control its use. This action can be taken against the owner's wishes through *condemnation* proceedings. Unlike the exercise of state police powers, the right of eminent domain requires that the landowner receive fair compensation for the land. Normally the public authority negotiates with the property owner to determine an acceptable price for the property. If an agreement cannot be reached, the price is determined by court proceedings, with acceptance mandatory upon the landowner. It is through this procedure that the government retains the ultimate right to acquire land for streets, freeways, schools, parks, public parking, public housing, and other purposes that serve the needs of the general public.

Sometimes the government permits the use of eminent domain by private and quasi-public companies which serve a public need. A right-of-way for a power transmission line, pipeline, or railroad may be acquired through the exercise of this governmental right.

What is "fair" compensation under eminent domain depends on the rights acquired and the damages that the property owner may suffer. If, for example, the desired right-of-way creates an obstacle to future work on an operating farm, an additional compensation called "severance damages" may be paid. If land suffers a loss of value due to the construction of a nearby public facility, such as an airport or a sewage plant, the landowner may be entitled to "consequential damages." Under some conditions, a landowner who feels damaged by a nearby facility can initiate a proceeding to demand that the government purchase that property. Such a case is called an *inverse condemnation.*

1987 *Property Rights Decisions*

After a half century of steady erosion of private property rights, in 1987 two landmark decisions that could alter the trend were handed down by the United States Supreme Court. Over the years, a number of regulations, zoning ordinances, and building permit requirements added restrictions on a landowner's right to use the land. Until 1987 there had been no clear distinction as to what local authorities could "take" from a property owner for their usage without fair compensation. Now the action of the U. S. Supreme Court may be considered a "first step" toward distinguishing between a noncompensable regulation and a compensable taking.

On June 9, 1987, the U.S. Supreme Court ruled that land use officials may be liable for damages if zoning regulations prevent landowners from using their property, even temporarily. The case involved the First English Evangelical Lutheran Church, of Glendale, California, which wanted to reopen its retreat and recreational area for handicapped children after a flood. The County of Los Angeles refused to allow the church to use its land for that purpose since the authorities wanted to use the land as a drainage channel. The church complained that this zoning, even though temporary, amounted to a "taking," requiring compensation under the Fifth Amendment to the Constitution. The Supreme Court agreed with the church, ruling that even a temporary taking, wherein the owner loses all use of the property, is the same as a permanent taking. There was no question that the government has the authority to "take" the property for flood control purposes but must compensate the owners if they do. The court expressed the opinion that this ruling "will undoubtedly lessen to some extent the freedom and flexibility of land-use planners and governing bodies," but, after all, "many of the provisions of the Constitution are designed to limit the flexibility and freedom of governmental authorities."

Later in the same month of June, 1987, the United States Supreme Court ruled in favor of landowners in another California case whereby the state sought to increase access to public beaches by placing conditions on a building permit. The dispute involved a couple with oceanfront property who wanted to tear down an existing house in order to replace it with a larger one. The State Costal Commission approved the plan on condition that the couple provide increased access for the public along the beach in front of their house. The Supreme Court reversed a California court's decision that favored the state's position. In effect, the Supreme Court said that while the state's idea might be a good one, coastal residents alone should not be compelled to contribute to its realization. If California needs more beach access, it may take the land by eminent domain and must pay fair compensation to the landowners.

Government Influences on Land Use

Completely removed from the categories of rights, laws, and requirements are several government subsidy and assistance programs that effectively direct how land is used. If the landowner expects to receive the benefits offered by the programs, the land use must adhere to the programs' guidelines. Foremost in this category are the FHA and VA loan underwriting programs. Both agencies stipulate land use and building standards that must be met in order to qualify for loan assistance.

A more recent program directed by the federal government subsidizes the purchase of flood insurance in designated areas. The National Flood Insurance Program has established flood plain zones along waterways and in coastal areas. The decision to join this program has been optional for local governments in the affected areas. If an area elects to join and meets certain minimum requirements, the federal government provides subsidy support for private insurance carriers to write flood insurance policies for property owners in the area. Further construction cannot be undertaken on flood-prone land (i.e., land that has been subject to flooding during the past 100 years of weather conditions) unless protective measures are taken. Enforcement is accomplished by forbidding any federally regulated lending institution from financing construction that is not in compliance. The result has been to remove large tracts of marginal land from possible development.

Land Restrictions Due to Lack of Service

In very recent years, a new form of land use restriction has developed due to (1) shortages of the basic utility services needed to sustain a modern community, and (2) rapid growth that, for some areas, has produced "unacceptable" problems. "No growth" laws have been enacted, producing an escalation in value for developed property and a sharp drop in value for surrounding land with potential development value.

Restrictions on Sewer and Water Lines

Sewage disposal facilities and drinking water are services usually supplied by a municipality, although in some communities water is furnished by a private utility company. Electricity and natural gas are usually—but not always—furnished by privately owned utility companies. Regardless of who furnishes the services, many areas of the country are encountering difficulties in sustaining the growth rates of recent years. A number of measures have been undertaken to adjust to shortages, particularly in areas where water is in short supply.

Some California and Arizona communities, for example, have enacted building restrictions that virtually forbid new developments. The reasons for these restrictive laws include (1) lack of sufficient water, (2) lack of adequate sewage disposal facilities and the money needed to build suitable plants to meet federal and state pollution control requirements, and (3) the simple desire of many residents to enjoy their community as it is and not to be overcrowded.

Land developers have frequently challenged the right of communities to enact building limitation laws, arguing that these laws are destructive of the landowner's rights to use the land. It will probably be many years before these legal questions are resolved. In the meantime, a potential investor in real estate must be aware of the utilities situation in the specific area of investment interest.

Water Restrictions. The most important utility-based limitation on land use is shortage of water.

Water rights have long been an essential part of landownership in the Western states. Indeed, without rights to water for such things as irrigation and use by livestock, ranch land can be worthless.

For development land in and near cities, the availability of good quality water has only recently become a matter of concern. The location of early settlements was often dictated by the presence of suitable water, and the quantity needed to satisfy community sanitary requirements was not great. But today that situation has changed. Many areas are finding that the cost of cleaning up the water is escalating more rapidly than the tax money available to do the job. As a result, many local governments cannot permit new water taps; in others, delays are increasing. The emphasis on growth—and the increase in jobs that growth can produce—are being forced to slow down.

Sewage Disposal. The construction of sewer lines and sewage treatment plants has struggled to keep pace with the surge in housing construction across the country. Many local governments have fallen behind in their efforts to improve sewage treatment facilities in order to meet federal and state standards governing the quality of effluent that may be released into waterways. The techniques for proper treatment of waste material are now available and local shortages of this utility service are being remedied. But time—and, as always, more money—will be needed.

Electricity and Natural Gas

It was barely 100 years ago that electricity first became available for limited household use. Only since World War II has natural gas been distributed on a national scale. Yet today many homeowners and almost all businesses would call electricity an absolute necessity and natural gas the cleanest and most convenient fuel.

Electric Power.   Even in the high-growth areas of the country, developers have traditionally had small cause for concern over the local power company's ability to furnish adequate electric power. This confidence in their ability to meet the increases in demand is now being shaken. The plans of many power companies to supply future demand with nuclear power plants have been substantially curtailed because of the difficulties in construction cost overruns and in obtaining regulatory agency approvals. Coal-fired plants are encouraged by various government agencies because coal is the most abundant of the fossil fuels. But coal-fired plants have to meet pollution restrictions that are both uncertain and costly. Plants using natural gas and oil for fuel are faced with possibly limited and more costly supplies. It is possible that new energy resources will be developed in the coming years, but if not, the future production of electricity is expected to fall a little short of meeting the growth in demand.

For the investor in real estate, the impact of any future electricity shortage would show up in an inability to tie new outlets into the local power grid. If this should happen, an alternative source of power would be a privately owned generator added to the building or the development—at an increase in the investment. Plans for future projects should be cleared with the local power company well in advance of starting construction.

Natural Gas.   The use of natural gas as a fuel has increased substantially since World War II. This is partly because it is clean, easy to transport, and relatively low in cost compared to alternate fuels. In the late 1950s, the production of natural gas was placed under the regulatory powers of the Federal Power Commission, and price ceilings were set on all gas moving in interstate commerce. For many years the ceilings remained stable while the cost of other fuels increased. A gas shortage developed in the late 1970s, resulting in partial deregulation of prices. New gas and deep gas (at depths below 15,000 feet) were deregulated and severe distortions occurred in the price structure. However, at this writing gas is in adequate supply at competitive prices.

Fortunately for the real estate investor, natural gas is rarely a necessity. Most energy needs that have been satisfied by natural gas can be satisfied by other means. Some new housing developments are using all-electric heating and cooling (let the power company worry about which fuel is most suitable!). Both solar heating and heat pumps are being used to augment more conventional systems.

Environmental Impact Statements

The National Environmental Policy Act of 1969 requires the preparation of an environmental impact study for any major federal project that will affect the environment. The idea appealed to state legislatures, almost all of which have adopted similar requirements. Many local governments have construed state requirements to include them or have added environmental statements to their local zoning or planning ordinances. The courts have generally supported the requirements as a prerequisite to land development.

The thrust of the National Environmental Policy Act is to require an environmental impact statement (EIS) for *government* projects. But in the idea's adoption at lower levels of government, the burden of preparing such statements has been placed on the private developer. Generally required is a report on the expected impact of a new project, or a requested change in zoning classification, on many hard-to-define areas such as noise, air quality, public health and safety, wildlife, and vegetation. The report also must estimate the impact on more easily measurable aspects of community life such as population density, automobile traffic, energy consumption, the need for sewer and water facilities, employment, and school enrollment. Not every project must first be studied—the laws generally specify how large a project must be to require an environmental statement. (This threshold varies with the locality.)

The information contained in an EIS is helpful to many agencies of the government. Copies of the statement are commonly submitted to the affected school district, water department, sewage control district, flood control district, and highway department. The EIS is also made available to the public, with open hearings held on the application. If federal or state money is involved in the project, additional federal or state hearings must be held.

Preparation of the statements is generally not subject to any qualification or competency standards. For a government project, the EIS is prepared by the agency involved with the project (sometimes with the help of a private consultant). If the development is privately owned, the statement may be prepared by the developer or by a private firm specializing in environmental studies.

The cost of preparing an EIS is usually the least of the new environment-based costs of a new project. The need to study the statement and process the application through prolonged public hearings has added many months to the preparatory time required before construction can commence. With inflation continuing, delay means cost escalation. An additional problem is that an EIS sometimes provides a major weapon to opponents of a project—even a mere handful of opponents—who wish to stop growth rather than control it.

The following section examines methods and theories of environmental control that can shape the future planning and, thus, the growth of land use.

Environmental Control Methods

The growing concern for the environment—and for all the living conditions encompassed by that word—has engendered a large and not yet clearly defined body of laws and regulations. The trouble derives from (1) lack of a clear definition of what the problem is, and (2) lack of agreement as to what should be done about it. As the environment has become a political issue, governments have looked first to their police powers as a means to improve or correct the problem. Earlier in this century, when land use in growing cities required some control, the states exercised their police powers first to regulate building construction. Then followed zoning ordinances, subdivision controls, and efforts to use police powers to protect the living environment. The first response to smog came under the authority of nuisance control laws. Next came emission control limits for automobiles and factories. Finally, requirements have been devised that make pollution abatement devices mandatory.

Cleaning up the environment is a problem involving more than just land use, but an essential thrust of the cleanup effort is directed at how the land is used. Four methods can be used to accomplish environmental goals, insofar as land use is concerned. These are (1) government police power, (2) private contract, (3) acquisition, and (4) social pressure. The first two methods were discussed earlier (in connection with land use restrictions) but are touched on again here in connection with efforts to improve the environment—a subject of interest not only to land investors, but also to present and potential landowners.

Police Power

Government police power arises from the need for social organization. It can be termed an expression of sovereignty. When used as a control technique in restricting land use, the government's restricting an individual's freedom *without compensation* is generally accepted by the public as necessary for the good of society. When the same police power is used to restrict the freedom of *most* individuals comprising the general public—as is necessary for an effective emission control regulation—the individual generally fails to see the restriction as necessary for the good of society. Probably nowhere else in the United States has police power been used more strongly for emission control than Los Angeles. Yet the city's air remains polluted; governmental actions have failed to clean it. This cannot be because the city lacks the police authority to enforce the regulations. Rather, the general public most likely feels that other economic considerations carry a higher priority than a clean environment.

Private Contract

A private contract is drawn between the local taxing authority and a landowner. The taxing authority agrees to limit property taxes to, say, a capitalized value of the open space usage, while the landowner agrees to forego any development. This type of agreement is effective in controlling the use of the land, but it has limited application. It requires a special set of circumstances wherein (1) the taxing agency is willing to forego the increased revenue that would result from an increase in land value, and (2) the landowner is willing to forego the gain that could result from developing the land. But situations do occur where both parties are best served by withholding development.

Contract programs do remove tax pressures that can produce an undesirable change in land use. And such programs can help to direct urban growth into outlying rural areas before land speculation upsets proper mechanisms for land use control.

Acquisition

When control of land use is essential to protection of the environment, the government can acquire land through purchase—which can be fee simple, a right to the land that is less than fee simple, or an easement. The obvious limitation to this alternative is that it can be very costly for the government. One way to reduce this expense is for the government to purchase, for example, a piece of farm land, and then resell the land with a restrictive clause in the deed that allows subsequent owners to use the land only for farming.

The use of easements is also an effective way to reduce the high cost involved in acquiring ownership rights. Many highways are constructed on easements, which allow the government to restrict highway signs. Special legislation has expanded the right to control signs along interstate highways. One state, Wisconsin, has acquired easements adjoining its major highways for the purpose of protecting the scenic beauty along the way.

More than the other methods of accomplishing environmental goals, the use of government power to acquire land from private owners for the primary purpose of preventing its use involves political and emotional questions. The heritage of this country is deeply rooted in the concept that private property is a basic right of the people. Strong arguments have been made that the security of private property is the very foundation of personal liberty. It is hard to deny the advantages that have accrued to this society under a system of private initiative and the right to own property. But as society has become less dependent on the land as a source of personal income, the concept of absolute rights to private property has been modified somewhat to meet society's needs.

Some of those who strongly support the environmentalists' goals consider the theory of property rights to be illogical. They say that only labor and capital create value, that the land itself was not made by an owner and is basically a social possession. Therefore, this theory concludes, the private property owner has no compensable rights in land itself (but does have compensable rights in the improvements) and should not be paid if the land is needed for the benefit of society as a whole.

Social Pressure

The fourth method of accomplishing environmental goals is through the attitudes of society. In our system, social priorities are determined by the laws and in the marketplace. Both the legislatures and the marketplace are strongly influenced by human conduct. And human conduct reflects a mixture of tradition, public opinion, habit, education, religious belief, and moral leadership. Changes in the law that reduce individual rights and freedoms to promote a safer and more liveable environment cannot be successful without the support of at least a sizable minority.

4

Financing Real Estate

Investment in real estate often involves borrowing a portion of the money needed. Indeed, mortgage loans today comprise the largest single demand on the nation's credit markets. To support this market, real estate offers excellent collateral. It has long life, a fixed location, a permanent record of title, and laws that fix methods of conveyance and the process for making claims against it. While some mortgage loans are for short terms, such as construction loans and warehouse lines of credit to mortgage companies, most are for terms of over 10 years and classify as long-term loans. It is this long-term nature of real estate financing that distinguishes it from other types of credit.

Because lending for long terms brings special risks, such as the effects of government monetary policies, the probability of continued inflation, and the future growth patterns of a given location, such loans command higher rates of interest. Many lenders have backed away from holding such long-term loans in portfolio, that is, as the lender's asset. Instead, the growing trend is to convert long-term loans into various classes of securities that are easier to sell; this alters the nature of the risk.

The mortgage loan market itself functions on two major levels—the primary market of loan origination and the secondary market that purchases and sells existing loans. Supporting this market is a rapidly growing trend toward federal underwriting of huge blocks of mortgage loans assembled by a variety of lenders and investment bankers.

To gain an insight into how this market functions and what it means to an investor in real estate, we will start with the primary market.

Primary Mortgage Market

The primary market is where loans are originated. There are a number of participants in this field, many of whom have stepped in since the early 1980s. Loan originators are no longer limited to those institutions with deposit assets or those who broker loans for them. Loan originators today include home builders, real estate brokerage firms, financial services companies, and automobile credit companies as well as mortgage companies and the institutional lenders. While the newcomers are gaining market share, the field is still dominated by savings associations, commercial banks, and insurance companies. However, these mortgage loan trends reflect mostly residential loans—those on one- to four-family dwelling units—that comprise two-thirds of all mortgage loan originations. It is the residential loan that has become more standardized in its qualification requirements and the documentation needed, thus enabling this kind of loan to be assembled in large blocks for conversion into securities. Loans for apartments, commercial buildings, and industrial plants are not so easily standardized, and most are handled on an individual basis.

While all loan originators benefit from the large volume and easier conversion to securities of residential loans, they also recognize the value of commercial loans of larger individual size and greater fees. So the investor seeking a mortgage loan today enjoys a broader range of money sources. If the local bank or savings association is not interested in the loan, the investor can try such alternatives as those offered by American Express, General Electric Credit Corporation, GMAC, Sears Roebuck, or Century 21, to name a few.

Secondary Market

What has made mortgage money readily available for a variety of loan originators is the expansion of the secondary market for these loans. At its beginning, the secondary market consisted of the Federal National Mortgage Association (FNMA or Fannie Mae), opened in 1938 for the sole purpose of providing a market for loans insured by the Federal Housing Administration. When the Government National Mortgage Association (GNMA or Ginnie Mae) was partitioned out of Fannie Mae in 1968, Fannie Mae held a grand total of $7 billion in its loan portfolio. By 1987 Fannie Mae held over $100 billion in its own portfolio and had issued an additional $100 billion in mortgage-backed securities. But Fannie Mae is only a portion of the secondary market—it handles about 8% of the mortgage debt outstanding.

What the secondary market does is buy loans from loan originators. In the early 1980s, the secondary market was following two separate paths in its loan acquisitions. One, and the original concept of the market, was acquisition for its own portfolio investments. This was the practice of such major investors as large savings associations, life insurance companies, and Fannie Mae. Mortgage loans were purchased and held as sound investments.

The second path followed by the secondary market was one spearheaded by the Government National Mortgage Association beginning in 1970, and the Federal Home Loan Mortgage Corporation (FHLMC or Freddie Mac) a few years later. The basic idea in this "second path" procedure was to either buy or assemble blocks of such loans as collateral for security issues. The securities are then sold to others. Thus the purchasers of the securities become the "buyers" of the loans and they benefit from the cash flows produced by the underlying block of mortgages.

The blocks of loans serving as collateral can be assembled by any loan handler, such as a commercial bank, a home builder, Sears Roebuck, or Prudential Life Insurance Company. The mortgage loans themselves are placed in the care of a trustee. Then, whoever is selected as the underwriter examines the block of mortgages to make sure each fulfills the requirements. If they do, the underwriter issues what amounts to an insurance certificate. The underwriter charges a fee for this certificate. In practice, it is the insurance certificate that becomes the security sold in the financial markets.

There is no requirement that the block of loans be insured or underwritten—after all, each mortgage loan must carry its own default insurance, be it FHA, VA, or private mortgage insurance. But what the market quickly learned is that a federal agency underwriting certificate could be sold in the financial markets more easily and at a better price than one issued by a private company or institution. The result has been that over 95% of mortgages converted to securities are federally underwritten. The huge market for mortgage loans has attracted investment bankers acting as "converters." These companies assemble blocks of loans in the hundreds of millions of dollars, obtain federal underwriting, and issue mortgage-backed securities. More recently, these mortgage-backed securities have been issued in the form of collateralized mortgage obligations (CMOs). In this design, the security is issued in several classes offering a variety of maturities. This practice was encouraged and given a big assist by the 1986 Tax Reform Act authorizing mortgage blocks to be placed in a new legal entity called a Real Estate Mortgage Investment Conduit (REMIC). A REMIC is essentially a method that clarifies the tax liabilities of those handling the cash flows of mortgage payments.

Who are the federal agencies underwriting blocks of mortgage loans? They become important, not only because they dominate the mortgage-backed securities market, but because as the system matures, the need for uniform loan practices becomes more important in successfully administering the mortgage pools. The largest underwriter in dollar volume underwritten is the Government National Mortgage Association. Ginnie Mae is a government agency under the Department of Housing and Urban Development. It carries an authority that is not normally found in government agencies: Ginnie Mae can issue a guarantee certificate for a block of loans that carries the full faith and credit of the United States Government. Stated another way, a "Ginnie Mae," as their certificates are called, carries the risk equivalent of a government bond, and passes through to the certificate holder the cash flows from mortgage loans that pay a return of 1 to 2% greater interest than the government bond of similar maturity. It is a very attractive investment for pension funds and some restricted trusts. There is a limitation in that Ginnie Maes only cover FHA, VA, and some FmHA mortgage loans—no conventional loans can be underwritten. In 1987, GNMA had underwritten over $300 billion in their guarantee certificates.

The second largest federal agency insuring blocks of loans is the Federal Home Loan Mortgage Corporation (Freddie Mac). Freddie Mac was created in 1970 as a part of the savings association system. It is a federally chartered corporation with 15 million shares of participating preferred stock owned by over 3,000 savings associations and 100,000 shares of common stock owned by the Federal Home Loan Bank. Its purpose when created was to purchase loans from member savings associations as a better method of providing liquidity to the associations. Selling loans in the secondary market had not been a very common practice for savings associations prior to that time. Almost from its inception, Freddie Mac opted to assemble blocks of geographically diversified mortgage loans, pledge them as collateral, and issue what they called a "Mortgage Participation Certificate," or a "P.C.," as the financial markets identify them. For many years PCs were straight pass-through type securities—the cash flows including both principal and interest payments generated by the underlying pool of mortgages was simply passed on in pro rata shares to the security holders. Then, in 1983, Freddie Mac opened the door to a new design when it issued the first collateralized mortgage obligation (CMO) in this country. An important point is that Freddie Mac does guarantee their certificates, but it is an "agency" guarantee. It is not the same as Ginnie Mae's guarantee. An agency guarantee carries weight in the financial markets simply because it is assumed the government will not let one of its agencies go into default—but it is not a government guarantee. By 1987, Freddie Mac had issued over $200 billion of their PCs and CMOs.

The first federal agency to enter the secondary market became the last to enter the field of underwriting mortgages for others. Their first effort came in 1982 when they offered several underwriting programs to their seller/servicers. The prime motive then was to earn underwriting fees. As the market escalated, Fannie Mae moved rapidly to a strong position in underwriting mortgage pools, yet still continued their outright purchase of mortgages for their own portfolio. When Fannie Mae was partitioned—part of its functions were transferred to the Government National Mortgage Association—in 1968, it became a private corporation with its stock openly traded on the New York Exchange. However, it retained certain unique ties to the federal government; for example, five of its 18 directors are appointed by the President of the United States, and it can borrow up to $2.5 billion from the U. S. Treasury. Because of these ties it is still classed in the financial market as a "federal agency." FNMA does guarantee some of its mortgage-backed securities and these are given the same treatment as Freddie Mac in the markets. Both Fannie Mae and Freddie Mac deal primarily in conventional residential loans. In 1987, Fannie Mae had issued well over $100 billion of its mortgage-backed securities.

How do federal mortgage pools affect an investor in commercial properties? For one, much of the credit demand for residential mortgage money has shifted from savings deposits and insurance company reserves to the financial markets. The historic participation of institutional lenders—savings associations, commercial banks, and life insurance companies—in mortgage lending for their own portfolios is more focused on commercial loans. And mortgage companies, with their great expertise in handling this kind of credit, benefit from the same market growth. They, too, have increased access to money sources for handling commercial loans. Also, there is a small, but growing, effort to pool blocks of commercial loans for the issuance of mortgage-backed securities.

While a review of where the mortgage money comes from provides some background and guidelines, investors are also concerned about how money can be obtained and how borrowed funds affect the investor's yield. The rest of this chapter is devoted to a comparison of yields, a review of mortgage repayment plans, and other financing techniques.

Why Borrow Money?

For an investor, the purpose of borrowing money is singular—to increase the return, or yield. Like any venture, the result might not always be successful, but the intent is always the same—to make a profit. A commercial loan differs from a residential loan in several ways, but for the investor as well as the lender, one key difference is that the property being acquired is expected to repay the loan. ("Commercial" loans are being defined broadly here as loans that are not classed "residential.") So both the lender and the borrower must examine the property being pledged as collateral to assure themselves that the loan can be repaid in a timely manner. In contrast to residential loans that look first to the borrower's personal income, unrelated to the property itself, for loan repayment, the commercial loan may not even hold the borrower personally liable. So the effect of borrowed money must be measured in direct relation to the property's income and what the result is on the borrower-investor's yield.

Impact of Mortgage Loans on Equity Return

While most real estate investors borrow money to meet acquisition requirements, the reasons for borrowing vary. Even a business firm with adequate cash reserves may elect to borrow money to acquire a new property. And an investor with insufficient cash to purchase a larger property seeks a mortgage loan to complete the acquisition. The underlying advantages of borrowing money to acquire property are called *leverage*, which can be illustrated as follows. If an individual can earn an 11% return on a property and can borrow money at 9%, there is a net 2% return on every dollar borrowed in addition to the 11% return on equity capital. Further support for mortgage borrowing arises from the expectation of making a larger return on one's cash through reinvestment in another business activity that provides a greater return than the interest cost for a mortgage loan. This expectation is undergoing a major re-evaluation as fixed interest rates give way to variable, or adjustable, rate loans. An increase in the interest rate diminishes the advantage formerly associated with "leverage."

The basis for leverage is the use of fixed-cost borrowed funds as a portion of the purchase price needed to acquire a property. Leverage may be defined as the ratio between the borrowed funds and the investment cost—the higher the ratio of borrowed funds to the purchase price, the greater the leverage. For example, if an investor can acquire a property for $100,000 that is capable of producing an income of $16,000 per year, a purchase with cash would yield 16% return on the investment:

$$\frac{\$16,000}{\$100,000} = .16 \text{ or } 16\%$$

If the investor borrows $75,000 at 12% interest and uses $25,000 equity cash to complete the acquisition, the return would be:

Return on total investment	$16,000
Less: Interest cost ($75,000 × 12%)	9,000
Return on equity invested	$ 7,000

Equity return converted to a percentage:

$$\frac{\$7,000}{\$25,000} = .28 \text{ or } 28\%$$

Obviously, an advantage accrues to the investor when the interest rate for borrowed money is less than the anticipated return from the property. Leverage that produces an increase in the return on equity invested is called *positive leverage*. When the rate of interest and the return from the property are at the same rate, the result is *neutral leverage*. Neutral leverage would have no effect on the rate of return on the equity investment but would reduce the amount of equity cash required to purchase the property. When the interest rate for mortgage money *exceeds* the overall rate of return from the property, the result is *negative leverage*. For example, if the interest rate for borrowed funds rises to 18% and the rate of return from the property remains at 16%, the return on the equity investment would be substantially reduced. Assuming a total investment of $100,000 with borrowed funds of $75,000 at 18% interest rate:

Return on total investment ($100,000 at 16%)	$16,000
Less: Interest cost ($75,000 at 18%)	13,500
Return on equity invested	$ 2,500

Equity return converted to a percentage:

$$\frac{\$2,500}{\$25,000} = .10 \text{ or } 10\%$$

Clearly there is a risk to the investor in properties that are over-leveraged. Few real property investments, with the possible exception of high-grade net leased properties, present the certainty of future income that can guarantee a margin of profit between the fixed-cost borrowed funds and the overall return from the property. A slight drop in the overall rate of return can sharply decrease the return on equity investment, or even produce a net loss. Obviously, an increase in the interest rate has the same negative impact on leverage as does a decline in profitability of the property.

Leverage Factor. Another method of expressing the leverage ratio is to compare equity to total investment. In the preceding examples, the ratio of loan to value was 75% ($75,000 ÷ $100,000 = .75). To obtain the reciprocal percentage, the following formula applies:

$$\frac{1}{1 - .75} = 4.0$$

Expressed another way, the equity investment of $25,000 goes into the total investment four times. So if an investor has $40,000 cash to invest and is capable of borrowing 75% of the property value, the leverage factor would indicate that the total size of the investment could be $160,000, as shown below:

4.0 × $40,000 = $160,000

Debt Service to Operating Income

In the evaluation of income properties, *lenders* show the greatest concern for the ratio between net operating income and annual debt service. This ratio is more important than the loan-to-value ratio or the appraised value of the property. The reason is that the lender looks *first* to the income stream as the source of repayment for the loan, rather than to foreclosure and resale of property. The lender's evaluation thus centers more on the accuracy of the estimates of future net operating income than on the present market value of the property.

The key elements to consider are:

1. Size of the income stream.
2. Time when the income will be available.
3. Duration of the income stream.
4. Stability, or assurance of continuity.

There are no fixed rules within the industry used to measure these key elements of analysis. Lenders develop their own criteria, using past experience to establish the guidelines for future evaluations. This is the reason lenders generally limit their loans to those categories of properties that have proven successful for them. For example, some lenders will make motel loans; others will not.

Coverage Ratio

Because of the variables that can affect income from real property, lenders normally require a protective margin between the net income available to repay a loan and the amount of the payment required. An easy way to express this requirement is to limit the repayment amount for the loan to, say, not more than 75% of the net operating income. This, of course, would provide a 25% safety margin. Such margins vary with the policies of the lender, the strength of the borrower, and the type of property offered as collateral. Generally, the margins vary from 5% up to 30%.

Another method of determining a required safety margin is to express it as a "coverage ratio." The requirement might be stated as "net operating income must be at least 1.3 times the debt service." Most investors simply convert the coverage ratio to a percentage. This is accomplished mathematically by dividing 1 by the coverage ratio number thus:

$$\frac{1}{1.3} = .77 \text{ or } 77\%$$

So if the coverage ratio requirement is 1.3, the debt service cannot exceed 77% of the net operating income in order to qualify for the loan.

To further explain the use of a coverage ratio, and how it is used to determine a maximum loan amount for a given income level, consider the following example.

Example

If a borrower has a property with a net operating income of $11,000 annually, what is the maximum loan that could be anticipated in compliance with the 1.3 coverage ratio? The above computations show that the debt service cannot exceed 77% for this ratio, therefore:

$11,000 × .77 = $8,470 (maximum annual debt service)

By referring to a loan amortization table, the investor can determine the approximate loan amount that can be repaid with an annual debt service of $8,470. For example, if the current market offers a 20-year loan at 12% interest, the calculation can be based on a monthly or annual payment amount. The following figures utilize a monthly payment amount. By referencing a financial table showing the monthly payment needed to amortize a $1,000 loan, we find the monthly payment required for a 20-year loan at 12% is $11.01. The first step is to convert the monthly payment to an annual amount as follows:

12 × $11.01 = $132.12 (annual payment per $1,000 of loan amount)

To determine $1,000 multiples that can be obtained for an annual debt service of $8,470:

$$\frac{8,470}{132.12} = 64.1084$$

To convert multiples:

64.1084 × $1,000 = $64,108.40 (maximum loan)

Interest Cost on Long-Term Loans

The interest cost of a long-term mortgage loan is calculated no differently from that of a short-term loan if both are using simple interest computations. The mortgage loan's large amount and longer repayment term create an impression of excessive interest cost. However, that impression is not quite accurate, as can be seen in the following example.

Example

Interest cost for a small loan of $1,000 for 10 years at an 11% simple interest rate:

Monthly payment: $13.78 × 120 months =	$1,653.60
Less: Amount of original loan	−1,000.00
Interest cost over 10-year term	$653.60

Interest cost for a mortgage loan of $40,000 for 30 years at an 11% simple interest rate:

Monthly payment (P & I) $380.80 × 360 months	$137,088
Less: Amount of original loan	−40,000
Interest cost over 30-year term	$97,088

While the interest rates are exactly the same, the shorter-term loan shows a much lower interest cost as a percentage of the loan amount. This is due to the term of the loan, not the way the interest is computed.

Interest cost for the short-term loan: $653.60 divided by $1,000 = 65.36%

Interest cost for the long-term loan: $97,088 divided by $40,000 = 242.72%

Participation by Mortgage Lender

Another question that faces investors seeking mortgage loans is the position of the lender in regard to participation in the project. In earlier times, when interest rates were quite stable, long-term loans presented little concern for lenders. Their earnings are based on the margin between cost of funds and what can be earned on the loan. And with both elements fairly well fixed, the risk was minimal. But as inflation escalated in the 1970s, and interest rates became more volatile, this comfortable assurance disappeared. One way to reduce this growing risk is to sell the mortgage loan as described earlier in this chapter. Another way to seek some risk protection is for the lender to participate in the mortgaged project. Still another way has been for lenders to forego such long-term loans altogether and undertake the risk of owning the property outright.

If the lender opts for participation, there are many ways to accomplish it, falling into two general categories: (1) income participation and (2) equity participation, as more fully described next.

Income Participation

The lender shares in the cash flow from the property for a limited period of time, usually the term of the mortgage loan. This type of participation takes the form of a percentage of the income from the property. This percentage may be based on gross rental receipts (the procedure subject to the least contention), or it may be based on net operating income. The base for percentage calculation varies; it may be either the before-tax or after-tax cash flow from the property. One example would be no participation payment from the borrower under the rental structure existing at the time of funding the loan but substantial participation (say, 25%) in all rental increases thereafter.

Equity Participation

The lender receives rights that may endure beyond the term of the loan and can represent a true equity share in the property. An equity participation may or may not require an additional investment by the lender on top of the mortgage loan. It is a method used by many large joint ventures between major lenders and property developers. An equity participation permits the lender to share in all the benefits that are derived from the property, including the residual value upon sale of the property, increases in net income from the property, and any tax advantages that may be available to the owners.

Mortgage Repayment Plans

How a mortgage loan is repaid directly affects an investor's cash flows. The type of mortgage used affects the overall cost of the loan itself, and thus the amount of the invested capital. So it is important to know the basics of mortgage loan terminology, what kinds of loans are available, and the normal procedures used in the industry.

The fully amortized, constant-level payment loan that once completely dominated the industry began to give way to new designs in the mid-1970s. The pressures to change came from two directions: (1) Lenders and their regulators became concerned that housing costs were escalating to the point that new buyers would be priced out of the market, and (2) the rapid increase in interest rates was creating a massive mismatch between lenders' cost of funds and their portfolio income. As an attempt to help with the first problem, regulators approved several plans of graduated payment mortgages. These permitted a borrower to qualify income based on a first year's lower payment amount rather than what it would take to amortize the loan. The answer offered for the second question was to allow adjustable rate mortgages to be written, giving lenders the right to change an interest rate at periodic intervals without altering other terms of the note and mortgage.

In the rather extensive language of mortgage lenders, a few key words might be identified for better understanding of this chapter. *Term* means the length of time over which there remains an outstanding balance on the loan. *Maturity* is that point in time when the loan must be paid in full. *Amortization* is the periodic repayment of the principal balance, plus interest as it comes due. How a loan is amortized is one way of classifying mortgage loans, as indicated below:

- *Straight mortgage loan.* The entire principal balance is due at maturity, with only interest paid during the loan's term. This method is also called a "term loan," or an "interest only" loan.

- *Partially amortized loan.* Periodic payments are insufficient to repay the principal during its term, requiring a full payment of the remaining principal balance at maturity. The method is sometimes called a "balloon note." A common plan for such payments might be a loan that matures in 10 years with payments calculated as if it were a 30-year term. With this plan, after ten years the balance due would amount to nearly 90% of the initial loan!

- *Fully amortized loan.* Periodic payments (usually monthly) include principal and interest computed (usually at a constant level payment amount) so that the loan is fully paid at maturity. This is the standard for almost all residential loans.

Mortgage Loan Amortization

The repayment of a mortgage loan is normally calculated as a constant level monthly payment for a specified number of years. The payment amount includes interest cost on the principal balance due each month plus a reduction of the principal itself. Since each payment reduces the principal balance, it necessarily reduces the interest cost for the next month. Thus, each successive payment comprises less interest cost with a larger amount applied to the reduction of principal. On a fully amortized loan, the payments over the term of the loan pay off the principal amount in full.

The monthly payments on a mortgage loan constitute an annuity. An annuity is annual, or monthly, payments designed to deliver a specified principal amount, plus earned interest, in equal payment amounts over a given time period. It is the kind of payment offered by an insurance company to policyholders on certain kinds of life insurance policies. In the case of a mortgage loan, the mortgage amount becomes the "present worth" of future monthly payments. Put another way, if we consider the present worth of each future monthly payment, as discounted at the interest rate required by the mortgage loan, the sum of the discounted future payments is equal to the mortgage amount. While the mathematics of mortgage, or annuity, payments is not offered in this text, present worth calculations are explained in Chapter 13, "Discount Analysis."

While the calculation of mortgage payment amounts as a monthly annuity is fairly common, there is another method sometimes used. It results in a slightly greater return to the lender and may serve to point out that a given interest rate can result in different *costs for the borrower*. The other method mentioned is to calculate the interest charge for one full year on the outstanding loan amount at the beginning of the year, then divide that interest into 12 payments, adding sufficient payment against principal to pay off the loan by the end of its term. The following example shows how the calculation works.

Example

$1,000 loan at 11% per annum, payable monthly over 30 years. Monthly payment is $9.52 (from amortization tables).

First year calculations	
Annual payments—12 × $9.52	114.24
Less: Interest charge—11% of $1,000.00	−110.00
Paid on principal balance	$ 4.24
At the end of the first year—	
Principal due $1,000.00 − $4.24	$995.76
Second year calculations	
Annual payments—12 × $9.52	$114.24
Less: Interest charge—11% of $995.76	−109.53
Paid on principal balance	$ 4.67
At end of second year—	
Principal due $995.76 − $4.67	−$991.09

The principal due at the end of each year can be readily converted to a percentage figure with the information found in a "Remaining Balance Table." Using the figures above, the principal due at the end of the first year is $995.76, or 99.58% of the original loan amount. At the end of the second year, the $991.09 principal due converts to a remaining balance equal to 99.11% of the original loan amount.

Alternative Mortgage Repayment Plans

Another method of classifying mortgage loans is by their repayment procedures. While the mortgage crunch of the early 1980s brought out many creative designs, there are only two basic mortgage plans involved. These two are (1) adjustable rate mortgages (ARM), and (2) graduated payment mortgages (GPM). These two plans class as alternatives to the fixed rate, constant-level payment plan that still is used in more than half of the loan originations. The basic designs and several of the variations are further described next.

ADJUSTABLE RATE MORTGAGES

Adjustable rate mortgages are long-term loans that allow a lender to adjust an interest rate at periodic intervals without altering the other terms and conditions. The purpose is to shift a portion of the loan risk—that of fluctuating interest rates—to the borrower. It was intended primarily for savings associations, who customarily hold some of their loans in portfolio, to provide them a closer match between their cost of funds and their loan income. For the borrower to accept the additional risk, a key inducement has been a lower interest rate, sometimes as much as 2 to 3 percentage points less than a fixed-rate loan. More commonly the differential is closer to a 1½ percent advantage for the adjustable design.

PRINCIPAL ELEMENTS OF ADJUSTABLE RATE DESIGNS

Change period.   With an adjustable rate mortgage, regulated lenders must disclose the time period between rate changes. This can vary from every six months to every five years. In practice, the standard has become one year for about 80% of the ARMs originated.

Index.   One of the protections for borrowers with an ARM is that the rate change must be tied to a regulator-approved index, one not under the control of the lender. The rate for the borrower must follow that indicated by the index, which must be disclosed in the repayment clause of the note. A number of approved indexes are in use, including:

1. Federal Home Loan Bank's average mortgage rate on previously occupied houses.*

2. Federal Home Loan Bank's average mortgage rate on new homes.*

*A national average of rates charged by insured savings associations for the previous month as published by the FHLBB.

3. Average Cost of Funds—FSLIC-insured institutions—all districts.

4. One-year rate on U.S. Treasury securities

5. Three-year rate on U.S. Treasury securities.

6. Five-year rate on U.S. Treasury securities.

Popularity of indexes varies a bit. For example, in California, it is the Cost of Funds for that region. The secondary market that follows Fannie Mae uses their preference for U.S. Treasury securities as indexes. Currently they are using a one-year Treasury security, weekly average, adjusted to a constant maturity.

What is the best index? Borrowers are not often given a choice, but if so, the less volatile ones are better in the long run. Cost of funds moves rather slowly, as do the longer term Treasury securities. Usually, the index ties to the change period; for instance, for a one-year change period, the lender would use a one-year Treasury security.

Application of an index. Even though the use of an index to set interest rates at a change point offers some protection for the borrower against substantial increases, the lender is free to set the pattern of how the rate is applied. And this can cause some variations—two lenders using the same index may easily come up with quite different rates for the borrower. Three methods of index application are explained:

1. *Direct.* If the index selected reflects market rates, such as the FHLB's average rate for the previous month, the index itself may become the new rate. These rates are often rounded to the nearest quarter of a percent.

2. *Margin.* Probably the most common way of applying an index is to use it as a base, such as the U.S. Treasury security rate, and add a reasonable margin of, say, 2 percentage points. The margin remains fixed for the term of the loan but the index changes periodically.

3. *Movement.* Using the movement of an index offers a chance for greater variation. With this method, the lender offers an initial rate at nearly any level that can be justified, which may be higher than market at the time. Then the index rate is noted at origination and again at the point of rate change. Whatever the movement of the index has been during that period is added, or deducted, from the rate for the next period. The result can be, through using the same index as explained above with a margin added, substantially different rates for the borrower.

It should be noted that regulations require lenders to reduce rates should an index go down, but leave increases optional with the lender should the index increase.

Payment Caps. One of the causes of massive foreclosures in the early 1980s was attributed to mortgage payment increases, generated by ARMs, that pushed borrowers beyond their limits. To avoid a repeat of this problem, many lenders, as well as secondary market purchasers, have added limitations, or caps, on how much a payment can be changed at any one change period and over the life of the loan. Three caps are in common use:

1. Interest rate at adjustment period cannot be changed more than 1%, and in some plans, 2%.
2. Interest rate over the life of the loan cannot be changed more than 5%, in some cases 6%.
3. Payment amount cannot be increased more than 7½% at any one change period.

Caveats. While regulations call for full disclosure of how payments are to be calculated, the index used, and any caps that apply for all residential loans, commercial loans may not be so protected. Careful reading of any mortgage agreement is most important.

Payment caps may be handled in two substantially different ways. With some loans, the cap limits the payment amount but *not the amount owed*. For example, if the monthly payment is $1,000 and the payment cap is 7½ percent, the next period's payment cannot be greater than $1,075. However, if the applicable index should indicate, say, that a payment of $1,125 is due, the lender may accrue the additional $50 each month, adding it to the principal balance due. This procedure is called "negative amortization"—an addition to the principal balance rather than a reduction in it. There is nothing illegal in the practice, but some secondary market purchasers decline to purchase such loans.

Another often overlooked feature of caps as limiting factors is that the limit can also apply to the downside. Regulated lenders are required to reduce interest rates on adjustable rate loans if the index calls for such an adjustment. However, the lender may limit the reduction if it is clearly a part of the rate adjustment agreement.

One more caution—some commercial banks use their own prime rate of interest as an index, which is common for their normal lending practices. When the prime rate is applied, it means the bank does not consider that particular loan as subject to residential mortgage loan restrictions. The bank's prime rate is *not* a regulated rate, nor is it an approved index for residential loans. Each bank is free to set its own prime rate by its own judgment standards. The publicized prime rate found in many financial publications is most often a New York prime, and is generally followed by regional banks. But there is no requirement to do so.

Graduated Payment Plans

Several of the new mortgage designs are intended to help the new home buyer by permitting a reduction in the monthly payment amount during the early years of the mortgage term. The purpose is to qualify the borrower's income with a lower first-year payment. This provides easier qualification for more buyers, or possibly the acquisition of a larger house than might otherwise be justified. Several methods are used to accomplish this purpose, as discussed below.

Graduated Payment Mortgage (GPM).   The GPM design as introduced initially by the FHA offers an arbitrary reduction in the early monthly payment amounts so calculated as to allow precise percentage increases for the first few years. The early payments are normally insufficient to pay any portion of the principal and pay only a part of the interest due each month.

Periodically, the unpaid interest is added to the principal balance and earns additional interest. Since amortization of a loan is the periodic *reduction* of the principal balance, when the balance is *increased*, it is termed "negative amortization." The payment amounts on a GPM design are increased each year for a period of 5 or 10 years until they reach a level that fully amortizes the loan within its original term. It is this method that has gained popularity through the FHA Section 245 program identified as "GPM's" (Graduated Payment Mortgage). When traded in the secondary market, this mortgage plan is known by the acronym "jeep" (not "gipem" as originally proposed!).

The down payment for a GPM-type mortgage is increased in a general proportion to the reduction of the initial monthly payments. That is, the lower the initial monthly payment, the higher the down payment that is required. The reason is to prevent the periodic additions to principal from increasing the loan amount to a sum greater than the initial value of the property.

While the concept of a graduated payment mortgage has given assistance to many home buyers, it is flawed by the need for continued inflation to make it work perfectly. While it has lost some of its original luster, the plan remains available to qualified buyers. Variations on the graduated payment design have also lost support from lenders because of lower inflation rates. But this can change, so they are worth reviewing next.

Pledged Account Mortgage (PAM).   The same purpose as the GPM design is achieved with PAM but without the negative amortization feature. This is accomplished by depositing what would otherwise amount to the down payment in a savings account pledged as additional collateral to the lender. The additional collateral allows the lender to make nearly a 100% loan (based on the property value) and to pay off the seller. The pledged account (which belongs to the borrower but is pledged to the lender) is then used as a source of supplemental funds to help make the monthly payments. Each month during the early years, the borrower makes a payment that is less than needed to fully amortize the loan. And each month the lender withdraws a portion of the pledged savings account, adds the interest earned for the month, and applies this amount to the borrower's payment to achieve a constant-level, fully amortized payment.

Buy-Downs.   A variation of the graduated payment design that gained popularity in the declining housing market of 1982–83 is the "buy-down" mortgage. Builders found it to be an attractive financing package that helped encourage home sales. The purpose is the same as with the FHA-GPM plan or the PAM design: Offer the buyer a lower initial payment amount to make loan qualification easier. Instead of making an arbitrary reduction in the initial payment amounts, the buy-down plan ties the payment reduction into an interest rate calculation. Home sellers have long used loan commitments (promises that builders purchase from lenders to assure themselves of mortgage money at a competitive cost for their buyers), to provide more attractive sales packages. With the buy-down, the builder, or any other seller, pays an up-front fee for mortgage money so that a dramatic reduction can be made in the early years of repayment. The older procedure is to use the up-front fee to reduce an interest cost for the life of the loan.

An example of a typical buy-down design is one that offers a reduction in the first year's payment amount at the equivalent of a 3% reduction in the interest rate, a 2% reduction for the second year, and a 1% reduction for the third year. By the fourth year, the buyer's payment is calculated at the normal market rate from which the original buy-down was determined. Market jargon identifies this design as "3-2-1." Technically, the rate has not changed: the note itself reflects only the one initial rate of interest. It is the payment amounts that are listed in the note that reflect the reductions in the effective interest rate. What the seller does is pay a portion of the interest cost in the early years; the seller may, or may not, add this cost to the price of the home.

Shorter Term Mortgages

The 30-year term for a mortgage loan has become so widely accepted that many have considered it an optimum time period. Enthusiasm for minimal down payments and monthly payments hit a peak a few years ago when government housing experts began pushing the 40-year mortgage term. The longer term saves very little. For example, in the payment chart below, the difference between a 30-year and a 40-year term payment amounts to $20.30 per month. The $1,028.63 payment is reduced to $1,008.33, and requires the payment for 10 years longer!

What has been overlooked is the effect of reducing, rather than increasing, the term of the loan. The results in total savings on interest costs are spectacular.

Example

For a $100,000 loan at 12% interest, the following table compares repayment costs over the full term of the loan.

Term	Monthly Payment	Months Paid	Total Cost	Interest Cost
40-year	1,008.33	480	483,998	383,998
30-year	1,028.63	360	370,307	270,307
20-year	1,101.12	240	264,269	164,269
15-year	1,200.22	180	216,040	116,040
10-year	1,434.81	120	172,177	72,177

What frightens many borrowers is the idea that shortening the term of a loan substantially increases the monthly payment. For instance, doesn't cutting a 30-year term loan to 15 years just about double the monthly payment? Not at all. Take a closer look at the chart above and compare the monthly payment amounts. The difference between payments on a 30-year and a 15-year loan amounts to $171.59, or an increase of 17% to cut the term in half.

The idea of paying more towards the reduction of principal and less to interest costs sometimes brings comments like, "—interest is tax-deductible and I would lose some of my write-off." But where is the advantage in paying a greater amount simply to be able to recover only 15% or 28% of the payment in a tax saving?

There are several other ways that can be used to expedite a loan pay-off other than committing to a shorter term. These are Growing Equity Mortgages (GEM) and the use of biweekly payments as explained further.

Growing Equity Mortgage. The plan is sometimes called a Graduated Equity Mortgage and offers some variations in its calculations. One popular design is to write the mortgage as if it were a 30-year term. Then each successive year the payment amount is increased by a fixed percent, say 4%. All increases are applied directly to a reduction of the principal balance. The result is a pay-off of the loan in 12 to 15 years (depending on the interest rate) instead of the initial 30-year term.

Biweekly Payment Plan. Some people are paid every other week and may prefer to make their mortgage payments at that interval. If the every other week payment amount is set at just half the monthly payment, the result is one additional monthly payment each year—26 biweekly payments instead of 12 monthly payments. Again, the result is a much quicker pay-off of the principal balance resulting from the extra month's payment each year.

A Negative View on Shorter Term Loans.   In economic terms consideration should be given to the opportunity cost of a faster loan pay-off. What this means is that the money given to accelerate loan repayment could be used for other investment that would earn a return. Therefore, that opportunity for additional return is lost when the money is used to pay off an existing loan prematurely or at a faster pace than necessary. It is an offset to the amount of interest saved.

Shared Mortgages

Two kinds of mortgages involve a shared position in the transaction, but they differ substantially.

Shared Appreciation Mortgage.   The shared appreciation mortgage offers some attractions in periods of high interest rates and continuing high inflation. What the plan does is to grant the lender a share of the property's appreciation in value as a portion of the interest, called "contingent interest." The lender accepts a lower interest rate plus a portion of the appreciation but acquires no ownership interest in the property.

For example, if market rates are at a 15% level, the lender could offer to make a loan at 10% and take one-third of any appreciation in property value over, say, the next 10 years. If the property is sold sooner, the lender is entitled to one-third of the appreciation at the time of sale. If the owner does not sell, the loan agreement could call for an appraisal at the end of 10 years. Based on the appraised value, the lender could then claim one-third of any net increase (additions to property not included). Payment to the lender could be made in a lump sum cash payment, or it could be added to the loan balance and a new note written.

Shared Equity Mortgage.   A shared equity transaction grants two or more parties an ownership position in the property and dual liability for the mortgage if there is one. The purpose would be to assist someone in the acquisition of a property. An example could be an employer joining with an employee to buy a house in a remote, or a high-cost, area to assist in a job transfer. Normally, the employee is given an option to buy out the employer's portion within a limited number of years. Or, in case of a transfer, the employer could purchase the entire property at the appraised value.

Junior Mortgages

A mortgage is a pledge of property as security for a loan. It may grant a conditional title to the property, or it may be a lien on the property, to secure a debt, obligation, or duty. There can be more than one mortgage claim against the same property as long as state laws or existing mortgage provisions do not prohibit it. Multiple mortgages present no real problems for a lender unless there is a default resulting in foreclosure. Then, under a foreclosure sale, the property may not produce enough money to pay off all the claims. Whatever the proceeds are from such a sale, distribution is made to the claimants in accordance with the priority of their claims, not in a pro rata share as might be found in a bankruptcy action. Thus, whoever holds the highest priority of claim is more likely to be fully covered.

Since its priority of claim represents a greater risk for the lender, a junior mortgage loan commands a higher interest rate, and probably a shorter term. A common limitation on the size of a junior mortgage would be that the sum of any prior mortgages plus the junior mortgage cannot exceed 80% of the property value. However, not all regulated lenders are authorized to make real estate loans secured by other than first mortgages.

While accurate statistics are not available, probably the largest group of holders of junior mortgages is made up of home sellers. They are mostly involuntary lenders, though, preferring cash rather than a note and second mortgage. When financing is handled by the seller of a property, some states permit a *vendor's lien* to be created, which is an implied lien even without a mortgage. Also, a mortgage accepted by a seller, regardless of lien priority, classes as a *purchase money mortgage* that carries a favored priority position in some states.

Another use of junior mortgages is as a method of obtaining additional cash from an investment property. A second, or junior, mortgage loan is taken on the investment property and the proceeds distributed to the owners. While this procedure certainly converts a portion of the property into cash, it also creates an additional obligation and a claim against the ownership. So long as property values increase, there may be no problem with this practice; but in the event of a decline, it could mean total loss for the owners.

Junior mortgages are openly traded to smaller investors and finance companies who usually require deep discounts to cover the added risk. There is also a market for second mortgages in the secondary market: Fannie Mae has several programs to purchase second mortgages. Fannie Mae will buy a second mortgage from a home seller *providing* the loan is originated and documented by a Fannie Mae approved seller/servicer. Fannie Mae will purchase such mortgages at no discount if the interest rate meets market yield requirements at the time the mortgage is sold.

Home Equity Revolving Loans

Pledging the equity in a home as security for an open line of credit gained impetus from the 1986 Tax Reform Act. This Act limited an individual taxpayer's interest deductions to that paid on mortgages secured by a first or second home. With this procedure, the borrower is granted an open line of credit, very much like a Visa or MasterCard, secured by a mortgage on the borrower's home. The mortgage remains in place so long as the credit line is in use. The limit on the credit extended can be as much as the difference between the sum of any existing mortgages and the value of the house.

Wrap-Around Mortgages

A wrap-around is a junior mortgage since there must be an existing one for it to "wrap around." There is a little confusion on this point because some banking regulations classify a wrap as a first mortgage, but *only if the lender involved also holds the existing first mortgage*. This is a banking rule and does not affect the claim status of the mortgage itself.

A wrap mortgage is a new mortgage that includes in its amount the balance due on any existing mortgage or mortgages. The wrap acknowledges the existence of prior mortgages but declines to accept liability for them so as to avoid a dual liability. Liability for payment of the existing mortgages remains with whoever held that responsibility before. To limit this liability as described, the buyer granting the wrap accepts the property "subject to" the existing mortgage, which acknowledges the existence but does not accept liability for anything other than payment on the wrap. The holder of the wrap is responsible for delivery of the money to cover any existing mortgages. So the grantor of the wrap (the buyer) makes payments to the holder of the wrap, who in turn makes payments to the existing mortgage holders.

In order for anyone to grant a mortgage, they must hold a valid title to the property being pledged. The same applies to a wrap mortgage—title passes to the buyer who is then able to grant the wrap-around mortgage as a junior lien.

What is the purpose of a wrap-around mortgage? It serves several purposes:

1. It is a way of obtaining additional financing while still holding the priority of an existing mortgage.

2. It presents an opportunity to utilize the value of a lower interest rate on an existing mortgage to make a more attractive sales package.

Comments on the Wrap. A wrap-around mortgage is a more complex instrument and should be prepared by a knowledgeable attorney. The buyer needs some protection to ensure that payments made on the wrap are properly passed on to the existing mortgage holder as may be required. One way to accomplish this is to make the payments to an escrow agent, who in turn makes payments to the existing mortgage holder and the balance to the wrap holder. Any escrowed funds allocated to taxes and insurance payments are usually handled by the first mortgage holder but should be acknowledged in the wrap instrument. The existing mortgage should be assumable, as are most FHA and VA loans and some commercial loans. If the existing loan is not assumable by its terms, permission will be needed from the lender. The wrap procedure does involve a transfer of interest in the property and can trigger a call of the existing loan unless the lender agrees to the transaction. A successful wrap is one that better serves both buyer and seller, including minimizing future problems.

The wrap procedure serves its purpose better when an older, lower interest rate can be used to enhance the sale of a property. It is best illustrated by an example.

Example

A commercial property is sold at a time when market interest rates for first mortgages are 12%:

Sale price	$150,000
Existing loan @ 9%	70,000
Equity	$ 80,000

To consummate the sale, seller agrees to accept:

Cash	$ 15,000
Wrap mortgage @ 11% (includes existing $70,000 mortgage PLUS $65,000 in new financing)	135,000
Consideration received	$150,000

The seller receives payments on the $135,000 wrap mortgage and makes payments on the $70,000 existing mortgage. Result: an 11% return on the $65,000 of new financing *plus* a 2% override on the existing $70,000 mortgage, thus a greater than 11% yield. The seller then has better control with the knowledge of how payments are made, as the seller would remain liable on the existing mortgage.

The wrap mortgage is an alternative to other methods of financing. A buyer might use an assumption of an existing mortgage and a new second mortgage to handle the financing, but the cash requirement might be greater and the interest rate on a second mortgage would be higher than for a wrap. If the wrap procedure fits a transaction, it is an effective tool that can benefit both buyer and seller.

While the example considers a seller-financed transaction as a wrap-around procedure, it is not so limited. Mortgage lenders undertake wrap mortgages when they are assured the existing mortgage is assumable. The incentive to do so is the greater yield that can be realized with an interest rate a bit higher than that on the existing mortgage, as illustrated in the example above. Another use of the wrap procedure by mortgage lenders is when additional money is advanced, as for an expansion, by the same lender holding the initial mortgage. A second mortgage could be used, but a wrap gives the lender a better tie to the priority lien position of the first mortgage.

Mortgage Foreclosures

The early 1980s brought a wave of property foreclosures unprecedented since the depression of the 1930s. There were many causes: a reversal of the economy in major areas of the country, a lack of concern for loan quality by both lenders and mortgage default insurers, and some mortgage designs that encouraged over-extension of a borrower's credit. The massive foreclosures that followed reacquainted many in the industry with the problems involved.

Lenders consider foreclosure a last resort procedure and generally prefer to work out problems with a troubled borrower before reaching foreclosure. A borrower who suffers setbacks should try to explain the problems to the lender. Some, but not all, lenders will try to renegotiate the terms to carry the loan through a slack period, retaining both a good loan and the borrower's good will.

Lender's Rights in Foreclosure

Contrary to a popular belief, a lender does not automatically acquire mortgaged property when it is posted for foreclosure. While the procedure varies among the states, the general practice is that such property must be sold at an auction—a sheriff's sale, a trustee's sale, or a court-administered sale. The auction is open to anyone with a bid to offer, and the highest bid takes the property. In practice, a foreclosure auction is not as open as it might be. For, instance, the lender's representatives may have the right to time the auction at their own convenience during the open auction hours. It is quite possible for other bidders to miss the precise time of sale. Further, the lender can offer its promissory note as consideration for the property; others must pay in cash. But all the lender is entitled to is recovery of its money, and that may come from any bidder at the auction.

Priority of Claimants

In a foreclosure auction, the proceeds from a property sale are distributed in accordance with state law. The priorities may vary somewhat but usually follow a similar pattern:

First: Administrative costs of the foreclosure proceedings, including attorneys' fees.

Second: Taxes, including property taxes and liens filed by the federal government.

Third: Secured claims, including mortgages, with priority based on time of filing or by contractual agreement.

Fourth: Unsecured claims.

Fifth: If any money remains after all rightful claimants have been satisfied, it belongs to the debtor.

In a foreclosure settlement, claimants are paid in full in order of their priority of claim. Once settled, the foreclosure action nullifies any further claims to that property.

Deficiency Claims

While a foreclosure action nullifies further claims against the property, it does not necessarily defeat an obligation to pay. If, for example, a lender forecloses on a loan of $500,000 and the property has declined in value to $400,000, the foreclosure action would result in a $100,000 loss to the lender. Depending on state laws, the lender may have a right to seek a deficiency judgment against the borrower to recover the $100,000 loss in foreclosure. In some states, like California, when the property securing a loan is a personal residence, the lender is not permitted to seek a deficiency judgment—the value of the property is all the lender can recover. Some interpret this as a "no personal liability" condition.

In cases where the mortgage lender negotiates a reduction in a loan balance, as might be arranged to avoid an undesireable foreclosure action, the reduction amounts to a *relief of debt*. Under IRS rules, any relief of debt is considered income to the debtor and is subject to income tax.

5

Property Taxes and Income Taxes

Two particular kinds of taxes are of special importance to the real estate investor.

- Property tax—sometimes called "ad valorem" tax, which is levied on the value of taxable property.
- Income tax—taxes on individuals and corporations based on the amount of eligible income.

The three major tax authorities—federal, state, and local—have in practice assigned the assessment of property taxes mostly to local authorities. The taxation of income, however, is dominated by the federal government, although most states and some municipalities do levy income taxes. This chapter begins with a review of property taxes, followed by an introduction to the complex world of federal income taxation.

Property Taxes

As a major source of revenue, property taxes support many local government programs and services. The range of these services includes governmental administration, fire and police departments, street construction and maintenance, airport improvements, public schools and libraries, parks, hospitals, flood control, and drainage. The state grants taxing authority to local districts and may participate in a portion of the revenues.

Determination of Property Taxes

Each authorized tax authority initiates three basic steps to determine the amount of taxes levied. First, the authority figures its budget requirements for the year. Second, the taxable property within the district is appraised. And third, the tax authority's needs are measured against the total value of property subject to tax, then allocated in such a manner that each parcel pays an equitable share. Following is a discussion of the three steps.

Budget Requirements. Each taxing authority prepares its own budget for the tax year. These authorities include counties, cities, towns, school boards, sanitation districts, hospital districts, flood control units, county road departments, and in some cases, the state. To determine the authority's needs, other revenue sources including sales taxes, federal revenue sharing, and business licenses and fees are calculated and then deducted from the budget requirements. The balance needed must come from property taxes.

Appraisal. Not all land within an authority's district is subject to tax, but whatever is must be appraised to determine its value. This work may be done by the county or state appraiser, or in some cases, by private appraisal companies under contract to the tax authority. While appraisal methods do vary among different authorities, the purpose is to establish a fair value for each parcel. To develop more equitable values, some states have taken steps to establish uniform procedures for their taxing authorities. These rules set appraisal standards and determine how assessments can be calculated. If property owners are not satisfied with their valuations, they have the right to challenge them and may find relief through special hearings or through the courts.

Assessment. With budget requirements known, and the total value of taxable property determined, it is a simple matter of mathematics to decide how much each parcel should be assessed. Practice varies as to how the assessment is determined—some districts use the appraised value as the assessed value; others use a percentage of the appraised value as the tax basis. For example, say the assessed value is set at 60% of the appraised value. In this case, a property appraised at $100,000 would be "assessed" at $60,000 for property tax purposes. Such a procedure obviously undervalues the property and would require a higher tax rate than if an appraised value were used as the tax basis.

However a tract of land is assessed, the assessment is the amount used to determine the tax rate. The tax rate is expressed as a percentage of the assessed value, usually in dollars or cents per a dollar amount of value, and is calculated to produce the income required. The tax rate itself can be quoted as a mill rate (one mill equals one-tenth of a cent—a 50-mill rate would be five cents tax on each dollar of assessed value). Or the rate could be expressed in dollars, or cents, per hundred dollars of assessed value.

Collection of Property Taxes

Property taxes carry a unique distinction as regards priority of claim on the land since they automatically become a specific lien* at the time a tax bill or ordinance is enacted. Payment of the tax releases the lien. Counties maintain separate records for property taxes as a matter of public record. This ensures recognition of any property tax liabilities whenever title is examined preparatory to a conveyance.

Failure to pay property taxes can result in a foreclosure and sale of the property at public auction. State laws control foreclosure procedures, but generally a property tax claim carries a very high priority, even exceeding that of a first mortgage claim that may have been recorded many years earlier. In some states, the maintenance assessments made by neighborhood associations may carry lien rights equivalent to a tax claim.

Property Tax Exemptions

In all tax districts, some land is exempt from property taxes. This includes government-owned property (states do not tax federal land and vice versa), parks, schools, churches, public roads, public hospitals, charitable organizations, military bases, and cemeteries.

Some communities offer a limited exemption from property taxes as an inducement to attract industry. The expectation is that jobs provided by the new business will be of greater benefit to the community than the limited loss of tax revenues. Other uses of tax exemptions include special exclusions extended to encourage needed development, such as low-cost housing. Senior citizens are sometimes granted benefits that limit their property tax increases. Another interesting example of tax limitation is found in California, where qualified elderly home owners are not required to pay property taxes when due, allowing them instead to accrue against the homestead for collection whenever it is sold.

---

*A specific lien is a claim against a designated parcel of land as contrasted to a general lien that is a claim against all assets owned by the target of the lien.

Special Assessments

The revenue from property taxes need not necessarily be used for the general welfare of all taxpayers. When the need arises for an improvement, such as pavement of a street, which is of special benefit to a limited area, it is possible to set up a special improvement district, or a special assessment district. In such a case, the cost of the improvement is borne by the taxpayers who directly benefit. This kind of assessment may be payable in full in one tax period, or possibly in a limited number of installments. Or the cost may be covered from the sale of a special bond issue secured by an assignment of the tax assessment revenues.

Tax Revenue Bonds

The state, and its locally authorized taxing districts, may raise money through the sale of bonds as long as they comply with state regulations and federal tax requirements. The purpose of such bond money is generally to build large facilities needed by communities, which cost more than can be paid using a single year's tax revenues. By means of borrowing money through the sale of a bond issue, the tax authority can build a hospital or a sewage treatment plant and spread its cost over the years needed to repay the bondholders. Repayment on the bonds is made through a pledge of anticipated revenue from the new facility, or from a tax assessment.

Bonds issued under state or municipal authority pay interest that is exempt from federal income taxes. This means investors can accept lower interest rates on "municipals" than other corporate-type bonds because the after-tax return may be better. It is this tax advantage that encouraged the use of "bond money" as a way to make lower-cost money available to home buyers. Recent federal tax law has placed limitations on the use of this kind of money by making a distinction between that used for private purposes and that for public purposes.

Deductibility of Property Taxes

Generally, property taxes are deductible for federal income tax purposes. Following are rules applicable in special situations.

Homeowner—Taxes are fully deductible (not limited to first and second home).

Business—Property taxes are fully deductible.

Mortgagee—A mortgagee cannot deduct property taxes paid for periods prior to acquiring title to the property as such payment is considered an additional loan. If paid after foreclosure, the payment represents an additional cost of the property.

Back Taxes Paid by the Buyer—A buyer is allowed no deduction for back taxes paid to close a transaction. The sum paid is added to the purchase price.

Federal Income Taxes

The enormous section of federal law covering income taxes is called the Internal Revenue Code. It consists of an accumulation of more than 70 years of laws, rules, and legal interpretations, which are constantly changing. For the real estate investor, a general knowledge of the major rules is important, together with an understanding of the basic language used in the tax world. The brief exposure to tax procedures in this text will not make anyone an expert, but it should serve to give the reader enough understanding to more effectively discuss questions with a tax counselor. Like many businesses, income taxation uses a specialized language. Such phrases as "basis of value," "realized selling price," "recovery period," and many others have a clear meaning in the Internal Revenue Code that are different from what might be found in a dictionary. For this reason, some emphasis is placed on definitions.

Another key element of the tax law is how "income" is determined. It is surprising to find that this has not changed so much in definition, but rather in its level of taxation, meaning the applicable tax rates. For instance, capital gain has always been a type of income subject to tax, but its level of taxation has been changed periodically. One of the more important changes in the Tax Reform Act of 1986 was the introduction of a new category of income called "passive income" that is treated differently than other kinds of income. Passive income, or loss, may be derived in a normal manner, but its use in determining the amount of tax due is subject to a number of restrictions.

How the Internal Revenue Service (IRS) interprets and implements the tax law is crucial in determining a taxpayer's liability. Tax law does not always clearly indicate how a particular tax provision should be applied, granting the IRS some leeway in its interpretations. So it becomes a combination of laws, IRS regulations, and court decisions that ultimately determine tax liability. To better explain income taxation, the text first examines business income and some problems a taxpayer has in determining proper expense deductions. This is followed by an explanation of the four kinds of income identified in the tax code and how each is treated for tax purposes. The next chapter, Chapter 6, explains depreciation deductions, and Chapter 7 examines special tax treatment accorded certain other real estate transactions.

Business Income

Real estate investors are often sole owners, or participants in the ownership, of an operating business organization. While the tax laws treat each type of organization differently as to reporting requirements and even levels of taxation (See Chapter 9), the determination of income that is subject to tax is fairly similar. Following is an examination of general business income.

Income

Business income has many sources, and the IRS identifies a few in the following general categories for reporting purposes:

1. Gross receipts less cost of goods sold and/or cost of operations, which includes labor costs.
2. Interest and dividends.
3. Rental and royalty income.
4. Net capital gain or loss.

DEDUCTIONS FROM INCOME

Most operating businesses handling income property deal with gross receipts and deductible costs of operations rather than the costs of goods sold. For this purpose, deductible expenses are defined by the IRS as "all ordinary and necessary" business expenses, including the following:

- Salaries and wages
- Management expenses
- Property taxes
- Repairs and maintenance
- Interest
- Insurance
- Utility costs
- Depreciation deductions

Capitalizing an Expense.   Under certain conditions, such as during a construction period, the taxpayer may elect, or be required, to "capitalize" an item that would otherwise be classed as an expense. What this means is that the expense, such as construction interest cost, must be added to the property value rather than deducted in the year the cost is incurred. The IRS identifies this procedure as an increase in the basis of value. Then the deduction for cost recovery is allowed to be taken over a period of years. There is a distinction between such deductions in their terminology. If the capitalized item is non-tangible, like interest, the recovery of the cost is "amortized" over a period of years. If the capitalized item consists of tangible property, such as a specific improvement, its recovery is taken as "depreciation" over a cost recovery time period.

Problem Areas of Deductions.   Most of the expense items listed above are easily identified and present no real problems for taxpayers. Such expenses as salaries, wages, taxes, and insurance costs are clearly defined. The more difficult expense deductions requiring definition are found in just three categories: (1) repairs and maintenance, (2) interest, and (3) depreciation, or cost recovery, deductions. Further discussion of the first two items follows while the more complex subject of depreciation will be considered in the next chapter.

Repairs and Maintenance

Repairs vs. Improvements

Tax law draws an important distinction as to what kind of work classifies as a repair and what is an improvement. The repair is deductible in the year it is made, while an improvement must be capitalized and its cost recovered over a period of years. The general rule that makes this distinction defines a repair as "something that maintains a property but does not increase its useful life," while an improvement is either an addition to the property (with a useful life of more than one year) or something that prolongs its useful life. It is a difficult rule to apply in practice. Faced with such a decision, the taxpayer is most likely to choose the classification that allows the greatest deduction. The IRS position is that they will examine the deduction on a case-by-case basis to determine whether or not it is justified.

Replacement vs. Maintenance

Another difficult distinction to make is whether or not an expenditure should be classed as a replacement item or as an ordinary maintenance cost. A replacement must be capitalized and depreciation taken over its proper recovery period, while maintenance is the same as a repair and thus deductible in the year it is made. If the replacement item is a complete unit, such as a refrigerator, rather than simply a maintenance part, it is more likely to be a capital expenditure and its cost should be recovered over a period of years. An example of a gray area for this kind of distinction would be the replacement of a major part: does it simply maintain the property without increasing its life, or does it prolong the useful life? If it is the latter, it must be treated as an addition to capital rather than a deduction.

Interest Expense

The Tax Reform Act of 1986 brought significant changes in the tax treatment of interest as a deduction. The following distinctions apply:

- Business interest is fully deductible.
- An individual's investment interest is deductible up to the amount of net investment income.
- Personal interest is deductible up to the cost plus improvements of a first or second home with certain limitations. (Chapter 8).
- Consumer interest is being phased out as deductible.

Thus, how the proceeds of a loan are used determines whether or not interest can be deducted as an expense.

Tracing the Use of a Loan. To justify a deduction, records must be kept that trace the use of all borrowed money. In some cases, it may be necessary to allocate interest costs as part deductible, and part nondeductible. Taxpayers must trace how they use a loan from the day they take it out until it's repaid. The tax deduction depends on how the loan is used each day. For example, a taxpayer borrows $10,000, puts it in a checking account, and later in the year uses it to invest in a limited partnership and to buy a car. The IRS considers this as generating three kinds of interest: (1) investment interest because of the checking account deductible only against investment income; (2) passive activity interest on the limited partnership deductible only against passive activity income; and (3) personal use interest for the car which is not deductible (subject to phase-out). Corporate debt is not affected by this rule.

Another complication comes from the "15-day rule." If the proceeds of a loan are not disbursed in the first 15 days after funding, the IRS bases deduction eligibility on the first purchase made from the account financed by borrowed funds. For example, a taxpayer borrows $1,000 with a stock investment in mind and puts the money into an account with other unborrowed money on May 1. On June 17 a check is written for $800 to buy a refrigerator for the home. On June 26 a check is written for $1,000 to make the stock purchase. Since the loan was not used in the first 15 days, the taxpayer can no longer designate its use (for tax purposes). The IRS considers $800 of the loan used for a nondeductible consumer purchase and only $200 eligible for deduction as investment interest.

Taxpayers should consider establishing separate bank accounts for each activity if borrowed money is involved.

Prepaid Interest.   In years past, an inducement to invest in real estate was that up to five years' interest paid in advance was allowed as a deduction in the current tax year. This is no longer permissible. The current rule is that the interest must be both due and paid within the tax year to qualify as a deduction.

Investment Interest.   The tax code treats investment interest differently from other kinds of interest. Investment interest is that paid on indebtedness used to purchase or carry property held for investment. This does not include interest paid on a personal residence or passive activity interest. (Passive activity is discussed later in this chapter.) Property "held for investment" includes that producing income defined as interest, dividends, annuities, or royalties, and any trade or business in which the taxpayer does not materially participate, so long as that activity is not treated as a passive activity. Also, property subject to a net lease is not treated as investment property because it is subject to the passive loss rules. (A net lease places responsibility for building and grounds maintenance and the payment of taxes and insurance on the tenant; this is more fully described in Chapter 14.)

Limitation under the 1986 Tax Reform Act is as follows:

> Investment interest expense is limited to net investment income for the tax year. In addition, the former $10,000 exemption was repealed (subject to phase-out). Amounts disallowed are carried forward indefinitely and are allowable against future net investment income.

Interest on Rollover Loans.   If an old loan, including interest cost, is settled with the proceeds of a new loan, what is the tax treatment for that portion representing interest? The IRS has the support of several court decisions in its contention that interest on the old loan, replaced by a new one, is not deductible because the previous loan interest has not been paid in cash or its equivalent. That is, the purported payment of interest is nothing more than a postponement of the taxpayer's interest obligation. A possible solution might be to pay the interest cost from another source—perhaps even to borrow from a different source—but this cannot be lumped together with a rollover of the loan if the interest is to be claimed as a deduction.

Accrued Interest. Interest that is not paid but added to the principal balance of a loan is not deductible. This handling of interest is sometimes found with both adjustable rate and graduated payment mortgage plans. In order to offer a borrower a lower initial payment amount, or perhaps to limit a payment amount, not all of the interest due is paid. Periodically, the lender adds the unpaid interest to the principal balance. This is also referred to as "negative amortization."

Loan Discount. To increase the yield on a loan, a lender will sometimes require the borrower to pay a discount in addition to whatever interest rate is agreed to. The discount is normally paid when a loan is closed, in cash or as a deduction from the loan proceeds. Since it is a cost of borrowed money, the same as interest cost, it is deemed deductible by the same rules that apply to interest. The discount is measured in points (one point is 1% of the loan amount). Some confusion occurs among those who consider all points as discount and thus eligible for deduction. However, this is not correct as there are other charges, such as origination fees and mortgage insurance premiums, also measured in points, that are costs of services and not tax deductible.

Types of Income for Tax Purposes

Previously, the IRS identified three basic kinds of income: (1) earned income resulting from the product of one's labor compensated for in salary or wages; (2) unearned income derived from rents, royalties, interest, and dividends—generally, the product of one's investments; and (3) capital gain.

These distinctions were significant in the payment of Social Security taxes—earned income being taxable, unearned and capital gain nontaxable for Social Security tax purposes. This is still generally true. The distinction once applied to a maximum tax: earned income having paid a maximum tax up to 50%, unearned income and capital gain, 70%, but has now been replaced by an "alternative minimum tax" briefly discussed in the next chapter.

The definitions of income have been expanded by the 1986 Tax Act with the addition of "portfolio income" and "passive activity income." The Tax Code now identifies four kinds of income: (1) active, (2) passive activity income, (3) portfolio income, and (4) capital gain. Further explanation of each kind follows.

Active Income

Also known as *earned income, active income* retains the same character as before—it is that earned by one's labor compensated for in salary, wages, commissions, fees, or bonuses. Active income is subject to tax at whatever graduated rates apply for that tax year.

Passive Activity Income

A new kind of income called *passive income* was introduced in the Tax Reform Act of 1986. For this class of income, passive-loss rules have been designed to limit write-offs to real economic losses. Giving separate definition to this kind of income directly affects those who invest in property primarily for tax benefits rather than for earnings from the property. The target of passive-loss rules is high-income investors who used accounting losses from unrelated activities to offset their earned income, thus reducing tax liabilities.

To prevent such accounting transfers, the Act disallows the deduction of passive activity losses and passive activity credits against other active sources of income. The rule has been phased in over five years. For property acquired on or before October 22, 1986, the disallowance was 35% of the losses for 1987; for 1988, 60%; for 1989, 80%; for 1990, 90%; and for 1991 and on, a total disallowance. Interests acquired after October 22, 1986 are not eligible for phase-in and are fully subject to the passive loss rules.

Losses may be carried forward indefinitely and applied against future passive income. However, carry-backs are not permitted. Any unrealized losses are allowed in full upon a taxable disposition of the activity.

Passive Activity. *Passive activity* means any activity involving a trade or business in which the taxpayer does not materially participate, or any engagement in rental activity. However, a number of exceptions and special rules apply.

Material Participation. Material participation is determined by an examination of the particular business as to what functions are typically considered operational, and then by making a decision as to whether or not the taxpayer is materially participating in those functions. The activity of a spouse is examined in terms of whether or not there is material participation.

IRS rules define *material participation* as spending more than 500 hours in the activity during the tax year. Or, if the taxpayer participates more than 100 hours, and not less than any other individual, it is considered material participation. Two additional tests are used that require a search of activity during prior years. It is material participation if one has done so for any 5 of the 10 years that precede the tax in question. Or, if the activity is personal service, such as law, engineering, or consulting, in which the taxpayer has materially participated in any three years preceding the year in question, the taxpayer is considered to be a material participant, and thus not engaged in a passive activity.

Passive Income Offset Only by Passive Losses. Income that is *not* classed as passive and thus not eligible for offsetting passive income is earned, or active, income and portfolio income. Portfolio income is generally considered to be unearned income including rents, royalties, interest, dividends, and other investment income more fully explained later in this section.

Limited Partners. A blanket classification is given to any interest held by a taxpayer as a limited partner and is automatically treated as passive income.

Real Estate Rental Activity. A special rule applies to real estate rental activity. Although such activity is generally deemed passive, there is a limited exception for a taxpayer who actively participates in the rental activity. An example would be owning and operating a motel or an apartment building. Such a taxpayer is not subject to the passive loss rules so long as the passive activity loss and the deduction equivalent of the passive activity tax credit does not exceed $25,000. The deduction equivalent of the passive activity tax credit for any taxable year is the amount that reduces the tax liability by an amount equal to that credit. Thus, the deduction depends on the taxpayer's tax bracket, as illustrated in the example below.

Example

A taxpayer's real estate activity produces no income, $18,000 of deductions, and $9,000 of tax credits. The taxpayer is in the 28% tax bracket and may claim the $18,000 in deductions. However, the taxpayer has only $7,000 of deduction equivalent available: $25,000 minus $18,000 equals $7,000. So the tax credit that can be claimed in that year amounts to 28% of $7,000, or $1,960.

If a taxpayer owns and operates more than one real estate rental property, the $25,000 offset allowance applies to the aggregate of deductions and credits. These must be allocated to each property on a pro rata basis, first against all losses, then against the credits.

The $25,000 exemption is phased out for higher income taxpayers. The $25,000 offset allowance is reduced by 50% (but not below zero) of the amount by which the adjusted gross income of the taxpayer exceeds $100,000 for the tax year (computed without regard to any passive activity losses).

Example

A taxpayer has an adjusted gross income of $130,000. The taxpayer's real estate rental loss of $25,000 must be reduced by $15,000 [50% × ($130,000 − $100,000)].

With this calculation, the taxpayer loses the benefit when adjusted gross income exceeds $150,000. An exception to this rule occurs whenever any portion of the passive activity credit is attributable to low-income housing or rehabilitation credit. If this is the case, then the phase-out does not begin until the taxpayer's adjusted gross income reaches $200,000. An additional special exemption applies to low-income housing: the housing credit, or rehabilitation credit, counts toward the $25,000 allowance whether or not the taxpayer actively participates.

Carry Forwards. While passive losses are generally disallowed, they are not lost indefinitely. Losses may be carried forward for deduction against future passive income. And the amount not eligible for deduction during the ownership period may be realized at time of disposition. The suspended deductions during the holding period may be used to reduce a capital gain in the year of sale. A loss realized in the disposition of a passive activity investment is *not* treated as a passive activity loss and is allowable as a deduction against other income. However, any suspended credits not used at the time of disposition are not allowed after the passive activity has been disposed of.

Portfolio Income

Essentially, portfolio income picks up a portion of what was formerly identified as unearned income and does *not* classify as passive income. It includes interest, dividends, rents, royalties and investment income that is not otherwise classified as passive activity income. It also includes the gain or loss from the disposition of any property producing such income. Expenses (other than interest) that are clearly and directly allocable to this kind of property must be applied to portfolio income.

Furthermore, any portfolio income of a taxpayer engaged in a passive activity must be separated from the passive gains or losses of the taxpayer. The purpose is to prevent a taxpayer from using passive losses to offset portfolio income. Allowing otherwise would permit those taxpayers with portfolio income an advantage not permitted those whose principal income is wages and salaries.

Example

A taxpayer holds a general partnership interest in a computer rental business that generates losses of $10,000. The taxpayer does not materially participate in the venture. The business also has $5,000 of portfolio income. The portfolio income may not be offset with the taxpayer's share of the rental losses.

Capital Gain Income

Profit realized in the sale, exchange, or other disposition of a capital asset is considered income to the taxpayer, and subject to income taxes. The tax on such a gain applies to both real and personal property. And the tax applies to property whether used for business purposes or for personal purposes. However, a *loss* in the disposition of any capital asset is deductible *only* if the property is used for business purposes. Thus, a loss in the sale of rental property is deductible, but a loss in the sale of a personal residence is not.

One of the most sweeping changes resulting from the 1986 Tax Act was the repeal of the preferred treatment previously granted long-term capital gain. For property disposed of prior to 1987, only 40% of a long-term gain ("long term" was measured then as an asset held for more than six months) was subject to income taxes. For property disposed of after 1986, any gain is treated as ordinary income regardless of how long the asset has been held. This means the gain is added in full to whatever other ordinary income the taxpayer may have that year and the total is subject to whatever tax rate may apply. There is no separate tax rate for capital gain.

As a result of this change, investors have no longer been given an incentive to convert ordinary income* into long-term capital gain because the tax liability is the same for both types of income. Since a large section of the tax code was written to make distinctions between long-term gain and ordinary income, this step did create some simplification.

What needs further explanation is the method used to determine capital gain. The applicable rules follow.

Determining Capital Gain

How a profit is determined on the disposition of an asset varies, but the only way that matters in terms of tax calculations is how the IRS defines it. A fairly common error among newcomers to this type of computation is to consider profit as the

---

*"Ordinary income" has been used to identify income other than capital gain—that subject to the tax tables.

difference between the sales price and what is owed on the property. The sales price is important, but the loan payoff has no bearing on this calculation.

To determine the amount of a gain, the taxpayer must first know and make use of just two figures: (1) the adjusted basis of value for the property and (2) the amount realized from the disposition of the asset. The gain or loss is simply the difference between the two figures. Exactly how the IRS defines these two items is the key to a correct result. First, consider the adjusted basis of value which is figured from the initial basis of value as follows.

Basis of Value

For tax purposes, the basis of value is determined by the method of acquisition. While most properties are purchased, with the purchase amount becoming the basis, not all properties are so acquired. The IRS recognizes many ways of acquiring property, seven of which are identified here to illustrate some of the differences.

Purchased Property. The basis of value for purchased property is the amount paid including cash, plus any acquired debt, and any other consideration given to purchase the property. Whether a loan is assumed, or a new loan obtained, makes no difference in regard to basis of value—so long as it is a part of the total consideration given for the property.

Property Purchased with Other Property. If a purchase consideration includes payment other than cash or a mortgage, such as a car, a diamond, or securities, the fair market value* of the property used to make the purchase is the value of the consideration. For example, a diamond acquired for $1,000, now worth $3,000, would represent a purchase amount of $3,000. Using other property as purchase consideration creates another tax situation. If the adjusted basis of value of the property offered as purchase consideration is less than its fair market value, the difference between its basis and fair market value becomes capital gain and subject to tax for the buyer. The reason is that conveyance of property as consideration is classed as disposition of that property. An example would be a buyer purchasing a $150,000 property with General Motors stock that had a market value of $150,000. Say the buyer had acquired the stock earlier at a cost of $120,000. Then the difference between the $120,000 basis of value and the $150,000 market value when conveyed as consideration, or $30,000, amounts to a capital gain subject to tax.

*Fair market value is the price at which property changes hands between a willing seller and a willing and capable buyer, when neither is forced to buy or sell, and both have reasonable knowledge of the relevant facts.

Property Exchanges. The tax code has a special section that offers certain tax benefits if like kind property is exchanged, rather than sold. The procedure is further described in Chapter 7. For real estate, "like kind" is broadly interpreted as any investment property. An example would be exchanging an office building for an apartment property. If the exchange qualifies, the basis of value is also exchanged. Thus, the basis of value of the property given up becomes the basis for the property acquired. So the basis of the previously owned property becomes the basis for the newly acquired property.

Inherited Property. If property is inherited, the basis of value generally becomes the market value as of the date of the grantor's death. If a Federal Estate Tax Return must be filed, the heir may elect to use a market value as of six months after the date of death.

Gift Property. The recipient of gift property assumes the donor's adjusted basis of value at the time of the gift. If the donor pays a gift tax on the property, the amount of the tax is added to the donor's basis and thus to the recipient's. However, the recipient's basis cannot be increased above the fair market value of the property at the time of the gift.

Property Purchased for Services Rendered. For property acquired in exchange for services rendered, the basis of value is the fair market value of the acquired property. Further, the fair market value of the acquired property becomes the value of the services rendered and is considered as ordinary income taxable to the recipient of the property.

Foreclosed Property. If a seller of real property holds a purchase money mortgage as a part of the consideration and is later forced to repossess the property, the basis of value is the sum of: (1) the amount of the unpaid obligation, plus (2) any recognized gain, plus (3) the cost of repossession. If the property to be repossessed is personal property, the market value becomes the basis of value because the seller's gain or loss occurs at the time of the repossession.

Adjustments to the Basis of Value

The basis of value as explained above is called the "unadjusted basis," the "original basis," or sometimes the "initial basis" of value. During a property holding period there are adjustments that may be needed. Property may be improved or added to, or it may be subject to depreciation or other reductions in value. These adjustments have nothing to do with the changes that may occur in the market value of a property. What counts are those adjustments that are permitted, or required to be made, by the tax laws. Each successive year a property is held, the basis of value for tax purposes may change and the newly established basis is called simply an "adjusted basis of value."

ADDITIONS TO THE BASIS

When a property is acquired, certain additions are allowable to the basis including any purchaser-paid commissions, legal fees to perfect or defend the title, and any title insurance costs paid by the buyer. Since additions to the basis ultimately reduce the amount of a capital gain upon disposition, it is important to include these permissible costs in the basis amount. It should be noted that a sales commission paid by a seller reduces the realized selling price, but not the basis of value.

During the holding period, any improvements to the property or replacements that are capitalized become additions to the basis of value. Also, additions or expansions may class as additions to the basis or may be treated as separate property with a new basis of value, depending on the nature of the change. If the addition is a parcel of land acquired at a different time, then it must be given a separate basis even though it may be contiguous to the existing property.

REDUCTIONS TO THE BASIS

Depreciation deductions must be taken as a reduction in the basis of value whether or not the deduction is taken by the taxpayer in that year. The kind of depreciation taken depends on the prevailing rules at the time the property was placed in service by the taxpayer. A reminder: depreciation deductions are not permitted for property used for personal purposes, such as a personal residence.

If a portion of the property is disposed of, whatever is realized from the disposition reduces the basis of value by that amount. Likewise, if the disposition is the granting of an easement, the basis must be reduced by the amount of any payment received.

If a property owner sustains a casualty, the loss is the difference between the property value immediately before and immediately after the casualty. If the property loss is insured, the basis must be reduced by the sum of the insurance proceeds received plus the amount of casualty loss deducted. However, the loss cannot exceed the adjusted basis at the time of the loss.

Realized Selling Price

The other key figure in the equation to determine capital gain is the realized selling price. *Realized selling price* is best defined as the total consideration received less certain permissible deductions. These are further explained as follows.

Consideration Received. The total consideration for the disposition of a capital asset is the sum of all the following items that may be received:

1. All cash received.
2. The fair market value of any property or services rendered.
3. Any liabilities of the seller assumed by the buyer:
    a. Liabilities that the property may be subject to such as property taxes.
    b. Liability on a mortgage loan assumed by a buyer.
    c. Any liability of the seller assumed by the buyer as a part of the transaction, even though not related to the property, whether or not the seller remains personally liable for the debt.

Permitted Selling Costs. The realized selling price is the total consideration less certain permissible deductions. These are essentially those costs incurred in the disposition of the property. Such costs include the sales commission, advertising, legal fees, any loan discount, and closing costs, as long as the item is paid by the seller.

Example of a Capital Gain Calculation

The following figures illustrate a hypothetical disposition of an asset for a sales price of $85,000, showing some typical changes in the basis of value over a limited holding period. The capital gain is the difference between the realized selling price and the adjusted basis of value.

Example

Sale price of asset		$85,000
Less: Sales commission		6,500
Realized selling price		$78,500
Initial basis of value		$56,000
Plus: Addition of storeroom	$8,400	
Replacement of fixture	6,800	
Additions to basis		15,200
Less: Depreciation deductions	$12,350	
Sale of an easement	1,800	
Reductions to basis		(14,150)
Adjusted basis of value		57,050
Capital gain		$21,450

6

Depreciation Deductions

For tax purposes, depreciation is an allowable deduction for owners of certain qualified assets. It is a method of allowing an investor to recover the cost of an asset over a period of years. Depreciation deductions are calculated as a percentage of the asset's basis of value.

For many years the tax law applicable to depreciation of both real and personal property remained relatively unchanged, allowing business to plan ahead with some assurance of the tax consequences. Even so, the previous tax laws were subject to some misinterpretation by taxpayers since they were expected to make their own determination of several key measures, including (1) the length of time over which a property could be depreciated (useful life); (2) the amount of salvage value for a property at the end of its useful life; and (3) the option to select from several different methods of taking depreciation deductions.

A major change in tax accounting for capital expenditures was introduced by the Economic Recovery Tax Act of 1981. This Act abolished some of the older procedures, replacing them with a new method identified as the Accelerated Cost Recovery System (ACRS), and simplified the calculation procedure. The new method substantially increased the rate of recovery, and thus increased the amount of deductions available for capital expenditures. The Act did this in two ways: (1) replacing the "useful life" concept with a series of shorter recovery periods and (2) offering accelerated percentage tables for calculation that allowed greater deductions in the early years of ownership.

The availability of these increased deductions attracted into real estate many investors seeking primarily tax benefits rather than returns from the operation of the property. The real estate industry responded with a resounding building boom through the early 1980s. Congress reacted in a series of revisions that require careful attention to the time a property is placed in service to determine which tax law applies.

In the 1981 Tax Act, real property, whether commercial or residential, was granted a cost recovery period of 15 years. Later changes increased the recovery period to 18 years for property placed in service after March 15, 1984 and to 19 years for property placed in service after May 8, 1985. The 1986 Tax Reform Act established still another set of recovery periods for property placed in service after December 31, 1986, as more fully described later.

Property Eligible For Depreciation

A taxpayer may claim depreciation deductions for both real and personal property so long as it meets the following qualifications:

1. It must be used in business or held for the production of income.

2. It must have a limited and determinable useful life longer than one year. Thus, land is not eligible for depreciation since it does not have a limited and determinable life.

3. It must be something that wears out, decays, gets used up, becomes obsolete, or loses value from natural causes.

If a property is used partly for business and partly for personal purposes, depreciation deductions are permitted, but must be allocated to only that portion used for business purposes. No personal usage property is eligible for this deduction. Also, if depreciable property is owned for a portion of the tax year, recovery is permitted for only that part of the year it is owned. Allocation of the time a property is in service for the taxpayer is incorporated in IRS Percentage Tables explained later in this chapter.

Depreciation is an allowable deduction only if claimed on the tax return. If an investor, for any reason, fails to take the deduction and allows the three-year period for amending a return to expire, the deduction is lost forever. Nevertheless, as explained in the previous chapter, in computing a gain or loss on the sale of an asset, the IRS requires a reduction in the basis of value by the amount of any qualified depreciation whether or not it is taken by the taxpayer as a deduction from income. Any reduction in the basis increases the amount of capital gain.

Explanation of Key Terms

By examining key words used in the tax language of depreciation, some insight can be provided as to previous practices, which may in fact still apply to presently held property. This information also shows how certain kinds of depreciation are calculated, and serves as an introduction to the most recent rules applying to the subject.

Basic Terminology

Basis of Value. The value of an asset eligible for depreciation deductions is its *basis of value.* This amount may, or may not, be what the asset is worth. How the IRS makes this determination is more fully explained in the previous chapter since it depends on how the asset is acquired. The basis of value used for depreciation calculations is the same as that used for capital gain determination. Depreciation deductions may not be taken in excess of the basis of value even though the property's market value may be much higher.

Adjusted Basis of Value. The value of property for tax purposes, after the inclusion of any applicable additions or reductions, is its *adjusted basis of value.* The taxpayer must use the adjusted basis of value at the time of property disposition as one determinant of the amount of capital gain (or loss).

Unadjusted Basis of Value. Another term having the same meaning as initial basis of value is identified by the IRS as the *unadjusted basis.* This is how the IRS designates the property value used in conjunction with the Depreciation Percentage Tables. The applicable percentage rate given in these tables is multiplied times the unadjusted basis (that is, it is not reduced by any previous depreciation deductions) to determine the amount of that year's deduction.

Salvage Value. The estimated value of an asset, at the end of its useful life to the taxpayer, is called *salvage value.* It is now an obsolete term in that it no longer applies to property acquired after 1980. For properties acquired prior to that time, the amount of eligible depreciation was limited to the difference between the basis of value and the salvage value. Salvage value is no longer used as a reduction in what a taxpayer may recover in depreciation of a capital asset.

Useful Life. An estimate of how long the depreciable property is expected to be useful in the taxpayer's trade or business is its useful life. Prior to 1981 this was the span of time over which depreciation deductions could be taken. Note that the definition does not limit useful life to how long the property will last but to how long it is "expected to be useful." It was not a clear limitation and has been replaced with prescribed mandatory *cost recovery periods*.

Cost Recovery Period.   This constitutes the time span over which eligible property can be depreciated, as set out by the Tax Act of 1981 and subsequent revisions. Separate series of cost recovery classes apply to real property and to personal property, as more fully detailed later.

Placed in Service.   The cost recovery period begins with the time a property is *placed in service*. This may be different from the time of acquisition.

Recapture.   A term used in several different sections of the Tax Code, *recapture* generally applies to income that has previously escaped taxation and then later becomes subject to a recovery of the tax payment if a gain is realized in the property disposition. As used in connection with depreciation deductions, "re-capture" applied to certain properties where accelerated depreciation rates were used. Any deductions claimed in excess of straight line rates were classed as *subject to recapture*. This meant that previous deductions taken subject to re-capture must be reported at the time of property disposition as additional ordinary income, rather than allowed as lower-taxed capital gain. Since the 1986 Tax Act eliminated the special treatment of capital gain, recapture has lost its purpose, except for property depreciated under prior rules.

Anti-Churning Rules.   Earlier rules designed to prevent an owner from trans-ferring ownership of property to another family member in order to qualify a particular property for larger depreciation deductions have not been repealed. However, these rules serve no useful purpose with regard to property acquired under the 1986 requirements. The newer rules result in much slower write-offs than the original ACRS rules, thus offering no incentive to "churn" the own-ership. Nevertheless, the rules remain in place and prevent a taxpayer owning real estate prior to 1981 from qualifying for the modified ACRS rules by engaging in a post-1986 churning transaction.

Methods of Calculating Depreciation

For many years the IRS had no fixed requirements on how depreciation must be calculated as long as it was reasonable and consistently applied. Over the years, four methods became more commonly used and influence the way present depreciation deductions are calculated. Following is an explanation of each.

Straight-Line. This method offers a constant level amount for each year of the allowable recovery period. The straight-line rate is that percentage of the asset value that may be claimed as a deduction each year. For example, if the allowable period is five years, the straight-line rate is 20% (100% divided by 5 years equals 20%). If the basis of value of an asset is $10,000, the amount depreciated each year is .20 times $10,000, or $2,000. Later rules have modified straight-line procedures to accommodate the half-month convention that applies to real property (half-year convention for personal property). This is accomplished by mandating the use of specially prepared IRS Percentage Tables.

Component. The component method is an interesting variation of the composite straight-line calculation. Its use has been prohibited since 1981, but may still be found in accounting systems for property owned prior to 1981. Instead of considering an entire building as a single unit for depreciation (the composite method), the component method dissects the building into its principal parts. Such parts as the roof, heating and air conditioning equipment, and the electrical and plumbing systems have much shorter useful lives than the walls, floors, and foundation. By setting up more suitable useful lives for each part and applying appropriate straight-line rates for each, the taxpayer achieves substantially larger deductions each year.

Declining Balance. This was the most popular method of taking accelerated depreciation deductions prior to 1981, since it allowed greater deductions in the early years of ownership. The concept has been included in certain percentage tables since the Tax Act of 1981. The calculation begins with an acceptable straight-line rate. The rate is then "accelerated" by an amount such as 150%, 175%, or 200% (the latter called *double declining balance*). Then the accelerated percentage is multiplied times the adjusted basis of value, meaning that basis resulting from the deduction of previous year's depreciation. Thus, each year the percentage rate is applied to a lesser basis of value, resulting in a smaller deduction.

Example

To compute the accelerated rate:

Straight line rate	4%
at 150% acceleration	× 1.50
Accelerated rate	6%

To apply accelerated rate:

Asset initial basis of value	$90,000
$90,000 × .06 (1st year's deduct)	5,400
Adjusted basis for 2nd year	$84,600

$84,600 × .06 (2nd year's deduct)	5,076
Adjusted basis for 3rd year	$79,524
$79,524 × .06 (3rd year's deduct)	4,771
Adjusted basis for 4th year	$74,753
$74,753 × .06 (4th year's deduct)	4,485

and continued in the same manner for each succeeding year.

It is possible with the declining balance method to reach the end of the asset's cost recovery time period without recovering the full amount of allowable depreciation. In such a case, the taxpayer may shift to a straight-line method at the appropriate point in order to obtain the full amount of recovery allowed. The proper shift to a straight-line basis is incorporated in the IRS Percentage Tables.

MODIFIED ACCELERATED COST RECOVERY SYSTEM

The Tax Reform Act of 1986 provided a modified accelerated cost recovery system (MACRS) that applies to all tangible property placed in service after December 31, 1986. MACRS altered the rules for calculating depreciation deductions from the prior accelerated cost recovery system (ACRS). MACRS offered new definitions for six classes of personal property and two classes of real property and changed several time periods for calculating the recovery amounts. The older ACRS rules apply to property placed in service after 1980 and before 1987. Property placed in service prior to 1981 and property that does not otherwise qualify for either MACRS or ACRS, must be depreciated by other methods. While "other methods" are not specifically limited by the IRS, the most common ones would be straight-line or declining balance methods using the taxpayer's estimate of useful life including a deduction for salvage value if applicable. However, if property qualifies for either ACRS or MACRS, no other method can be used. The method used must be selected at the time the property is placed in service. Generally, any change in the method of depreciation requires IRS approval as it is a change in the taxpayer's method of accounting. No change is permitted if MACRS methods are applied.

Cost Recovery Explained

The Tax Act of 1981 introduced a new concept for taking depreciation called *cost recovery*, and identified it as the *Accelerated Cost Recovery System*, or ACRS. It allows a taxpayer to recover the entire basis of value of an asset over a period of years. But unlike the previous useful life method, the new concept established certain "cost recovery periods" creating a set number of years for each period. The different kinds of property were defined and assigned to specific *classes*, each with a specified cost recovery period. For example, a car used for business purposes is assigned to the five-year recovery class, meaning its cost recovery may be taken over a five-year period with the amount of deduction for each year figured from the applicable IRS Percentage Table. (Special limitations now apply to automobile depreciation.)

IRS Percentage Tables.   Since the Tax Act of 1981, the IRS has assisted taxpayers with the calculation of depreciation deductions by preparing a series of percentage tables. These tables list the proper percentage of an asset's basis of value that may be deducted each year. The percentage figures incorporate the half-month convention applicable to real property. For personal property, the tables incorporate both the half-year convention and the accelerated rates that are optional for a taxpayer. Examples of the tables are given later in this chapter.

Tax law treats depreciation for personal property quite differently than it does depreciation for real property. These distinctions are further explained next.

Cost Recovery for Real Property Assets

For property placed in service after 1986, the Tax Act of 1986 allocated real estate investments to two MACRS classes:

1. Residential rental property eligible for recovery over 27.5 years.
2. Nonresidential property eligible for recovery over 31.5 years.

Further, accelerated methods are no longer available, as all deductions must now be taken by the straight-line method using the mid-month convention.

The *mid-month convention* considers the property as placed in service at the middle of the month regardless of the actual date of the month it is placed in service. The mid-month convention also applies to the year of disposition. Its purpose is to simplify the counting of time in service during the first year and the last. Rather than count the days in order to allocate the time, the mid-month convention makes it possible for the time to be incorporated in the Percentage Table figures.

Residential property is defined in this section of the tax code as one whereby at least 80% of the property's gross rental income is derived from dwelling units. This does not include property rented to transients, such as hotels and motels, which are classed as nonresidential. The determination must be made *each year* and may alter the amount of depreciation allowable for that year.

Depreciation Deductions for Real Property

Tables 6–1 and 6–2 show the IRS Percentage Tables applying to real property placed in service after 1986.* To apply the table, the taxpayer selects the month that the property is placed in service. Then the taxpayer uses the vertical column beneath that month; for the first year in service, the percentage number is multiplied times the initial basis of property value. As can be seen, the percentage number already allows for the half-month convention. For the second year, and successive years, the tax payer should use the next number down the column in the proper order, multiplied each year times the unadjusted basis of value (same as the initial basis of value).

Example of Percentage Table Method

A taxpayer owns a $200,000 nonresidential building (not including land) placed in service during the third month of the tax year. Calculations for permissible depreciation deductions each year are (Percentage figures from Table 6-2):

1st year: $200,000 × .02513 = $5,026
2nd year: $200,000 × .03175 = $6,350
3rd year: $200,000 × .03175 = $6,350

The same calculation continues for each successive year of ownership using the appropriate percentage figure each year.

Alternative Depreciation System

Under certain conditions, an *Alternative Depreciation System* (ADS) must be used for real property. The ADS must be used to calculate that portion of depreciation treated as a tax preference for corporate and alternative minimum tax. And it must be used for property that is leased or otherwise used by a tax-exempt entity, if used outside the United States, or if it is financed with the proceeds of tax-exempt bonds. If such conditions apply, real estate depreciation must be figured using straight-line recovery over 40 years, with the mid-month convention, as detailed in the applicable IRS Percentage Tables (not illustrated). This rule applies to both residential and nonresidential real property.

*Complete Tables and further information can be found in IRS Publication 534, *Depreciation*.

TABLE 6-1
IRS Percentage Table for 27.5-Year Residential Real Property Straight-Line Percentages

If the Recovery Year Is:	And the Month in the First Recovery Year the Property Is Placed in Service Is: the Depreciation Rate Is:											
	1	2	3	4	5	6	7	8	9	10	11	12
1	3.485	3.182	2.879	2.576	2.273	1.970	1.667	1.364	1.061	0.758	0.455	0.152
2	3.636	3.636	3.636	3.636	3.636	3.636	3.636	3.636	3.636	3.636	3.636	3.636
3	3.636	3.636	3.636	3.636	3.636	3.636	3.636	3.636	3.636	3.636	3.636	3.636
4	3.636	3.636	3.636	3.636	3.636	3.636	3.636	3.636	3.636	3.636	3.636	3.636
5	3.636	3.636	3.636	3.636	3.636	3.636	3.636	3.636	3.636	3.636	3.636	3.636
6	3.636	3.636	3.636	3.636	3.636	3.636	3.636	3.636	3.636	3.636	3.636	3.636
7	3.636	3.636	3.636	3.636	3.636	3.636	3.636	3.636	3.636	3.636	3.636	3.636
8	3.636	3.636	3.636	3.636	3.636	3.636	3.636	3.636	3.636	3.636	3.636	3.636
9	3.636	3.636	3.636	3.636	3.636	3.636	3.636	3.636	3.636	3.636	3.636	3.636
10	3.637	3.637	3.637	3.637	3.637	3.637	3.636	3.636	3.636	3.636	3.636	3.636
11	3.636	3.636	3.636	3.636	3.636	3.636	3.637	3.637	3.637	3.637	3.637	3.637
12	3.637	3.637	3.637	3.637	3.637	3.637	3.636	3.636	3.636	3.636	3.636	3.636
13	3.636	3.636	3.636	3.636	3.636	3.636	3.637	3.637	3.637	3.637	3.637	3.637
14	3.637	3.637	3.637	3.637	3.637	3.637	3.636	3.636	3.636	3.636	3.636	3.636
15	3.636	3.636	3.636	3.636	3.636	3.636	3.637	3.637	3.637	3.637	3.637	3.637
16	3.637	3.637	3.637	3.637	3.637	3.637	3.636	3.636	3.636	3.636	3.636	3.636
17	3.636	3.636	3.636	3.636	3.636	3.636	3.637	3.637	3.637	3.637	3.637	3.637
18	3.637	3.637	3.637	3.637	3.637	3.637	3.636	3.636	3.636	3.636	3.636	3.636
19	3.636	3.636	3.636	3.636	3.636	3.636	3.637	3.637	3.637	3.637	3.637	3.637
20	3.637	3.637	3.637	3.637	3.637	3.637	3.636	3.636	3.636	3.636	3.636	3.636
21	3.636	3.636	3.636	3.636	3.636	3.636	3.637	3.637	3.637	3.637	3.637	3.637
22	3.637	3.637	3.637	3.637	3.637	3.637	3.636	3.636	3.636	3.636	3.636	3.636
23	3.636	3.636	3.636	3.636	3.636	3.636	3.637	3.637	3.637	3.637	3.637	3.637
24	3.637	3.637	3.637	3.637	3.637	3.637	3.636	3.636	3.636	3.636	3.636	3.636
25	3.636	3.636	3.636	3.636	3.636	3.636	3.637	3.637	3.637	3.637	3.637	3.637
26	3.637	3.637	3.637	3.637	3.637	3.637	3.636	3.636	3.636	3.636	3.636	3.636
27	3.636	3.636	3.636	3.636	3.636	3.636	3.637	3.637	3.637	3.637	3.637	3.637
28	1.970	2.273	2.576	2.879	3.182	3.485	3.636	3.636	3.636	3.636	3.636	3.636
29	0.000	0.000	0.000	0.000	0.000	0.000	0.152	0.455	0.758	1.061	1.364	1.667

IRS Percentage Table for 31.5-Year Non-Residential Real Property Straight-Line Percentages

If the Recovery Year Is:	And the Month in the First Recovery Year the Property Is Placed in Service Is: the Depreciation Rate Is:											
	1	2	3	4	5	6	7	8	9	10	11	12
1	3.042	2.778	2.513	2.249	1.984	1.720	1.455	1.190	0.926	0.661	0.397	0.132
2	3.175	3.175	3.175	3.175	3.175	3.175	3.175	3.175	3.175	3.175	3.175	3.175
3	3.175	3.175	3.175	3.175	3.175	3.175	3.175	3.175	3.175	3.175	3.175	3.175
4	3.175	3.175	3.175	3.175	3.175	3.175	3.175	3.175	3.175	3.175	3.175	3.175
5	3.175	3.175	3.175	3.175	3.175	3.175	3.175	3.175	3.175	3.175	3.175	3.175
6	3.175	3.175	3.175	3.175	3.175	3.175	3.175	3.175	3.175	3.175	3.175	3.175
7	3.175	3.175	3.175	3.175	3.175	3.175	3.175	3.175	3.175	3.175	3.175	3.175
8	3.175	3.174	3.175	3.174	3.175	3.174	3.175	3.175	3.175	3.175	3.175	3.175
9	3.174	3.175	3.174	3.175	3.174	3.175	3.174	3.175	3.175	3.175	3.175	3.175
10	3.175	3.174	3.175	3.174	3.175	3.174	3.175	3.174	3.175	3.174	3.175	3.174
11	3.174	3.175	3.174	3.175	3.174	3.175	3.174	3.175	3.174	3.175	3.174	3.175
12	3.175	3.174	3.175	3.174	3.175	3.174	3.175	3.174	3.175	3.174	3.175	3.174
13	3.174	3.175	3.174	3.175	3.174	3.175	3.174	3.175	3.174	3.175	3.174	3.175
14	3.175	3.174	3.175	3.174	3.175	3.174	3.175	3.174	3.175	3.174	3.175	3.174
15	3.174	3.175	3.174	3.175	3.174	3.175	3.174	3.175	3.174	3.175	3.174	3.175
16	3.175	3.174	3.175	3.174	3.175	3.174	3.175	3.174	3.175	3.174	3.175	3.174
17	3.174	3.175	3.174	3.175	3.174	3.175	3.174	3.175	3.174	3.175	3.174	3.175
18	3.175	3.174	3.175	3.174	3.175	3.174	3.175	3.174	3.175	3.174	3.175	3.174
19	3.174	3.175	3.174	3.175	3.174	3.175	3.174	3.175	3.174	3.175	3.174	3.175
20	3.175	3.174	3.175	3.174	3.175	3.174	3.175	3.174	3.175	3.174	3.175	3.174
21	3.174	3.175	3.174	3.175	3.174	3.175	3.174	3.175	3.174	3.175	3.174	3.175
22	3.175	3.174	3.175	3.174	3.175	3.174	3.175	3.174	3.175	3.174	3.175	3.174
23	3.174	3.175	3.174	3.175	3.174	3.175	3.174	3.175	3.174	3.175	3.174	3.175
24	3.175	3.174	3.175	3.174	3.175	3.174	3.175	3.174	3.175	3.174	3.175	3.174
25	3.174	3.175	3.174	3.175	3.174	3.175	3.174	3.175	3.174	3.175	3.174	3.175
26	3.175	3.174	3.175	3.174	3.175	3.174	3.175	3.174	3.175	3.174	3.175	3.174
27	3.174	3.175	3.174	3.175	3.174	3.175	3.174	3.175	3.174	3.175	3.174	3.175
28	3.175	3.174	3.175	3.174	3.175	3.174	3.175	3.174	3.175	3.174	3.175	3.174
29	3.174	3.175	3.174	3.175	3.174	3.175	3.174	3.175	3.174	3.175	3.174	3.175
30	3.175	3.174	3.175	3.174	3.175	3.174	3.175	3.174	3.175	3.174	3.175	3.174
31	3.174	3.175	3.174	3.175	3.174	3.175	3.174	3.175	3.174	3.175	3.174	3.175
32	1.720	1.984	2.249	2.513	2.778	3.042	3.175	3.174	3.175	3.174	3.175	3.174
33	0.000	0.000	0.000	0.000	0.000	0.000	0.132	0.397	0.661	0.926	1.190	1.455

TRANSITION RULE

The original ACRS rules continue to apply in the case of residential rental property and nonresidential realty constructed, reconstructed, or acquired under a written contract binding as of March 1, 1986 and placed in service by January 1, 1991.

EXCLUDED REAL ESTATE

Not all real estate is included in the two MACRS real property classes for calculation of depreciation. That is, the 27.5-year residential class and the 31.5-year nonresidential class do not list many important land improvements such as sidewalks, roads, parking lots, fences, landscaping, and others. Even though property may be considered real by state law, it may not be so classified for tax purposes. Such improvements depreciated in accordance with personal property rules would qualify for larger deductions. One example is that certain agricultural structures, such as silos, remain in the MACRS 7-year class. It is this kind of tax detail that the Congress easily changes in periodic "technical corrections" bills and an important reason why tax counseling is advocated.

TAX TREATMENT OF SEPARATE REAL PROPERTY

For real property, taxpayers are free to select different classes or recovery periods for each separate property regardless of time acquired. Separate property can be either new buildings on the same tract of land, or it can be the substantial rehabilitation of an existing building. A low-income housing improvement added to another class of building is eligible for tax treatment as low-income housing.

TAX TREATMENT OF BUILDING IMPROVEMENTS

If a taxpayer makes a substantial improvement to a building, it is treated as a *separate building*. An improvement is defined as "substantial" if (1) the amounts added to the capital account over a two-year period are at least 25% of the adjusted basis (disregarding depreciation and amortization adjustments), and (2) the improvement was made at least three years after the building was placed in service.

Allocation of Land Cost and Building Cost

When existing buildings are acquired, it is necessary to allocate the cost between nondepreciable land and the other depreciable assets. This is not a problem with new buildings as the land would be acquired separately and achieves its own basis from the method of acquisition.

As long as the allocation of property cost between land and building is fair and reasonable, the IRS can accept the taxpayer's determination. But it is prudent to obtain supporting evidence of how the allocation was made to prevent a tax audit reallocation of the cost that might reduce the depreciable portion of the asset. There are several methods that help support a land-building cost allocation:

1. The purchase contract may specify the prices for major components of the property. If the allocation is reasonable, is negotiated without undue pressure, and is not an "inside family" transaction, a solid justification is provided.

2. An appraisal by a professional (but not the taxpayer) gives good evidence of a proper allocation.

3. The taxpayer may use a property tax (ad valorem tax) assessment of the property. The tax appraisal usually distinguishes between the value of the land and the value of its improvements. From these values, a ratio between them can be obtained and applied to the acquisition cost of the property.

In the acquisition of an existing building, the purchaser is very likely to acquire some assets that can be classified as "personal property," which could include some of the land improvements. Such personal property assets must be assigned a separate cost recovery period as may be appropriate for each one. Under the 1986 Tax Act, personal property used for business purposes is eligible for accelerated cost recovery deductions or straight-line deductions as elected by the taxpayer. With either method, the deductions would be greater than that allowed for real property.

Cost Recovery for Personal Property Assets

Under prior ACRS law, most tangible personal property was assigned to either a three-year or a five-year class Special recovery classes were provided for 10-year property such as mobile homes, 15-year public utility property, and 15-year low-income housing. The Tax Reform Act of 1986 separates personal property into six classes, identified as MACRS. It retains the declining balance method of calculating deductions, thus allowing accelerated depreciation for these classes. There is also a straight-line calculation available for each of the six classes as an optional alternative.

Recovery Classes—Tangible Personal Property

The 1986 Tax Reform Act modifies the Accelerated Cost Recovery System to provide for 3-, 5-, 7-, 10-, 15-, and 20-year classes for tangible personal property. The 3-, 5-, 7-, and 10-year classes calculate cost recovery deductions with the 200% declining balance method, while the 15- and 20-year classes use the 150% declining balance method. The Percentage Tables for both methods switch to straight-line at the appropriate time so as to fully recover all available depreciation.

The six recovery classes are briefly outlined below with reference to an "ADR" guideline in years. This is derived from the Revenue Act of 1971, when Congress established some guidelines for determining depreciation amounts. It was implemented by the IRS publication of an Asset Depreciation Range (ADR). This document defined an upper time limit, a lower limit, and an average time for an assets's useful life, called an *Asset Guideline Period*. While there was no requirement for taxpayers to use the prescribed limits, the ADR became the basis for current rules defining classes of assets in the different cost recovery periods.

Following is a brief description of property contained in each of the six classes:

3-year 200%	Property with an ADR midpoint of 4 years or less, except for automobiles and light trucks.
5-year 200%	Property with an ADR midpoint of 4.5 to 9.5 years including automobiles and light trucks. This class also includes trailers and trailer-mounted containers, typewriters, computers, adding machines, copiers, and most construction equipment.
7-year 200%	Property with an ADR midpoint of 10 to 15.5 years, and all other property with no ADR midpoint or class. Examples are office furniture and fixtures, single-use agricultural buildings, and most farm equipment.
10-year 200%	Property with an ADR midpoint of 16 to 19.5 years. Example: machinery used to convert grain into flour.
15-year 150%	Property with an ADR midpoint of 20 to 24.5 years including depreciable land improvements such as roads, fences, and landscaping. Also includes industrial steam and electric

generating plants, pipelines, sewage treatment plants, and telephone distribution systems.

20-year 150% Property with an ADR midpoint of 25 years or more, other than real property with an ADR midpoint of 27.5 years or more. Includes sewer pipe and farm buildings.

Depreciation Deductions for Personal Property

It is important to note that, for tax purposes, several important assets, such as land improvements, that might otherwise classify as real property are included in the above listed classes for depreciation. Thus, it is possible to identify separate components of a real property investment and apply shorter lives that offer an increase in qualified deductions. For instance, a residential building that is assigned to a 27.5-year class may comprise separate components including roads that qualify for a 15-year class (and accelerated depreciation), and sewer pipe that lists in the 20-year class. Also, all personal property, such as office furniture, qualifies for the shorter term classes and accelerated depreciation if desireable.

To calculate depreciation deduction for the various classes of property that are used for business purposes, the IRS offers a series of Percentage Tables similar to those used for calculating real property depreciation. However, for personal property classes as listed above, the taxpayer may elect either accelerated or straight-line methods. Either one is permissible. But once a method is selected, the taxpayer may not switch to another method for that particular property during its life.

In determining deductions for real property, the IRS applies a half-month convention: for personal property the IRS applies either a *half-year* or a *mid-quarter* convention. The distinction is made as follows.

Half-Year Convention.   If property is acquired throughout the year, rather than through heavy purchases in the last quarter, the taxpayer may use the figures illustrated in Table 6–3, that include the half-year convention calculation. That is, no matter when the property is acquired or disposed of during the tax year, it is deemed to be acquired or disposed of at the midpoint of the year. For example, an asset purchased in the last month of the tax year is entitled to the same depreciation deduction for the first year as one acquired in the first month of the tax year. The same is true for the year of disposition. However, if purchases are concentrated in the last quarter, then the *40% Rule* applies.

40% Rule—Mid-Quarter Convention.   If more than 40% of the tangible personal property eligible for depreciation is placed in service during the last quarter of the year, a mid-quarter convention applies. If the convention applies, property acquisitions are grouped by the quarter they were acquired and depreciated accordingly. Acquisitions during the first quarter receive 10.5 months of depreciation; the second quarter, 7.5 months; the third quarter, 4.5 months; and the fourth quarter, 1.5 months. The mid-quarter convention also applies in the year of disposition: disposition in the first quarter receives 1.5 months of depreciation; the second quarter, 4.5 months; the third quarter, 7.5 months, and the fourth quarter, 10.5 months. (See IRS Publication 534 for Tables.)

TO CALCULATE DEPRECIATION DEDUCTIONS

As with real property, there are IRS prepared Percentage Tables to be used for calculating the proper deductions for personal property The steps needed are first to determine the proper MACRS recovery class (3-year, 5-year, etc.), then to locate the proper column in the Percentage Table. By working vertically downward, the proper percentage amount of deduction is indicated for each year of ownership. The percentage figure is multiplied times the *unadjusted basis of value*. This means times the initial basis, unchanged by previous depreciation deductions.

The following example illustrates an MACRS personal property calculation.

Example

A company acquires a computer for $25,000 and places it in service during the eighth month of the tax year. Calculate each year's deduction amount. (The "eighth month" is irrelevant for this example as the deduction amount is predetermined by the tax table as if the property is placed in service at the midpoint of the tax year). Since a computer is in the 5-year class of property, refer to that column in the Percentage Table (Table 6–3) and work downwards.

1st year:	$25,000 × .20	= $5,000
2nd year:	$25,000 × .32	= 8,000
3rd year:	$25,000 × .192	= 4,800
4th year:	$25,000 × .1152	= 2,880
5th year:	$25,000 × .1152	= 2,880
6th year:	$25,000 × .0576	= 1,440
Total depreciation deductions		$25,000

TABLE 6–3
IRS Percentage Table for Tangible Personal Property
MACRS Declining Balance Method: 200 or 150 Percent
(Half-year Convention Applies)

If the Recovery Year is:	and the Recovery Period Is:					
	3-year	5-year	7-year	10-year	15-year	20-year
	the Depreciation Rate Is:					
1	33.33	20.00	14.29	10.00	5.00	3.750
2	44.45	32.00	24.49	18.00	9.50	7.219
3	14.81	19.20	17.49	14.40	8.55	6.677
4	7.41	11.52*	12.49	11.52	7.70	6.177
5		11.52	8.93*	9.22	6.93	5.713
6		5.76	8.92	7.37	6.23	5.285
7			8.93	6.55*	5.90**	4.888
8			4.46	6.55	5.90	4.522**
9				6.56	5.91	4.462
10				6.55	5.90	4.461
11				3.28	5.91	4.462
12					5.90	4.461
13					5.91	4.462
14					5.90	4.461
15					5.91	4.462
16					2.95	4.461
17						4.462
18						4.461
19						4.462
20						4.461
21						2.231

*Switchover from 200% Declining Balance to Straight Line
**Switchover from 150% Declining Balance to Straight Line

STRAIGHT-LINE DEPRECIATION FOR MACRS CLASS PROPERTY

The 1986 Tax Act allows taxpayers to elect straight-line depreciation for one or more MACRS classes in the year of acquisition. The election applies to *all property in that class for that year* and is used throughout the life of the property. Table 6–4 shows the straight-line percentages to be multiplied times the original depreciation base (the unadjusted basis of value).

TABLE 6–4
Straight-line Percentage Table
For Tangible Personal Property
(Half-year Convention Applies)

ACRS CLASS	First Recovery Year	Middle Recovery Years	Year %	Last Recovery Year	Year %
3-year	16.667	2–3	33.333	4	16.667
5-year	10	2–5	20	6	10
7-year	7.14	2–7	14.29	8	7.14
10-year	5	2–10	10	11	5
15-year	3.333	2–15	6.667	16	3.333
20-year	2.5	2–20	5	21	2.5

PASSENGER AUTOMOBILE DEPRECIATION LIMITS*

Passenger automobiles used either full or part time for business purposes are subject to special limitations in eligible deductions. For passenger automobiles placed in service after 1986, the depreciation deduction, including the Section 179 deduction (the one-time option to expense certain depreciable assets up to $10,000 in the first year; see Chapter 7) may not exceed the following amounts:

First tax year	$2,560
Second tax year	$4,100
Third tax year	$2,450
Succeeding years	$1,475

If the car is used less than 100% in a trade or business, the deduction limits are reduced by the percentage of applicable business usage. For example, if the car is used 60% for business purposes during the first year of service, the $2,560 limit must be reduced to 60% of that amount, or $1,536.

---

*For additional information on passenger automobiles, see IRS Publication 917, *Business Use of a Car*.

7

Special Income Tax Rules

Chapters 5 and 6 examined basic tax procedures including Tax Code definitions of income, the calculation of a capital gain, and how depreciation is figured. This chapter explains other sections of the Tax Code that offer special treatment for certain kinds of transactions including some that provide tax savings. For instance, the 1986 Tax Act continued a deduction to encourage investors in the purchase of tangible personal property. Also, the Act allows tax credits for certain building rehabilitation expenses and for low-income housing. Further, the tax advantages of a property exchange have been retained as well as favorable treatment for installment sales, although new rules have been added. It is these special tax applications that are considered in this chapter.

Alternative Minimum Tax

The *Alternative Minimum Tax* is a very complex calculation designed to make sure that high-income taxpayers do not escape a share of the tax burden. Calculation of the tax is beyond the scope of this text and mentioned primarily to point out that it can affect an investor's tax liabilities. Under prior law, individuals were subject to an add-on minimum tax that was generally payable as an addition to the taxpayer's regular tax liability. A flat 20% was levied on alternative minimum taxable income in excess of the allowed exemption amount. Under the revised procedures, the alternative minimum taxable income is subject to a separate tax computation with its own MACRS, basis, gain or loss computations, and other special requirements. The taxpayer must now make two separate income calculations and pay whichever results in the higher tax.

The key difference between the two procedures is the disallowance of many tax preference items when calculating an alternative minimum taxable income. For example, accelerated depreciation is considered a preference item to the extent that it exceeds depreciation computed on a 40-year straight line basis. Also, passive losses are simply disallowed in the alternative tax computation. The rules on minimum tax are subject to frequent changes and require expert tax counseling to determine proper liability.

Option to Expense Certain Depreciable Business Assets

As a means of encouraging the purchase of additional equipment, the tax laws for a number of years have offered special incentives. The 1986 Tax Act enhanced this incentive by allowing a taxpayer to deduct up to $10,000 of the cost of eligible property in the year of acquisition. Eligible property is identified as "Section 179 property" by the IRS.

Eligibility for this deduction is limited to tangible personal property purchased for use in a business but *not* held for investment. Examples of qualifying property include machinery, office equipment, transportation equipment, refrigerators, individual air conditioning units, grocery counters, and more. Such property is eligible even if local law terms it a "fixture."

The cost of a qualified capital investment can be expensed up to the aggregate dollar limitation allowed in any one tax year. The taxpayer must specify the property on which the expense deduction is claimed and the portion of the cost of each item so claimed. The total deduction for all items in any one tax year cannot exceed $10,000.

The expense deduction can be claimed *only* in the first year of an asset's use. The deduction is taken instead of depreciation and reduces the asset's basis of value by the amount of the deduction. Depreciation is then taken on the newly adjusted basis of value.

There is a limit on this deduction for large purchasers. If a company buys more than $200,000 of eligible property during the year, the allowable deduction is reduced on a dollar-for-dollar basis for purchases in excess of $200,000.

The dollar limitation for each year applies to partnerships and to the partners. If an individual is involved in a partnership and a separate business, care must be taken to avoid a combined expense amount from exceeding the limits. The penalty could be permanent disallowance of the expense deduction.

Tax Credits

The most powerful tax incentive is the tax credit. It reduces the tax payment itself dollar-for-dollar. In a practical sense, a tax credit is something paid for by the government for the benefit of the taxpayer! It is a concept borrowed from several European countries and was first added to our tax law as an investment tax credit in 1962. Since then, the investment tax credit has been added to and then rescinded from the tax law several times, currently being disallowed. But the concept of tax credits has been used for a number of other purposes, such as encouraging political contributions, supporting energy conservation, and attracting investment into low-income housing.

Two kinds of tax credits are of particular interest to the real estate investor: (1) investment tax credit for rehabilitation and (2) low-income housing tax credits. The rehabilitation tax credit has been revised from prior law, while the low-income housing credit was first offered in 1987.

Investment Tax Credit for Rehabilitation

To encourage restoration of certain existing buildings, the 1986 Tax Act continued, although with modifications, the investment tax credit for rehabilitation introduced by the 1981 Tax Act. The credit is allowed for rehabilitation of older nonresidential buildings and certified historic structures.

Rehabilitation Defined.   To qualify for the tax credit, there must be *substantial* rehabilitation of the building. For this purpose, substantial is defined as an amount of expenditures during the current tax year, plus those made in the preceding year, exceeding the greater of the adjusted basis of value of the property, or $5,000. Rehabilitation expenditures do *not* include the costs of acquiring or enlarging a building.

A further requirement for qualification of the rehabilitation credit refers to the external walls and requires at least the following:

Fifty percent of such walls retained in place as external walls

Seventy-five percent of the external walls retained in place as either internal or external walls, *and*

Seventy-five percent of the building's internal structural framework retained in place.

Allowable Tax Credits.   The tax credit is permitted on a two-tier basis as follows:

	Tax Credit Percentage
Qualified rehabilitation for:	
Nonresidential buildings placed in service before 1936	10%
Certified historic structures, residential or nonresidential	20%

Additional Requirements. Additional requirements are as follows:

- Rehabilitation expenditures must be treated as new property with a separate tax basis of value.
- No expenditure is eligible for credit unless the taxpayer recovers the costs of rehabilitation using the straight-line method of depreciation.
- The basis of value for the property must be reduced by the full amount of the credit taken.

Low-Income Housing Tax Credits

Previous tax incentives to encourage construction of low-income housing included preferential depreciation rates, five-year amortization of rehabilitation expenses, and special treatment for construction period interest and taxes. These have been replaced with three new tax credits.

To qualify for low-income housing tax credits, the project must meet certain "set-aside" requirements (explained below) and is subject to a 15-year compliance period. The tax credit is allowed for each of 10 taxable years beginning with the year the building is placed in service. The credit is available on a per dwelling unit basis since a single building may have both units that qualify and those that do not.

Qualification of Building. To qualify for a low-income housing credit, the building may be part of a multiple building project that serves the function of providing residential rental units to the general public on a nontransient basis. *General public* means that tenants are not limited to members of a social organization or to employees of an employer who is providing the housing. *Nontransient* means generally that the basis of the initial lease term extends to six months or more.

The building must meet the minimum "set-aside" requirements during the time that the buildings are subject to the 15-year compliance rule.

Set-Aside Requirements. Residential rental projects providing low-income housing qualify for the credits only if they meet the following tests:

- Twenty percent or more of the aggregate residential rental units in a project are occupied by individuals with incomes of 50% or less of area median income, as adjusted for family size (the 20-50 test), *or*
- Forty percent or more of the aggregate residential rental units in a project are occupied by individuals with income of 60% or less of area median income, as adjusted for family size (the 40-60 test).

The minimum set-aside requirements must be met within 12 months of the date the project is placed in service.

Rent Restriction. The gross rent charged to a tenant cannot exceed 30% of the qualifying income level for the tenant's family size. Gross rent includes utilities paid by the tenant (other than telephone), but does not include payments under Section 8 or similar rental assistance payments received by the tenant.

Rehabilitation Expenditures. Rehabilitation expenditures are eligible for the tax credit provided they equal at least $2,000 per rental unit. The $2,000 figure is an average based on all qualifying expenditures in the building, rather than on a unit-by-unit determination. Rehabilitation expenditures are aggregated over a two-year period begining on the date the rehabilitation is commenced.

Federally Subsidized. Lesser credits are given to owners of buildings that operate with federal subsidies. Such subsidies include HUD Section 8, Section 221(d)3, and Section 236 programs, or the Farmers Home Administration Section 515 program.

Credits Allowed. The tax credits are claimed each year over a 10-year period, not all at once. The credits are determined each year by the U. S. Treasury so that over a 10-year period they will equal 70% of the basis of a new building if not federally subsidized. If the building is existing, or federally subsidized, the credit percentage is 30%.

It is possible for the allowable credits taken over the 10-year period to exceed the cost of the building. The basis of the building is *not* reduced by the credits taken.

The tax credit also applies to qualified rehabilitation expenditures as indicated in the following chart of buildings and credits allowed. The percentages are applied to the amount of qualified expenditures.

Type of Expenditure	Credit Allowed
	Adjusted periodically by U.S. Treasury based on Applicable Federal Rates (AFR), applied to:
New construction and rehabilitation expenditures not federally subsidized	70% of present value of "qualified basis"
New construction and rehabilitation expenditures federally subsidized	30% of present value of "qualified basis"
Acquisition costs for existing buildings	30% of present value of "qualified basis"

Qualified Basis. The qualified basis of a Low Income Housing (LIH) building is the *lesser* of:

1. Eligible basis $\times \dfrac{\text{LIH units in building}}{\text{All units in building}}$

OR

2. Eligible basis $\times \dfrac{\text{Total floor space in LIH units}}{\text{Total floor space in all units}}$

Other Requirements. All of the requirements must be satisfied over a compliance period of 15 years. The penalty is recapture of the tax credits. If all units are not used for low-income housing, or some of the tenants don't meet the low-income requirements, the credit is prorated. Special provisions deal with tax-exempt bonds and state volume limitations.

While low-income housing credits are subject to the passive activities' rule, meaning the credit may only be used to offset passive income, there is a special rule. If the credits are more than the tax on passive income, the excess can qualify for a $25,000 offset against other active income without the taxpayer actively participating in the management.

Tax-Deferred Exchange of Property

The tax law covering property exchanges applies to more than real estate transactions. For example, the Tax Code recognizes no taxable gain or loss when bonds are converted into stock under a conversion privilege, or when a life insurance contract is exchanged for an endowment or an annuity. Section 1031 of the Tax Code allows certain types of property to be exchanged for similar property, with any gain *deferred* until the property is sold. Since capital gain no longer offers a tax advantage, this method of deferring tax liability has become more important to an investor. Another inducement to considering the deferral advantages of a property exchange is the large "phantom" gain resulting from earlier methods of accelerated depreciation. Under these methods, greater depreciation deductions result in greater capital gain that becomes taxable on the sale of such property.

To be eligible for deferred tax treatment, the property exchanged must be of "like-kind." For a real estate investor, *like-kind* is broadly defined as any real property used for business purposes.

To defer tax on a property exchange, the basis of value of the property given up must become the basis of the property acquired. This means that the property acquired in a tax-deferred exchange also acquires the basis of the property given up, thus limiting depreciation deductions to the older basis amount. An investor considering such an exchange must determine whether or not it would be better to sell the property and pay the capital gain taxes and then purchase the desired property, as opposed to making an exchange. The purchase price would probably provide a higher basis of value for the newly acquired property and allow greater future depreciation deductions. The answer depends on the taxpayer's tax situation.

The following example illustrates the immediate tax consequences of a simple trade:

Example

Owner Smith has a building worth $100,000 with an adjusted basis of value of $25,000. Smith exchanges the building for another also worth $100,000. As a like-kind exchange, no gain is recognized and no tax is due. However, Smith's basis for the newly acquired building becomes the same as that given up, namely, $25,000. Smith pays no tax on the $75,000 gain ($100,000 realized less $25,000 basis equals $75,000 gain) and must transfer the $25,000 basis of the property given up to the newly acquired $100,000 property. Note that if the newly acquired property is later sold for, say, $200,000, the capital gain is the difference between that realized sales price and the $25,000 basis. Thus, the capital gain tax is *deferred*, not *excluded* in such a transaction.

In order to qualify for tax-deferred treatment, an exchange must meet certain requirements.

1. The property traded and the property received must both be *held by the taxpayer for business or investment purposes*. It cannot be property for personal use, such as a home or an automobile. It cannot be stock in trade or property held for sale in an inventory. Dealers who trade in land or sell lots as a business do not qualify for tax-deferred property exchange treatment. The property can be any kind used in the taxpayer's business for a productive purpose. It can be machinery, office equipment, cars, buildings, or land. It can be a leasehold for real estate if the leasehold has 30 years or more to run.

2. The properties traded must be of *like kind*, which depends on the *nature* of the property rather than its grade or quality. Real estate has an advantage in meeting the like-kind requirement, in that any real property held for business or investment purposes classes as like kind. However, an exchange of investment real estate for machinery would obviously not qualify as like kind.

3. If the trade is a combination of like kind and *unlike* property, as most are, any unlike property *received* is subject to capital gain tax in the year of the transaction. Unlike property is usually exchanged in order to equalize the equities involved.

4. To be eligible for tax deferral, the property exchange must occur between principals in the transaction. If one of the parties must purchase additional property to satisfy the trade, care must be exercised so that title is taken by the proper party, then conveyed to the other as a part of the transaction. To bypass this step in an effort to simplify the transaction can result in disqualification of the tax deferral.

Unlike Property

If a like-kind exchange includes unlike property to balance the trading of equities, a capital gain tax is due from the *recipient* of the unlike items. There are three kinds of unlike property identified in these transactions, which are described next.

Cash. If any cash is received in the transaction, it is taxable as unlike property. Instead of cash, the money might be used to purchase another piece of like-kind property for use in the trade, if this is agreeable.

Other Property. Unlike property, other than cash, is called *boot.* The expression derives from an old German word, *bute,* meaning exchange or to obtain as booty. An example of boot would be a car or a mobile home as a part of the consideration in a real estate exchange. Boot is taxable to the recipient. However, the grantor may also face a tax consequence in that the conveyance amounts to a disposition and may therefore be subject to a capital gain tax. This would be true if the market value of the boot at the time of the trade is greater than its adjusted basis of value. Such a difference amounts to a gain and is subject to tax. For example, say a mobile home used as boot in a real estate trade had been acquired for $3,000 and had a market value of $5,000 at the time of the trade. The difference of $2,000 would be treated as capital gain to the grantor of the mobile home.

Net Loan Relief. Another kind of unlike property in an exchange is the *relief of debt.* Relief of debt in this section of the tax code means the debt given up on the property exchanged. Say Owner Smith owes $50,000 on property conveyed to another in a property exchange. The conveyance itself is deemed to include relief of the debt for Smith. Such relief is subject to a capital gain tax *whether or not liability for the debt is assumed by the recipient of the property subject to the debt.*

A special rule applies to debt relief in exchanges where *both* properties have mortgage debts. The rule is that the two mortgages are "netted out," and the amount of unlike property "received" is the amount that the mortgage debt on the property given up *exceeds* the amount of the mortgage on the property received.

Transaction Costs. When unlike property is a part of the exchange, the recipient of such property is liable for capital gain taxes. However, the amount subject to tax is reduced by the amount of any transaction costs. Such expenses as brokerage commissions, taxes, filing fees, and escrow costs, if paid by the recipient of the unlike property, can reduce the amount of gain recognized by the amount of expenses paid.

Example of a Property Exchange

Owner A's Property	Item	Owner B's Property
$70,000	Market Value	$90,000
$45,000	Mortgage Debt	$55,000
$25,000	Equity	$35,000
$50,000	Adjusted Basis of Value	$60,000

In an exchange transaction, Owner A would have to add $10,000 to the conveyance of property to equalize the difference in equities ($35,000 less $25,000 equals $10,000). Since Owner B is exchanging a $55,000 mortgage for one of $45,000, Owner B also receives net loan relief of $10,000. Following is the tax result of the transaction in terms of *unlike property received*.

Owner A:
Pays in cash (or other)	$10,000	
Assumes additional debt	$10,000	
Owner A receives	*No unlike property*	

Owner B:
Receives in cash (or other)	$10,000	
Receives net loan relief	$10,000	
Owner B receives	$20,000	in *unlike property*

If a gain has been realized in the transaction, any unlike property received is subject to a capital gain tax. The amount of gain is the difference between the market value at the time of the transaction and the adjusted basis of value. For Owner A the gain would amount to $20,000 (the difference between the $70,000 market value and the $50,000 basis of value), but since no unlike property was received, there is nothing subject to tax. For Owner B, the amount of gain was $30,000 (the difference between the $90,000 market value and the $60,000 basis of value). Owner B received $20,000 in unlike property, so the entire amount is subject to a capital gain tax. Owner B may reduce the amount subject to tax by deducting all transaction costs paid by Owner B as described earlier in this chapter. The gain subject to tax is identified as "recognized gain" in this section of the Tax Code.

Involuntary Exchange

An involuntary exchange is also called an *involuntary conversion,* and occurs when property is converted into cash or other consideration through (1) condemnation by a governmental authority, (2) a natural disaster such as a fire where an insurance company pays the loss, or (3) any other conversion contrary to the wishes of the owner. If the proceeds from the conversion exceed the basis of value of the property lost, a gain results. Under these circumstances, the taxpayer can postpone liability for the capital gain tax by acquiring a replacement property before the end of the second year after the year in which the gain was realized. If the taxpayer elects to postpone the tax on the gain, then the basis of value for the replacement property must be reduced by the amount of the untaxed gain. If all the proceeds from an involuntary conversion are not used to acquire a replacement property—that is, if the replacement property costs less than the proceeds—then the unspent portion of the gain is subject to tax in the current year.

In order to qualify for a tax deferment, a replacement property must offer approximately the same function as the property it replaces. However, there is a helpful exception to this rule for real estate investors. When real property is held for the production of income or for investment, replacement property need only be expected to do the same. It is immaterial that the properties are unrelated in use or service. Thus, unimproved property would be an acceptable replacement for improved property since both are held for investment purposes.

Installment Sales Method

The Tax Code generally considers the receipt of a promissory note as income, just as if it were cash. If any taxes are due from the transaction, the amount due is expected to be paid in cash that same year. However, a special section of the Code details requirements that permit different treatment for a qualified installment sale.

The IRS defines an installment sale as one in which the taxpayer *receives at least one payment after the year of sale.* The tax treatment for the installment method applies only when the transaction results in a gain, whether or not the property sold was used for personal purposes or for business purposes. However, use of the installment method is limited for certain kinds of sales, such as those by dealers holding property in inventory and related party transfers.

Loss incurred on an installment sale of business assets cannot be spread over future years but must be deducted in the year of sale. A capital loss on the sale of property held for personal use is not deductible under any rule.

Under older rules, if an installment sale included receipt of 30% or more of the total consideration in the year of sale, the entire transaction would be subject to capital gain tax. This rule was later modified to permit a taxpayer to pay the capital gain tax on the amount actually received during the tax year. The 1986 Tax Act retained this general concept but added certain limitations if money is borrowed by pledging an installment note.

Reporting Gain on the Installment Method

When property is sold on the installment basis, the amount of gain subject to tax must be determined. This is done by figuring what percentage of the sales price is capital gain. Remember, capital gain is the difference between realized selling price and the adjusted basis of value. For example, if the seller realizes $100,000 in the sale of an asset with an adjusted basis of $60,000, the difference amounts to $40,000 of capital gain. The $40,000 gain represents 40% of the $100,000 sale. So for each payment received by the seller, 40% must be reported as capital gain. If the down payment amounts to $20,000, 40%, or $8,000, is capital gain. If the next installment is $10,000, 40%, or $4,000, is capital gain. Whatever is received each year is subject to a similar calculation of gain.

IRS Installment Sale Terminology

For an installment sale transaction, the IRS calls the capital gain percentage a *gross profit percentage*. It is calculated as a percentage of the total *contract price*. In general, the gross profit percentage, once determined, remains unchanged and is applied to each installment payment as it is received. Further explanation of the tax terminology follows:

1. *Selling Price.* The entire cost of the property to the buyer, including cash; the fair market value of other property conveyed to the seller; and any of the seller's debt the buyer pays or assumes. The selling price is not reduced by commissions or other selling expenses since this reduction is allowed against gross profit.

2. *Gross profit.* In this section of the tax code, the IRS uses the term *gross profit* to indicate a capital gain. The two terms mean the same since gross

profit is defined as "the selling price, less commissions and other selling expenses, less the adjusted basis of value for the property." It means the same as "the difference between realized selling price and the adjusted basis of value," which is the way capital gain has previously been defined.

3. *Contract price.* The amount the seller receives, not reduced by selling expenses. This constitutes the equity—the selling price less any mortgage debt the buyer assumes. If no debt exists, the contract price would then be the same as the selling price.

The above terminology is used in a formula as follows to illustrate how the gross profit percentage is figured:

$$\frac{\text{Gross profit}}{\text{Contract price}} = \text{Gross profit percentage}$$

The following examples use figures to show how the gross profit percentage is determined and then applied to each payment:

Example 1

A property is sold at a contract price of $2,000 and shows a gross profit of $500. What is the capital gain taxable on receipt of a down payment of $700?

$$\frac{500}{2,000} = .25 \times 700 = 175 \text{ (taxable gain)}$$

Example 2

A property is sold for $25,000 including a mortgage loan of $15,000 assumed by the buyer. The property had an adjusted basis of $20,000 at time of sale. What is the taxable gain on a $2,000 payment?

Gross profit: 25,000 − 20,000 = 5,000
Contract price: 25,000 − 15,000 = 10,000
Gross profit percentage: $\frac{5,000}{10,000} = .50$

Taxable gain on $2,000: .50 × 2,000 = 1,000

Example 3

A property is sold for $100,000 with an assumed mortgage of $45,000. The adjusted basis is $49,000, and sales costs amount to $5,000. The buyer pays $25,000 down and grants a second mortgage to the seller for $30,000, payable in six annual installments of $5,000 each plus 14% interest. What is the amount of taxable gain on the first installment payment with interest due for that year? To determine gross profit:

To determine gross profit:

Sale price		$100,000
Less: Adjusted basis	$49,000	
Sales costs	5,000	
		54,000
Gross profit		$ 46,000

To determine contract price:

Sale price	$100,000
Less: Mortgage assumed	45,000
Contract price	$ 55,000

Gross profit percentage: $\dfrac{46,000}{55,000} = .8364$

Taxable gain on first installment: .8364 × 5,000 = 4,182

Interest earned subject to tax: .14 × 30,000 = 4,200

The amount subject to ordinary income taxes for the year on this transaction totals $8,382 ($4,182 plus $4,200 equals $8,382).

Exceptions to Treatment as an Installment Sale

The Revenue Act of 1987 introduced some special rules for certain kinds of installment sale transactions in an effort to limit its use. The same Act also eliminated a complex calculation from the 1986 Tax Act called the "proportionate disallowance rule."

In general, the installment method of tax treatment is *not* available to dealers who sell from an inventory, such as building lots, as a normal method of transacting business. Also, a taxpayer does have the option of electing out of the installment method which would mean payment of the entire capital gain tax in the year of sale.

Borrowing Money on an Installment Note.   If an installment obligation is pledged as collateral for a loan, the proceeds of that loan are treated the same as a payment received. For example, if an installment note was pledged by the holder as collateral to obtain, say a $50,000 loan, the entire $50,000 would be treated as a payment received for calculation of tax. In such a case, subsequent payments received would be used to offset the tax paid on the proceeds of the loan. The intention is to tax cash as it is received, not to increase the total amount of tax due.

Interest on Deferred Tax Liability.   If the property sold on an installment contract was used in the taxpayer's trade or for the production of income at a sales price of more than $150,000, another rule applies. In such a case, in addition to the normal capital gain tax due on payments received each year, the taxpayer must pay further taxes calculated as interest on the balance of the capital gain remaining in the unpaid installments. In effect, what the rule says is that since you are not paying the tax on that deferred gain, you must pay interest on it. The interest rate applied for this purpose is the *Applicable Federal Rate*. (See further detail under "Imputed Interest" in the next section.) However, this interest need not be paid if installment obligations total less than $5 million at the end of the year and the sale is by a nondealer.

Additional Rules for Installment Sales

There are special rules for tax treatment of installment sales to related parties. For instance, a sale to a spouse, child, grandchild, parent, and certain related business organizations may be disallowed as an installment sale if the related party sells or otherwise disposes of the property before all payments have been made on the first sale. Special tax rules apply in these circumstances.

As regards installment sales treatment, prior law permitted no sales contingencies. Current law allows greater flexibility since it is possible to leave such questions as total sale price and terms of sale open, dependent upon later developments. Parties to the transaction may negotiate a deal utilizing such contingencies as future profits, cost of living escalators, and others. The key element is that whatever amount is received in payment on principal, the capital gain on that amount must be reported in that tax year. Adequate records must be maintained on the entire transaction when reporting an installment sale.

Recapture. Prior law had special rules that applied to recapture of depreciation deductions. At that time, the law was designed to tax that portion of a gain subject to recapture as ordinary income in the year of sale, rather than as a lower-taxed capital gain. The rule regarding recapture remains in effect. However, the tax rates for capital gain and ordinary income are the same after 1987, significantly reducing the effect. Nevertheless, depreciation recapture is still recognized in the year of disposition in the case of an installment sale.

IMPUTED INTEREST

In an installment sale, the seller might set an interest rate well below a market rate and increase the sales price to offset the lower interest charged. In this way, under prior law it would be possible to reduce the tax liability by making a larger portion of the sale qualify as capital gain and a lesser portion (the interest amount) treated as ordinary income. To offset this possibility, the IRS applied an *imputed interest rule*. If the taxpayer did not use a certain minimum interest rate for the installment note, the IRS could recalculate the transaction imputing its minimum required interest rates in determining tax liability. Since the 1986 Tax Act eliminated the special treatment for capital gain, the incentive to convert ordinary income into capital gain became meaningless. Nevertheless, the need to distinguish interest income from capital gain remains in effect. The reason is that interest as income (or as a tax deduction) requires definition in order to know how it should be treated. For instance, is it passive or portfolio income? Also, in the disposition of property, capital gains and losses are not subject to the same tax treatment as other income. (See Chapter 5.)

The continuing need to identify the interest portion of an installment sale has been clarified by the imputed interest law applicable to seller-financed transactions. Transactions that fall under these rules must apply interest rates known as *Applicable Federal Rates* (AFR) as determined periodically by the IRS.

Applicable Federal Rates (AFR).   In 1985, Congress established a system for the IRS to set minimum permissible interest rates and distinguished several different kinds of transactions for application of these rates. The published rates are for the purpose of determining tax liability and are not intended as a form of credit control or as required contract rates. These rates are determined in accordance with market conditions by the IRS and are released each month.*

For seller-financed transactions involving more than $2.8 million, the installment note must carry a rate equal to or higher than the AFR. Transactions of less than $2.8 million may carry the lesser of 9% or the AFR. For a sale-leaseback transaction involving seller financing, the rate must be 110% of the AFR. The rates are determined for four different compounding periods and for three loan terms as shown in Table 7–1.

Sale-and-Leaseback of Real Property

A sales transaction that can produce immediate benefits for both parties involves a property owner selling to an investor. The selling owner then leases the property back from the investor for continued occupancy. The sale and leaseback transaction offers an investor acquisition of an income-producing property while the former owner receives cash, or other consideration, and the continued use of the premises. The transaction can be considered a financing procedure inasmuch as it converts a fixed asset into cash.

---

*AFR rates are also available in the Vital Statistics Update of REALTOR NEWS, published by the National Association of Realtors.

TABLE 7–1
Example of Applicable Federal Rates
(As applied in May, 1988)

	Period for Compounding			
	Annual	*Semiannual*	*Quarterly*	*Monthly*
Short Term (less than 3 years)	7.22%	7.09%	7.03%	6.99%
Mid-Term (3 to 9 years)	8.34%	8.17%	8.09%	8.03%
Long Term (more than 9 years)	8.86%	8.67%	8.58%	8.52%

Sale-and-Leaseback in Leveraged Buy-Outs

A *leveraged buy-out* is one wherein the purchaser uses a high percentage of borrowed money to acquire a piece of property or a going business. A fairly common way of borrowing a portion of the money needed for acquisition is to pledge as collateral certain property yet to be acquired. This can be arranged through a letter of intent.

Another method of financing the acquisition of an operating company is through a sale and leaseback of its buildings and/or equipment. To accomplish this, the purchaser of the company arranges to sell certain company property at the time the transaction is to be closed. Simultaneously, the property is leased back to the company for continued use. In this way the purchaser of the company receives cash from the sale of certain property that can be used to pay for the company itself without losing the use of the property. This reduces the need for borrowing money.

What makes this possibility more interesting is when there is a substantial difference between the "book value" of property an older company owns (which would normally be the cost of acquisition years ago less all depreciation deductions) and the present higher market value. By offering to sell a company's land and buildings (or other tangible assets) to an investor at a fair market value, the people proposing a takeover may realize more cash than the target company's balance sheet shows for the value of that particular asset.

At-Risk Rules

Deductible losses generated by a taxpayer's business activities are generally limited and cannot exceed the amount the taxpayer has at risk in that particular activity. The amount at risk is determined at the close of the tax year. *At risk* is defined as the sum of three contributions by the taxpayer to the activity: (1) cash, (2) the adjusted basis of other property contributed, and (3) any amounts borrowed for use in the activity for which the taxpayer is personally liable.

Under prior law, real estate investments held a special exception from this rule that allowed mortgage debt to be treated as an at-risk contribution even though the taxpayer was not personally liable for it. The 1986 Tax Act extended the at-risk rules to include real estate investment losses for property placed in service after 1986, subject to certain exceptions.

The most important exception allows certain nonrecourse debt secured by real estate to be treated as an amount at risk. (Nonrecourse means the borrower is not liable for the obligation.) To be acceptable under this rule, the loan must be made by a party regularly and actively engaged in real estate lending. The loan may even be made by a related party provided the terms of the loan are reasonable and substantially the same as could be obtained from an unrelated lender. Except in unusual circumstances, seller financing of real property of any type would generally not be considered at risk.

If losses in the activity exceed the amount at risk, the excess losses are disallowed. However, disallowed losses under the at-risk rule are carried forward indefinitely for deduction in a succeeding tax year to the extent that the taxpayer increases the amount at risk in that activity.

Real Estate Reporting Requirements

The 1986 Tax Act added some tax reporting requirements that are important for real estate investors. The requirements apply to residential one-to-four–family houses, including condominiums and stock in a cooperative housing corporation.*

The gross proceeds from a sale or exchange of such property must be reported to the IRS by the filing of Form 1099-B after December 31 of the year of closing, but before February 28 of the following year. Responsibility for filing the information is placed on the Settlement Agent as may be listed in the HUD Uniform Settlement Statement. If no one is listed as the settlement agent, or that statement is not used, the duty to report falls to that person preparing the closing statement.

*Rules apply to 1987 tax year and will probably be expanded to include other types of property.

If no closing statement is prepared, then the duty falls to the buyer's attorney, then the seller's attorney, or if none, to the title or escrow company significantly involved in the disbursal of the gross proceeds. If no person is responsible for closing the transaction, then the duty falls to the mortgage lender, the seller's broker, the buyer's broker, or the buyer.

Penalties may be assessed for failure to comply.

8

Single Family Dwellings and Condominiums

One of the largest and most important investments that the average person makes is a house to live in. In past years, it was an acquisition of living accommodations and was expected to decline in value as it grew older and more outdated. In today's inflationary climate, a house is often purchased with a view to capitalizing on the growth in value. Indeed, it has been this speculative interest in housing that has helped sustain housing sales in spite of high interest rates. Nevertheless, a distinction needs to be made between property purchased as an investment and property purchased for the personal purpose of living accommodations.

The purchaser of a home wants a property that will meet the living requirements of an individual or a family. The size of the home, the number and arrangement of the rooms, and its proximity to schools, churches, shopping centers, and recreational facilities are all important.

The economic difference between investment property and residential property is crucial: residential properties are purchased with the buyer's *personal* income, which is unrelated to the property; investment properties are expected to produce income that will provide the principal source for repayment of a loan.

Those physical characteristics of a residential property that are so important to the prospective homeowner are of small concern to the investment purchaser. A home buyer might see some value in a high-cost amenity, e.g., a beautiful swimming pool; the investment buyer would look only to the amenity's contribution to the property's income.

This chapter considers the special tax treatment accorded a homeowner, which is quite different from the rules applying to rental houses. Certain deductions are permitted to the homeowner while living in the house. And if the personal residence is sold for a profit, there are some tax deferments and an exclusion that may be available. Also, some special tax rules apply to personal dwelling units that are rented for part of the time. Another major area of concern for homeowners is the distinctive nature of condominium ownership with its joint use and responsibility for common areas separated from the dwelling unit itself. It is these aspects of residential property that are examined next.

The Principal Residence

A taxpayer is permitted only one principal residence—the place where he or she lives. The tax status cannot be assigned by the taxpayer, such as claiming a vacation home as a principal residence. The portion of a multi-family residential unit that is owned and occupied by the taxpayer qualifies as a principal residence. The purchase of an accommodation in a retirement home does not qualify because no title passes.

Allowable Tax Deductions

A homeowner can deduct certain costs of the principal residence from ordinary income. These are:

1. *Interest*. Interest paid on mortgage debt during the taxable year.
2. *Taxes*. All property taxes applicable to the residence.
3. *Casualty losses*. Limited to the lesser of (1) the decrease in fair market value of the property resulting from the casualty or (2) the adjusted basis in property. The first $100 of loss is *not* deductible, and any insurance proceeds that are received must be used to reduce the amount of the loss. Further, personal casualty losses must be reduced by 10% of the taxpayer's adjusted gross income.

LIMITS ON INTEREST DEDUCTIONS

While the 1986 Tax Act retained almost all the benefits available to home ownership, limitations were placed on the deductibility of mortgage interest. One reason for these restrictions was the disallowance of other consumer interest deductions. Without such restrictions, Congress felt that taxpayers might substantially increase the use of residential debt for other purposes. Hence, mortgage interest eligible for deduction is now identified as *qualified residential interest*. The rules for deductibility apply to a first or second residence. And such debt must be secured by a security interest as required under local law on the taxpayer's principal or second residence.

The 1986 rule was modified so that, effective after December 1987, individuals may deduct the interest on residential mortgage loans used for the purpose of *acquiring* qualified residences (principal residence plus one other), provided the total residential debt does not exceed $1 million ($500,000 for each married taxpayer filing separately). *Acquisition debt* is defined as that incurred in acquiring, constructing, or substantially improving any qualified residence and which is secured by that residence. Acquisition debt is no longer limited by the fair market value of the property. This is particularly important in cases where the fair market value of a home is not increased by as much as the cost of substantial improvements.

In addition to the acquisition debt, interest is deductible on a loan of up to $100,000 ($50,000 for each married taxpayer filing separately) on the equity in the residence regardless of how the proceeds are used. Prior law restricted the usage of equity debt, but since 1987, those restrictions no longer apply. *Home equity debt* is defined as debt other than acquisition indebtedness secured by the home, to the extent that the aggregate amount of debt does not exceed the fair market value of the home reduced by the acquisition indebtedness. Thus, a home with a fair market value of $120,000 and acquisition debt of $70,000 could justify a home equity loan up to $50,000 ($120,000 minus $70,000 = $50,000) on which the interest is deductible.

Also, interest on mortgages for mobile homes, boats, or vacation cabins used as second homes still qualify for the interest deduction within the overall $1 million limit. To qualify a living unit for this purpose, it must have sleeping accommodations, kitchen facilities, and a toilet.

DISCOUNT AS A DEDUCTION

A discount paid by the borrower for a mortgage loan in the acquisition of a personal residence is deductible the same as interest. If the loan is for the *purchase* of the residence, it is deductible in full in the year it is paid. However, if the discount is for *refinancing* an existing loan, the discount is deductible over the life of the loan, not in the year paid. For example, if the cost of discount for refinancing is $2,400, and the term of the loan is 20 years, the taxpayer may deduct only $120 each year.

PROPERTY TAX DEDUCTION

Property taxes are deductible for taxpayer-owned residences without limitations. While mortgage interest deductions are limited to only two "qualified residences," there is no such limitation for state and local property taxes.

Tax Treatment on Gain from Sale

Capital gains taxes have always applied to gains made by the taxpayer on the sale of a principal residence or personal property. But it is the persistent inflation of recent years that has made the sale of a residence an important tax consideration. Before the mid-1960s, existing residences rarely sold for more than had been paid for them. Only a few exceptionally strong growth areas of the country, such as California and Florida, regularly witnessed this type of gain on personal homes. With the relatively small tax revenues available from the sale of personal residences, the IRS did not actively pursue records of house sales, relying instead on the integrity of taxpayers to report all gains and pay required taxes.

Inflation has now changed this attitude of routine acceptance, and the IRS has issued form #2119 specifically for reporting a "Sale or Exchange of Personal Residence." The special requirements of the tax law are of interest to the homeowner, the investor, and the professional real estate person.

The calculation of a gain upon the sale of a personal residence follows the same pattern as investment property, with two major exceptions: (1) a homeowner may *not* deduct depreciation which reduces the basis of value and (2) the tax code does *not* permit a homeowner to deduct any *loss* on the sale of a personal residence.

The capital gain from the sale of a personal residence is the difference between the *adjusted basis* of the property value and the *realized selling price*. The important point to consider is how the tax code defines these two figures.

Basis of Property Value.　The basis of value for a personal residence is determined no differently from any other property investment. It is the *method of acquisition* that determines the basis. While most residences are acquired by purchase, there are tax rules that apply to acquisitions by gift, by inheritance, and for services rendered. (Please refer to Chapter 5, under "Basis of Value.")

Adjusted Basis.　The basis can be increased by the value of any improvements. ("Improvements" must add to the value or prolong the life of the property. Ordinary maintenance, therefore, is not permitted as an increase in the basis.) Another permissible increase to the basis is an *addition* to the property, such as a new room or additional adjoining land. *Decreases* in the basis come from casualty losses (reduced by the amount of any insurance recovery), disposition of any part of the property, or the sale of easement and similar rights. As pointed out earlier, depreciation is not permitted as a deduction against the homeowner's income and is therefore *not* a required reduction in the property basis for capital gains calculation. (A possible exception should be noted here. If a dwelling unit is used partly for rental purposes and partly for personal use, an allocation of depreciation must be made in accordance with the special requirements of rental property that are discussed later in this chapter.)

The *adjusted basis* applicable to a personal residence is the original basis of value (determined by the method of acquisition), plus any improvements or additions, less any losses, dispositions, or sale of rights to the property. The IRS requires reasonable proof that the adjusted basis has been adequately calculated, so it is important that the taxpayer keep adequate records of all applicable transactions. Remember that any increase in the adjusted basis *reduces* the amount of taxable capital gain when the property is sold.

Realized Selling Price

Since the capital gain is the *difference* between the adjusted basis of the property value and the amount *realized* from the sale of that property, the next step is to determine how to calculate the realized selling price. The calculation starts with the total consideration received from the sale.

Total Consideration Received.   This includes cash, notes, mortgages, and the fair market value of any real or personal property received in the transaction. If the taxpayer is moved by an employer, any payment from the employer as reimbursement for a decline in property value or as payment in excess of fair market value is *not* included in the selling price in the calculation of capital gain. Any such money received from an employer must be reported as ordinary income for services rendered. The sales price for any *personal* property is not included in total consideration received.

Deduct Selling Expenses.   The expenses that the homeowner can deduct from the sales price in calculating the realized selling price are:

1. Sales commission.
2. Advertising paid for by the seller.
3. Legal fees incurred in the sale.
4. Loan placement fees or discount points paid by the seller.

Deduct Fixing-Up Expenses.   Fixing-up expenses are not deductible from ordinary income, nor can the deduction be used in calculating a capital gain if the tax is deferred. Fixing-up expenses are *only* deductible in determining the gain on which taxes are *payable*. They *cannot* be deducted in figuring actual profit or the reduction in basis for the replacement home. (See Example 1, page 130.)

For tax purposes, fixing-up expenses include decorating and repair costs incurred solely to assist in the sale of the property. These expenses must have been incurred for work performed within 90 days before the sales contract was signed and must have been paid no more than 30 days after the sale. Capital expenditures or improvements cannot be included in fixing-up expenses. Incidentally, the IRS offers no clues for the taxpayer in determining just when "90 days prior to the sale" actually begins!

Tax Deferral on Personal Residence Sale

The capital gains tax, as originally assessed, placed the taxpayer-homeowner in a dilemma. To replace an existing home required at least as much money—often more—than could be realized from the inflated value of the old house. On top of this, the taxpayer would have to pay a portion of the increased value in a capital gains tax, thus substantially reducing the ability to maintain a standard of living after the sale. To provide relief for this problem, Congress approved a plan that allows the capital gains tax on the sale of a personal residence to be deferred—but *not* eliminated—when a replacement property is acquired within a specified period of time. The tax is deferred by adjusting downward the basis of the acquired property by the amount of the gain postponed on the property sold. Deferral is permitted whether the new residence costs more or less than the selling price of the old residence as long as any part of the gain is reinvested.

Time Limits to Qualify

The tax code specifies deadlines for the purchase and occupancy of a replacement home in order to qualify for postponement of the capital gains tax on the sale of the old house. The time period allowed to acquire and occupy the new home is 48 months. This means that to qualify for the deferment, a taxpayer must buy or build a home and occupy it as a principal residence *within two years before or up to two years after* selling the old house.

Armed Forces Eligibility. Time limits to acquire a replacement residence were extended in 1986 for members of the armed forces. The time allowed to replace, occupy, and postpone gain on the sale of the old home has been extended until one year after the last day the person is stationed outside the United States or required to reside in quarters on base. The replacement period is still limited to eight years from date of sale of the old home and applies to any gain on a residence sold after July 18, 1984.

Tax Basis of the New Residence

The tax relief offered under the rollover, or replacement residence rule, is a deferment of the taxes, not a release from payment. The deferment is achieved by requiring that the *basis* of the new residence be *reduced* by the exact amount of the *gain* on the sale of the old residence that is deferred, i.e., that portion of the capital gain on which the taxes can be postponed. When the house is eventually sold, and no replacement residence is acquired, the lower adjusted basis will result in a higher capital gain.

Special Rules

Frequency of Use. The homeowner is not limited as to the number of replacement transactions, or rollovers, permitted. However, they must be at least 18 months apart unless a move to commence work at a new principal place of employment is necessary. To qualify as a new place of employment, the move must be at least the former distance traveled to work plus 35 miles. For instance, if the homeowner presently lives 12 miles from work, the move must be at least 47 miles (12 plus 35 equals 47).

Moving Expenses. One of the permissible deductions in a qualified move is the *selling cost of the old house.* There is a limit of $3,000* for this kind of deduction. Since moving expense is an allowable deduction from taxable income, this means that 100% of the qualifying expense reduces taxable income. An alternative option for the taxpayer is to take the selling costs (or that amount in excess of the moving expense limit) as a reduction of the *realized selling price* of the old house. This reduces the capital gain and amounts to a tax benefit for the taxpayer. Then, of course, the capital gain tax may be deferred! It is a choice for the taxpayer and depends on which procedure is most beneficial.

Improvements to Replacement Residence. Tax rules allow homeowners to include the cost of major improvements added to the replacement residence as a part of its purchase cost, as long as the changes are made within the qualifying time period (24 months prior to date of sale of the old house and up to 24 months after). Thus, improvements added to the house are the same as money *reinvested* and reduce the capital gain that could be recognized as taxable. In the example below, a homeowner purchases a house of less cost than the one sold, resulting

---

*The $3,000 limit is subject to change but applies to *all indirect* moving expenses (including travel to find a new residence, temporary living costs away from home, and others). The limit is halved if spouses file separately. The text does not consider moving costs further. Reference: IRS Publication 521 *Moving Expenses.*

in a part of the gain being subject to tax. Note that any increase in the purchase cost reduces the amount of gain subject to tax. (The capital gain itself is unaffected—only the amount that may be taxable in the year of sale.)

Example 1

Following is an example illustrating the calculations needed to report gain on the sale of a personal residence. The difficult factor to work with is the fixing-up expense. This item reduces the adjusted sales price, thus effectively reducing the amount of gain that is taxable in the year of sale. However, it should be noted that there is no reduction allowed for fixing-up expenses in the calculation of the adjusted basis of value for the *new* residence. To better understand the problems entailed, the chart below proceeds through the calculations needed for reporting the gain on a transaction where the replacement residence is of less value than the house sold (sometimes known as "buying down"). This best shows the proper handling of fixing-up expenses. Next, a completed IRS Form 2119, "Sale or Exchange of Principal Residence," is reproduced, showing how the figures are entered for the sale transaction (Figure 8–1).

REPLACEMENT OF LESS VALUE (BUYING DOWN)

Adjusted sales price of old residence		
Sales price	$72,000	
Less: Selling costs	6,000	
Amount realized	$66,000	$66,000
Less: Fixing-up expenses	3,000	
ADJUSTED SALES PRICE	$63,000	
Gain on sale of old house		
Original purchase price	$35,000	
Plus: Closing costs	1,000	
Original basis	$36,000	
Plus: Improvements	5,000	
Basis of residence sold		$41,000
GAIN ON SALE		$25,000
Gain to be reported		
Purchase price, new residence	$49,750	
Plus: Closing costs not otherwise deductible	1,250	
Cost of new residence		$51,000
GAIN TAXABLE THIS YEAR		$12,000
(Adjusted sales price minus Cost of new residence		

Adjusted basis of new residence

Cost of new residence	$51,000
Less: Gain postponed (Difference between Gain on sale and Gain taxable this year)	($13,000)
ADJUSTED BASIS OF NEW RESIDENCE	$38,000

Example 2

To illustrate the tax effect of buying a larger replacement residence, the following chart uses the same "old" house as Example 1, then shows a more expensive replacement. In this example, all of the gain is eligible for tax deferment.

REPLACEMENT OF GREATER VALUE (BUYING UP)

Adjusted sales price of old house

Sales price	$72,000	
Less: Selling costs	6,000	
Amount realized	$66,000	$66,000
Less: Fixing-up expenses	3,000	
ADJUSTED SALES PRICE	$63,000	

Gain on sale of old house

Original purchase price	$35,000	
Plus: Closing costs not deductible	1,000	
Original basis	$36,000	
Plus improvements	5,000	
Basis of residence sold		$41,000
GAIN ON SALE		$25,000

Gain to be reported

Purchase price, new residence	$81,000		
Plus: Closing costs not otherwise deductible	1,300		
Cost of new residence		$82,300	
GAIN TAXABLE THIS YEAR		0	0
(Cost of new residence is greater than adjusted sales price of old)			

Adjusted basis of new residence

Purchase price, Cost of new residence	$82,300
Less: Gain postponed	($25,000)
ADJUSTED BASIS OF NEW HOUSE	$57,300

FIGURE 8–1 IRS Example of Buying Down

Form **2119**	**Sale or Exchange of Principal Residence**	OMB No. 1545–0072

Form **2119**

Department of the Treasury
Internal Revenue Service (O)

Sale or Exchange of Principal Residence

▶ See instructions on back.

▶ Attach to Form 1040 for year of sale (see instruction B).

OMB No. 1545–0072

1987

Attachment
Sequence No. **22**

Name(s) as shown on Form 1040. *Frank and Evelyn Harris*

Your social security number *000 00 0000*

Do not include expenses that you deduct as moving expenses.

1 a Date former residence sold ▶ *May 6, 1987*

   b Enter the face amount of any mortgage, note (for example, second trust), or other financial instrument on which you will receive periodic payments of principal or interest from this sale ▶ *N/A*

		Yes	No
2 a If you bought or built a new residence, enter date you occupied it; otherwise enter "None" ▶ *May 5, 1987*			
b Are any rooms in either residence rented out or used for business for which a deduction is allowed? (If "Yes," see instructions.)			X
3 a Were you 55 or over on date of sale?			X
b Was your spouse 55 or over on date of sale? If you answered "No" to 3a and 3b, do not complete 3c through 3f and Part II.			X

   c Did the person who answered "Yes" to 3a or 3b own and use the property sold as his or her principal residence for a total of at least 3 years (except for short absences) of the 5-year period before the sale?

   d If you answered "Yes" to 3c, do you elect to take the once in a lifetime exclusion of the gain on the sale?

   e At time of sale, was the residence owned by: ☐ you, ☐ your spouse, ☐ both of you?

   f Social security number of spouse, at time of sale, if different from number on Form 1040 ▶ (Enter "None" if you were not married at time of sale.)

Part I **Computation of Gain**

4 Selling price of residence (Do not include personal property items.)	**4**	62,000
5 Expense of sale (Include sales commissions, advertising, legal, etc.)	**5**	3,700
6 Subtract line 5 from line 4. This is the amount realized	**6**	58,300
7 Basis of residence sold	**7**	43,000
8 Gain on sale (subtract line 7 from line 6). If zero or less, enter zero and do not complete the rest of form. Enter the gain on this line on Schedule D, line 3 or 10,* unless you bought another principal residence or checked "Yes" to 3d. Then continue with this form	**8**	15,300

If you haven't replaced your residence, do you plan to do so within the replacement period? ☐ Yes ☐ No
(If "Yes" see instruction B.)

Part II **Age 55 or Over One-Time Exclusion**

Complete this part only if you checked "yes" to 3(d) to elect the once in a lifetime exclusion; otherwise , skip to Part III.

9 Enter the smaller of line 8 or $125,000 ($62,500, if married filing separate return)	**9**	
10 Gain (subtract line 9 from line 8). If zero, do not complete rest of form. Enter the gain from this line on Schedule D, line 10,* unless you bought another principal residence. Then continue with this form	**10**	

Part III **Gain To Be Postponed and Adjusted Basis of New Residence**

Complete this part if you bought another principal residence.

11 Fixing-up expenses (see instructions for time limits)	**11**	500
12 Adjusted sales price (subtract line 11 from line 6)	**12**	57,800
13 Cost of new residence	**13**	57,200
14 Gain taxable this year (subtract line 13 plus line 9 (if applicable) from line 12. If result is zero or less, enter zero. Do not enter more than line 8 or line 10 (if applicable). Enter the gain from this line on Schedule D, line 3 or 10*	**14**	600
15 Gain to be postponed (Subtract line 14 from line 8. However, if Part II applies, subtract line 14 from line 10.)	**15**	14,700
16 Adjusted basis of new residence (subtract line 15 from line 13)	**16**	42,500

***Caution:** If you completed Form 6252 for the residence in 1a, do not enter your taxable gain from Form 2119 on Schedule D.*

For Paperwork Reduction Act Notice, see back of form.

Form **2119** (1987)

Example 3

One more example is offered to illustrate the possible result if the home seller buys way down, perhaps a small mobile home as a replacement residence. The taxable gain is limited to the *actual* gain on the sale of the old house, NOT the amount not reinvested. The following chart uses figures from the previous examples:

REPLACEMENT OF LESS VALUE (BUYING WAY DOWN)

Amount realized from sale, old house		$66,000
Adjusted sales price, old house	$63,000	
(Realized price less fixing-up expense)		
Basis of house sold		41,000
GAIN ON SALE		$25,000
Purchase price, new residence	33,000	
Amount NOT reinvested	$30,000	

In Example 3, it is the actual gain, the $25,000, that must be reported as capital gain in the year of sale, not the $30,000 which was not reinvested. The $5,000 difference is a tax-free return of the homeowner's original capital investment in the old house.

Age 55-or-Older Exclusion

The 1981 Tax Act permitted a taxpayer age 55 or older to exclude from taxable income up to $125,000 in *capital gain* on the sale of a principal residence. There is no limit on the sales price of the house eligible for qualification, and the rules remain essentially unchanged.

The election to take the exclusion offered under this rule is allowed only once in a lifetime—and the rule allows married couples only one such election. That is, if either spouse has previously exercised this option, as a single person or during a prior marriage, the other spouse is denied the use of this rule. However, there is no "recapture" if a couple married after each has independently taken advantage of the tax-free gain.

There are several provisions in the age 55-or-older exclusion that should be noted:

1. The house must have been owned and occupied as a principal residence for three out of five years preceding the sale in order to qualify.

2. If either the husband or wife is 55 or older, the exclusion may be claimed.

3. The right is for the exclusion of *one gain* up to the amount of $125,000. There is no right to use a portion of the gain for one sale, and carry over

the balance for a later sale. (If a gain is small, it might be beneficial to use the rollover rule until a larger gain is available.)

Residence Converted to Rental Use

If a taxpayer's personal residence is converted (in whole or in part) for use in the taxpayer's business or for the production of rental income, it is necessary to determine the basis from which the property may be depreciated. This basis is the *lesser* of:

1. The fair market value of the property on the date of conversion, or
2. The adjusted basis of the property (as explained earlier in this chapter).

The income and expenses of rental property are subject to IRS rules, which are examined next.

Rental Income

Regular Payments. The money received for the normal use of the rental property is income when it's received.

Advance Rent. Advance rentals must be included as regular income in the year they're received, regardless of the time period covered and the accounting method used by the taxpayer.

Payment for Lease Cancellation. Such a payment must be treated as rental income in the year it's received, regardless of the taxpayer's accounting method.

Expenses Paid by Tenant. If a tenant pays any of the landlord's expenses, these payments are rental income to the landlord and must be reported. However, the landlord may deduct those expenses that are normally deductible.

Rental Expenses

Cost Recovery. After determining the basis of the building and of any personal property included as rental property, it is necessary to determine the cost recovery period for each class of property. (See Chapter 6.)

Repairs and Maintenance. Any repairs to maintain the buildings and equipment or other rental property in an efficient condition are considered operating expenses and are deductible. Anything that adds to the value of the property or prolongs its useful life is considered an improvement, which is capitalized and then recovered over the appropriate recovery period.

Handicap Exception. The taxpayer may elect to deduct up to $25,000 each year for an improvement or alteration (such as a ramp) that assists a handicapped or elderly person's access to the building. This rule applies to all kinds of rental property, not just to residential units.

Other Expenses. All normal operating expenses for the property are deductible. These include advertising, trash collection, maintenance services, employee's wages, utilities, fire and liability insurance, taxes, interest, and commissions paid to rent the property or to collect the rents.

Rental of a Room

A room may be rented in a personal residence and is eligible for the same deductions available for renting an entire house. However, the deductions must be allocated only to that portion of the house that is rented. That is, the percentage of the property rented is applied to the deduction amounts. For example, if a room comprises 15% of the total living area, only 15% of the eligible business deductions, such as depreciation, repairs, maintenance, utilities, and insurance, can be taken. Taxes and mortgage loan interest are deductible for both a personal residence and a business property, so are taken in full for this calculation. NOTE: Any depreciation taken reduces the basis of value in the personal residence.

Business Use of the Home

If a portion of the personal residence is used by the owner for business purposes, it may justify greater tax deductions. To qualify, a specific part of the residence must be set aside (it need not be a separate room) and used exclusively on a regular basis as (1) the principal place of *any* business, or (2) a place where the taxpayer meets with patients, clients, or customers. Also, an employee is allowed a home-office deduction if its use is for the *convenience of the employer*. Managing a personal investment portfolio does *not* qualify as a separate business for this purpose.

Permissible deductions include depreciation, maintenance, insurance, and utility expenses as allocated to the portion of the house used for business purposes. The tax code does not specify, but the allocation can most likely be made on a basis of square feet. Any deduction taken for depreciation reduces the basis of value for the principal residence.

Prior law limited deductions for business use of the home to the amount of gross income from that use, reduced by otherwise allowable expenses, such as taxes, interest, and casualty losses from the business use and allowed no carry-forward of any excess losses. The 1986 Tax Act altered this restriction to permit deductions disallowed by the gross-income limit to be carried forward for deduction against future years' income. But the gross income limit for each year still applies, disallowing deductions that exceed income.

Taxpayers may no longer lease a portion of a home to an employer and claim deductions as a business usage.

If the taxpayer occupies rental housing, it may qualify for office-in-home deductions. There are some rather stringent guidelines, but eligible renters may deduct a proportionate share of their rent and utilities.

Part-Time Rental Units

If the same dwelling unit is used part-time for rental purposes and part-time as a personal residence, it is necessary to allocate expenses between the rental use and the personal use. Special tax rules apply to this allocation. The rules apply to any type of dwelling unit so used, but they are most commonly used for vacation homes. If the taxpayer owns a partial interest in such property, the deduction is only the proportionate share of ownership expenses, even if more than a proportionate share was paid.

The changes in defining income and the limitations of the passive loss rules contained in the 1986 Tax Act may alter the way a taxpayer treats part-time rental units. One option would be to claim the dwelling unit as a second home and deduct the interest and tax expense associated with it. As an alternative, the taxpayer may use the home less than the required time as a vacation home (less than 15 days), and potentially be subject to passive loss rules.

Tax Definition of "Dwelling Unit." For tax purposes, a dwelling unit may be a house, apartment, condominium, mobile home, boat, or other similar property. The term does not include hotels, motels, and inns that are operated as businesses.

Tax Definition of "Personal Use." Personal use occurs any day or part of a day when a dwelling unit is used by:

1. The taxpayer, a member of the family, or any other person with an interest in the property, unless a fair market rental is paid.

2. Anyone under a reciprocal arrangement that enables the taxpayer to use some other dwelling unit.

3. Anyone at less than a fair rental.

Allocation of Expenses

Expenses must be allocated between personal use and rental use. However, the allocation method and the deductible expenses vary with the number of days of personal use during the year. There are three categories of use, each of which is governed by its own tax rules:

1. Used primarily as a personal residence, and rented for less than 15 days during the year.

2. Used as a personal residence for more than the greater of (a) 14 days, or (b) 10% of the number of days during the tax year when the property was rented for a fair price.

3. Used as a personal residence, but for *not* more than the greater of (a) 14 days, or (b) 10% of the number of days it was rented at a fair price.

CATEGORY 1—RENTED LESS THAN 15 DAYS

A personal residence rented for less than 15 days during the year is excluded from the rule permitting deduction of expenses (other than interest, taxes, and casualty losses). Any rent received under this category is *not included* in personal gross income. The normal deductions permitted for a personal residence—interest, taxes, and casualty losses—are deductible only if the taxpayer itemizes deductions (Schedule A, Form 1040).

CATEGORY 2—PART RENTAL, PART PERSONAL USE

If the dwelling unit is substantially used both as a residence and for rental purposes, expenses must be allocated between the two. The allocation is based on the number of days that the property is used during the year, not on the 365-day year. The number of "days used" includes those for both rental and personal purposes but not those days on which the unit was held out for rent. To count as a rental day, the unit must be rented at a fair price. For example, if the taxpayer owns a beach cabin that has been rented for 120 days during the tax year and used for personal purposes for 30 days, the total "days used" would be 150. To allocate:

For rental: $\dfrac{120}{150} = .80$ or 80% of expenses

For personal use: $\dfrac{30}{150} = .20$ or 20% of expenses

Limits on Allocation of Expenses. Under this category, the amount of deducted expenses may not exceed the unit's gross rental income. However, the income from rental property is classed as passive: if a profit is made, it may be used as an offset for other passive activity losses. If a loss is incurred, it may be carried forward indefinitely for write-off against future income from the property, or claimed as a deduction when the property is disposed of.

For tax reporting purposes, the taxpayer must first deduct from gross rental income that portion of total expense for interest, taxes, and casualty losses that is allocated to rental use. Next, the taxpayer deducts the portion of operating expenses allocated to rental use. Finally, the allocation for depreciation is deducted. The following example will illustrate the steps in allocating deductions.

Start with the following expenses for the beach cabin for a year:

Interest	$1,400
Taxes	$1,000
Utilities	$ 750
Maintenance	$ 300
Cost recovery	$1,200

As calculated above, the cabin was used for rental purposes 80% of the time it was in use and 20% for personal purposes. Assuming that gross rental income is $3,300 the results are as follows:

Gross rental income		$3,300
Interest (80% of $1,400)	1,120	
Taxes (80% of $1,000)	800	
Less: Interest and taxes		$1,920
Rental income exceeding interest and taxes		$1,380
Utilities (80% of $750)	600	
Maintenance (80% of $300)	240	
Less: Utilities and maintenance		$ 840

Rental income exceeding interest, taxes, and operating expenses	$ 540
Less: Cost recovery (limited in this example to the lesser of 80% of $1,200 [$960] or the remainder of the gross rental income not already deducted [$540]	$ 540
Net rental income	0

Rental income and expenses should be reported on Schedule E (Form 1040). Interest and taxes allocated to personal use (20% of each, in the example above) are deductible on Schedule A (Form 1040), *provided* that the taxpayer itemizes deductions (rather than taking the standard deduction).

CATEGORY 3—PERSONAL USE, LESS THAN 15 DAYS

If a dwelling unit is used primarily for rental with the expectation of making a profit, it is not considered the taxpayer's personal residence. To qualify in this category, use as a personal residence during the year must not exceed the greater of (a) 14 days, or (b) 10% of the number of days it was rented at a fair price.

As rental property, this class is considered a passive activity, but losses are not limited to the unit's income as with Category 2. However, any losses sustained can only be offset by other passive activity income.

Even so, as personal use property for only a portion of the time, it is still necessary to calculate total days of use and to allocate expenses between rental use and personal use, as in Category 2.

Time-Sharing Ownership

While the concept of time-sharing lacks the quality of ownership embodied in the other forms of ownership discussed here, it is growing in importance and needs to be understood.

Time-sharing ownership means the holding of rights to exclusive use of real estate for a designated length of time (such as two weeks or a month) each year. It is practical primarily in resort areas. There are two basic methods used to create time-sharing arrangements: one is through a long-term lease, and the other is through condominium-type ownership.

Long-Term Lease

Under the long-term lease arrangement, the developer or promoter acquires a hotel, motel, or an apartment building in a suitable resort area. For each unit in the building, the developer sells, say, 25 two-week leases out of each year for 30 years. That leaves a two-week period unallocated that can be used for general maintenance work. The sale of the leases is calculated to pay for the building, and the lessee pays a proportionate share of the cost of the management, maintenance, and any services that are commonly provided. A specific unit may be assigned to the lessee, or the lessee may be allowed to use any unit available on a first come, first served basis. In an arrangement of this kind, the leasehold interest should have the right to sell; thirty years is a long time for one vacation spot.

Condominium

The purpose of a condominium with this plan grants the owner the right to use the unit for a specified period each year. An example might be the sale of a unit to 24 buyers as tenants in common. Each holds the right to use the unit for two weeks out of each year. Or the arrangement could be a sale to 12 owners, each of whom has the right to use the unit for two weeks in the summer and two weeks in the winter.

Management and maintenance problems are somewhat more difficult with time-sharing as compared with full-time occupancy of a condominium. An ownership agreement is necessary to define user priorities, assign responsibilities for maintenance (probably a professional management company), and detail the procedures to be used if an owner wants to sell his or her interest. Another matter of concern is the allocation of expenses and debt service if one or more of the owners fail to pay their share.

Condominiums

The ownership of a condominium as a dwelling or as a business property is of fairly recent origin. It has taken enabling legislation in each of the 50 states to properly define a condominium as a piece of real estate. Through this type of legislation, an owner holds title to a particular apartment or unit in a larger building or building complex (an improved "cube of airspace"). He or she also holds title to an undivided interest—usually as a tenant in common with other unit owners—in the land on which the building stands and in the other elements of the property that are used by the owners as a group. Condominiums may be residential or commercial (shopping centers or office buildings, for example).

Condominiums did not appear in large numbers on the housing market until the early 1960s. It was not until 1967 that all 50 states had enacted the necessary legislation to permit condominium ownership as it is known today.

The Unit Owner

In general, the owner of a condominium unit holds the same tax status of any other real property owner. That is, if the property is occupied as a personal residence, the same rules as to deductibility of interest and taxes and the non-deductibility of maintenance costs and depreciation apply to the owner of a condominium as to the owner of a single family residence. If the condominium is used for business purposes—either all or a part of it—the same rules apply as with other forms of property. Several aspects of condominium ownership are unique and should be considered.

MORTGAGE INTEREST

The owner of a condominium may mortgage the unit, and the interest paid on such a mortgage is deductible. Since the unit owner's undivided interest in common elements is inseparable from the unit, this too would be included in the mortgage.

In most instances, the lender furnishing financing for the construction of a condominium project provides for the release of a portion of the construction mortgage as the individual units are sold, and the construction mortgage is repaid from the proceeds of the sale. Thus, there is no overall mortgage to concern the unit owner. However, there are situations—especially when an existing building is converted to a condominium—when the unit purchaser assumes a specified dollar amount of an existing overall mortgage on the premises. Under these circumstances, the *share* of interest paid on such a mortgage is deductible.

If the condominium is used as a business property, the interest is fully deductible. There is a slight possibility that a portion of interest costs could be reallocated to the unit owner's association, which is discussed later in this chapter.

REAL ESTATE TAXES

A condominium owner may deduct real estate taxes paid, or accrued, for the property the same as for any other real estate.

However, assessment procedures do vary from state to state. In some states each unit owner is assessed separately along with his or her corresponding percentage of ownership in the common elements. That is, a single assessment is made against each owner. In other states, the assessment is made only against the unit with no mention of the common elements. In such a case, a single assessment could be made against the common elements as a whole to be paid for by the unit owner's association. The association then assesses each unit owner his or her proportionate share of the taxes, which would be deductible when paid by the owner. If some of the unit owners should default in paying their share, the other owners, as tenants in common, could deduct the share of the deficit that they paid.

In states that permit condominiums to be created on long-term leaseholds, there is often a provision for the tax assessment to be made against individual units, which creates no problem for deductibility. In states that have no such provision and where the tax assessment is made against the landowner (the owner of the leased land), it is doubtful that unit owners can deduct any share of the taxes. The theory is that a lessee may not deduct taxes imposed on the lessor because this should be treated as a part of the rental payments. Such rental payments are deductible only if the property is used in business and not as a personal residence.

MAINTENANCE, REPAIRS, INSURANCE

If a condominium is occupied as a personal residence, expenses for repairs, maintenance, or insurance are not deductible whether or not the payment is made individually or as an assessment levied by the unit owner's association. These are considered personal expenditures of a homeowner. If the unit is used, all or part, for business purposes, the same rules of prorated deductibility for expenses apply as to other real estate.

An overassessment for common expenses by a unit owner's association is generally not deductible, particularly if the association has agreed to refund such overpayment or apply it to the following year's assessment. There are administrative complications in properly informing the unit members of the time when each expenditure was paid. Thus, an overassessment can be a normal result of prudent management.

DEPRECIATION OR COST RECOVERY

The unit owner may *not* deduct depreciation if the unit is occupied as a personal residence. It is deductible if the unit is used as rental property.

While the IRS distinguishes between residential and commercial rental property in determining qualification for cost recovery class, the rule was not clearly designed with condominiums in mind. To qualify as *residential* rental property, the building must have at least 80% of its gross rental income from dwelling units. The most logical interpretation is that the unit itself comprises the building and, therefore, should qualify under its own usage category.

There is one small problem in condominium depreciation. If the unit owner's association is considered to be a taxable entity, like a corporation, and it is considered to be the owner of the common areas, there could be a question if any part of the common area is used to produce income. The IRS might attempt to allocate a portion of any depreciation claimed by a unit owner to the corporation.

CAPITAL IMPROVEMENTS

An assessment for capital improvements would normally be capitalized and depreciated over its useful life if the unit is rental property. This is not permitted if the unit is used as a personal residence. Care should be taken that such an assessment is not handled as contribution to the capital of the owners' association corporation. As such, it would be neither deductible nor depreciable for the unit owners because the corporation would hold the depreciable interest in the improvements.

SALE OR EXCHANGE OF A UNIT

The owner of a condominium unit used as a personal residence qualifies for all of the normal tax benefits available in the sale of this type of property. The unit is a capital asset and, if sold at a gain, the gain is taxable, but a loss is not deductible. Any gain is subject to the same tax deferral rules applicable to a personal residence (see previous section in this chapter "Tax Treatment on Gain from Sale"), and qualifies for the age 55-or-older exclusion of up to $125,000 capital gain on the sale of a personal residence. A personal residence is not eligible for a deferment of the capital gain tax under the rules of a property exchange.

If the unit is used for the production of rental income (or used in the owner's business), it is eligible for the same tax provisions that apply to other commercial real estate—taxes can be deferred through a property exchange, and losses in a sale may be deducted as a Section 1231 asset.

The Sponsor or Developer

A sponsor or developer may engage in the new construction of a condominium project or convert an existing building to this use. The owner of an existing building may desire to convert his or her own building, or may prefer to sell it to a developer who can handle the conversion. There are tax questions involved: principally, how is a gain (or loss) calculated?

First, consider the decision of an owner to sell or convert the building. From a practical standpoint, the building would have to be worth more as condominiums than as rental property. The decision to sell or convert finds most owners opting to sell for some of the following reasons:

1. Conversion can be expensive and may require a considerable amount of the owner's time.

2. The owner will have to pay for conversion costs, legal fees, advertising, and promotion expenses, which can be considerable.

3. Income to be realized from a conversion will take longer than it would if the property is sold to a developer.

4. The converter must help obtain financing for tenants and others who want to purchase the units.

5. There is a risk in that the total projected profit may not be realized.

TAX QUESTIONS IN CONVERSION BY AN OWNER

Determining Capital Gain. Remember that a capital gain is the difference between the adjusted basis of the property sold and the realized selling price (as reduced by selling expenses). To figure the basis of each unit sold, the basis of the entire property must be equitably apportioned to each unit. While the tax rule is that the basis should be allocated in accordance with the relative fair market values of the different portions at the time of *purchase*, as a practical matter, the allocation is more likely to be made with relative values at the time of sale. Conversion was probably not a consideration at the time of purchase of the property, and anyway, the relative values would not change that much.

Example

An apartment building is converted to a condominium, and the owner sells one unit plus a 5% interest in the common area for $50,000. The adjusted basis of the property is $600,000, and the present value (as determined by the total asking price for all units) is $1,000,000. To determine the allocation to one unit:

$$\frac{50,000}{1,000,000} \times 600,000 = 30,000 \text{ (basis of unit)}$$

The gain is:

$$\$50,000 - \$30,000 = \$20,000$$

The Developer

A developer who buys an existing building and rebuilds it for the sale of condominium units is normally in the business of selling condominiums, and thus any gain is considered ordinary income. About the only possible exception to this rule would be the case of a developer converting a building and selling all of the units to one individual.

A gain on the sale of an individual unit (even though taxed as ordinary income) is the difference between the realized selling price and the *unrecovered cost of each unit*. In determining the cost of each unit, the developer is expected to use the *cost apportionment* method of accounting. That is, the cost of the entire condominium conversion must be equitably apportioned to each unit and a gain reported for each sale. The IRS has refused to permit the *cost recovery* method of accounting in reporting gain from the sale of units in the conversion of an existing rental building. The cost recovery method allows the taxpayer to defer reporting a gain on the sale of individual units until the cost basis for the whole building is recovered.

Example: *Cost-Apportionment Method*

A condominium project of 60 units is constructed for a cost of $2,460,000. Total square footage of salable space amounts to 48,400 sq. ft.

Cost per square foot:

$$\frac{2,460,000}{48,400} = 50.83$$

An 840 sq. ft. condominium is sold for $55,000:

Net	$55,000
Cost apportion = 840 × 50.83 =	42,697
Gain on Sale	$12,303

The Investor

Investors are often sought by condominium developers to provide equity funding for their projects. Most often the arrangement is handled as a limited partnership (the developer, usually as a corporation, is the general partner and the investors, limited partners). Or it could be arranged as a development corporation with the investor receiving shares of stock in the corporation in exchange for funding. The corporate form offers two drawbacks: (1) profits are taxed twice, as corporate income and as dividends to stockholders, and (2) losses are available to the corporation but cannot be passed through to shareholders for deduction against other passive income.

An individual invests in a condominium project for the same reason a developer does—the expectation of a share of the profits. The development of condominium projects never has been a tax shelter kind of activity inasmuch as the sale of units is classed as a sale of inventory and, under prior law, was not eligible for capital gain tax treatment. Since it is a real estate investment classed as passive activity, income can be offset only by other passive activity losses.

9

Business Organizations

An investor in real property can choose among several methods of holding and operating the investment. The investor may prefer a business organization—a sole proprietorship, general partnership, limited partnership, or corporation. Or the property may be held by a trust, or by an individual, or a group of individuals. Each method carries its own advantages, disadvantages, and income tax reporting requirements. State laws govern both business organizations and landownership. Income tax laws are set by the federal government and generally followed in those states which have their own income tax requirements.

This chapter considers the major forms of business organization, the responsibilities and benefits that can accrue from each, and the various federal tax reporting requirements. The next chapter examines property held in trust or by individuals and reviews the various classes of estates in land that are found under modern law.

Sole Proprietorship

The simplest form of business organization is the sole proprietorship. An individual can own land and/or operate a business in his or her own name, under a trade name, or under an assumed name. Most states require that a trade name or an assumed name be publicly registered or recorded if it differs from the individual's name, thereby reducing the possibility of misrepresentation to creditors or others. An advantage of the sole proprietorship is that the owner has absolute control over management decisions and an absolute right to dispose of profits or assets as may best suit the purpose. However, the sole proprietorship offers an owner no protection against financial losses or claims that may arise from the operation of the business. In some states, any non-business assets that belong to the owner may be attached in satisfaction of a judgment or lien. (The laws which govern are those of the state of residence, or of the state in which the business operates).

Income Tax Reports. All taxable income of a sole proprietorship must be reported as part of the individual owner's income or loss. It must be reported for the same calendar year (or fiscal year) used for the personal income tax return. The business report is submitted on Schedule C, Form 1040, "Profit (or Loss) from Business or Profession" of the federal tax forms.

Accounting Period Used. Individual tax returns normally cover a calendar year, i.e., the 12-month period from January 1 through December 31. However, individuals may choose to use a "fiscal year" accounting period, i.e., a 12-month period ending on the last day of any month except December. The election of an accounting period must be made when the first tax return is filed. Changing the period requires IRS consent.

Accounting Method Used. The individual may select any accounting system but is required by law to keep all records needed to prepare a complete and accurate income tax return. These records include receipts, cancelled checks, and other evidence to support the records. The most common accounting methods are the cash method and the accrual method. (See Chapter 11.) The taxpayer must select one method for each business when it begins to operate. (The *same* accounting method need not be used for all of a taxpayer's businesses.) Once a method has been selected, any change requires IRS consent.*

Disposition of a Sole Proprietorship. If the assets of a sole proprietorship are disposed of, they must be classified into four separate categories. The gain or loss for each category must be computed separately. Guidelines† are as follows:

1. *Capital assets.* Sale results in a capital gain or loss.

2. *Depreciable property used in the business.* Sale results in a gain or loss from adjusted basis as a Section 1231 transaction.

3. *Real property used in the business.* Sale must be reported separately, but the tax treatment is the same as for depreciable property.

4. *Property held as inventory or stock in trade.* Sale results in ordinary income.

---

*Further information may be obtained from IRS Publication 538, *Tax Information on Accounting Periods and Methods.*

†Further information may be obtained from IRS Publication 544, *Sales and Other Dispositions of Assets.*

Partnership

The laws of partnerships stem from civil law, common law, equity, and law merchant. In 1914, the Commissioners on Uniform State Laws drafted the Uniform Partnership Act, which codified the general rules prevailing at the time. The Partnership Act is the basis for all state laws regarding partnerships.

The Partnership Act defines a partnership as "an association of two or more persons, who carry on a business as co-owners for profit." Partnerships can be classified as "trading" and "non-trading." Non-trading partnerships are those formed by professionals, such as lawyers, accountants, and physicians. But it is the trading partnership that this text discusses. These trading partnerships can be further classified as "general" or "limited." (Limited partnerships are discussed in a separate section of this chapter.)

Formation of a Partnership

A general partnership can be formed by either oral agreement or a written contract between (or among) the partners.

By Oral Agreement. A valid partnership can be formed with an oral agreement, although some states limit the life of such a partnership to one year. Courts have held that a partnership formed by oral agreement may hold title to land even though state laws require land transfer agreements to be in written form. The reason is that courts have interpreted the law to govern the form of the land *transaction*, not the form of the *partnership*.

By Written Agreement. Even though oral partnerships are valid in some states, a written understanding is preferable. A written agreement should obviously contain the name of the partnership, the names of the partners, the duration of the agreement, and the partnership's place of business. Not so obviously, it should also clearly indicate the capital contributions of each partner, their duties, a method for settling disputes, a procedure for cash withdrawals required by the partners, the way in which profits or losses will be divided, and a method by which the partnership may be dissolved. Some states have statutory requirements regarding the names that can be used for a partnership, and most require that any fictitious or assumed name be published or filed with a designated authority. The Partnership Act does not prevent a corporation from becoming a partner. On the contrary, the Act defines the word *persons* as "individuals, partnerships, corporations, and other associations."

Partnership Operations

In a general partnership, the partners determine the responsibility for management. Each partner might have a specific area of management responsibility, with major policy decisions made by a majority vote of the partners. The partnership agreement should define the duties of each partner, as well as any shared responsibilities.

Liabilities.   In a general partnership, each partner is liable for all obligations incurred on behalf of the partnership by any of the partners. The partnership agreement can limit liabilities *among* the partners themselves, making partners responsible for their own commitments. But, the responsibility of each partner to the general public and to the partnership's creditors cannot be limited by internal agreement among the general partners.

Disadvantages of a Partnership

The most obvious disadvantage of the general partnership is each partner's unlimited liability for the partnership's losses. Insurance coverage is rarely available to protect the partners against bad management or poor judgment. Another disadvantage of a partnership is the limited life of the partnership agreement. Unlike a corporation, a partnership may be terminated by the death of any one partner, or by the withdrawal of a partner. Termination can also result from mutual agreement among the partners, an act in default of the partnership agreement by one or more of the partners, or through bankruptcy.

The partnership form does not provide an investment interest that is easily liquidated or readily sold. Each partner has, in effect, both undivided interest in the partnership's property and an equal right of possession. The close relationship among the partners, which is all-important for successful operation, is not readily replaced. Generally, partnership agreements contain restrictions on each partner's right to sell an interest to outsiders.

Advantages of a Partnership

A partnership is formed primarily to combine the capital and expertise of two or more people, and it does so effectively. All partners have a voice in the management; all participate directly in the success of the partnership's operation. Partnerships are not required to file reports or pay franchise taxes to the state, while corporations must. And the partnership is not a taxable entity for income tax purposes.

Partnership Income Tax Reports

Although a partnership pays no income tax, it must file an information return —Form 1065—each year. This return shows the results of the partnership's operations for the tax year, separating the items of income, gain, loss, deduction, or credit that affect each partner's individual income tax return. (These items are the partner's "distributive share.") Since 1987, a partnership is required to conform its tax year to the same as the tax year of either its majority partners (owning more than 50%), its principal partners (holding 5% or more interest), or a calendar year, in that order, unless it can establish a business purpose acceptable to the IRS for using a different tax year. The deferral of income to partners is not considered a business purpose. Partnership income is treated by the partners as having been distributed on the last day of the partnership year. Each partner must include the distributive share of partnership items on his or her individual return for the tax year in which the last day of the partnership year falls. A partner reports his or her share of the partnership's ordinary income or loss on Schedule E, Form 1040.

The manner in which profits and losses are distributed is usually set out in the partnership agreement. If there is no agreement on sharing a specific item of gain or loss, each partner's share is determined in accordance with that partner's proportional interest in the partnership. Partnership income and gains are taxable to each partner—to the extent of the individual's share—*whether or not they are distributed*. This is an important point to consider when selecting a form of business operation, particularly if cash flows must be retained in the business for a number of years while operations are getting off the ground. The distributive share of partnership losses is *limited* to the adjusted basis of each partner's interest at the end of the partnership year in which the losses occurred. Partnership income or losses may be allocated to each partner only for that portion of the year that the taxpayer is a member of the partnership. The IRS claims the right to reallocate the distributive shares of partnership income, losses, or other items to the proper parties if the allocation lacks substantial economic justification.

When a taxpayer-partner has the right to exercise an election, the partnership—not the taxpayer-partner—makes the decision. These decisions include the method of accounting, the method of computing depreciation, the use of installment sales provisions, and others. The elections apply to all partners collectively. (There are exceptions to this procedure, notably when foreign taxes are involved or certain exploration expenditures are incurred.)

Guaranteed Payments. If a partner is paid a salary for services rendered or interest for the use of capital, these guaranteed payments are generally deductible as business expenses to the partnership. But guaranteed payments for a partner's services in forming the partnership, selling interests in the partnership, or acquiring property for the partnership are *not deductible* as a business expense to the partnership. Any guaranteed payments to a partner must be reported on that individual's return as salary or interest income.

Distributive Items. When the IRS uses the term "distributive item," it means the various forms of income and loss that may be taxed in different procedures for the individual partners. Schedule K of Form 1065 contains a list of partnership's distributive share items. A copy of this list (Schedule K-1) shows each partner's share of the distributive items. Items commonly reported on Schedule K include:

1. Ordinary income or loss.
2. Partner's salary and interest.
3. Gains and losses from property used in trade or business, and from involuntary conversions.
4. Qualifying dividends.
5. Contributions.
6. Net self-employment income.
7. First-year asset expense option.
8. Expense account allowance.
9. Tax preference items.

Each partner's distributive share of the partnership's income, gain, loss, deduction, or credit must be shown *separately* on his or her own Form 1040. These items are treated generally as if each partner had realized or incurred them personally. If a partner itemizes deductions on Form 1040, the distributive share of items such as partnership's contributions may be included. These are not deductible in computing partnership income.*

---

*Further information may be obtained from IRS Publication 541, *Tax Information on Partnership Income and Losses.*

Joint-Stock Companies

Some states permit the joint-stock company as a form of business ownership. It has some features of a corporation but is actually a general partnership. Management is placed in the hands of trustees or directors, but the partners retain unlimited financial liability for company operations. Under the organization's constitution and bylaws, certificates are issued that represent ownership shares. Transferring shares does not cause dissolution of a joint-stock arrangement. So the death of a shareholder does not dissolve the organization, as it does in the case of a partnership. In many states, suit may be brought against a joint-stock company as a separate entity, just as with a corporation.

Limited Partnership

The limited partnership puts a ceiling on the financial liability of each person designated as a *limited partner*. It has become a popular method of organizing real estate investments and raising equity capital. The limited partnership can be formed only by written agreement, which must be filed with the state authority charged with its regulation.

The origin of the limited partnership is the Uniform Limited Partnership Act, which has been adopted by every state except Louisiana (which has its own Act covering limited partnerships). The essence of a limited partnership is that it consists of one or more persons, known as limited partners, who do not participate in the management of the business and are personally liable to creditors only for the amount of their capital investment in the partnership. The limited partnership also has one or more persons, known as *general partners*, who are responsible for the management of the business and are personally liable for financial obligations of the partnership without regard to their investment.

The Limited Partnership Act states that a general partner possesses all the rights—and is subject to all the restrictions and liabilities—of a partner, in a general partnership. However, the Act provides additional restrictions on the general partner, e.g., he or she cannot act contrary to the partnership certificate, and cannot admit someone as a general or limited partner. The death or retirement of a general partner generally terminates the limited partnership, but this can be overcome through a specific provision in the partnership agreement.

According to the provisions of the Act, a limited partner does not become financially liable as a general partner *unless* the limited partner participates in the management and control of the business. The limited partner is authorized to inspect the books of the partnership and to receive, on demand, full information on all matters affecting the partnership. The limited partner may lend money to the partnership and can transact other business with the partnership. The limited partner may make a capital contribution of cash or property to the partnership, but cannot contribute services.

Courts have held that a limited partnership may be dissolved if it is operating at a loss. The Limited Partnership Act establishes priorities for distributing assets upon dissolution of a partnership, giving general creditors first rights over limited partners, and limited partners priority over general partners.

Disadvantages of a Limited Partnership

Problems that can arise in a limited partnership are like those found in a general partnership, including the difficulty of selling a partnership interest and the possibility of early termination of the business through death or withdrawal of a general partner. The general partner takes the same risks as in a general partnership, plus the possibility of challenge by the limited partners if management decisions are less than prudent.

Limited partners, who generally contribute most of the capital, have very little voice in the management of the partnership. This may be an advantage or a disadvantage, depending on the quality of the general partners. The capability of the general partners is so important in this form of business organization that the limited partner-investor should investigate very carefully the experience and management track record of each potential general partner.

One of the more important changes in tax accounting from the 1986 Tax Reform Act was the introduction of a new kind of income identified as *passive activity*. The Act consigned *all limited partnerships* as creating passive activity income or losses. This means that any losses from a limited partnership interest may only be offset against passive activity income. It prevents the transfer of losses against other active income and substantially reduces the tax shelter attraction of this form of business organization.

Advantages of a Limited Partnership

For both general and limited partners, the limited partnership offers the same direct pass-through of profits and losses for taxation purposes that is found in a general partnership. The limited partnership is not a taxable entity and files only an information return.

For the limited partner, there is the added advantage of limited liability. The limited partner has minimal management responsibility, which may release his or her time for other endeavors. The general partners can also provide expertise in a specialized form of business activity that might otherwise be beyond the reach of the limited partner.

Limited Partnership Income Tax Reports

The limited partnership—like the general partnership—files the Form 1065 information return. Each partner, general or limited, must report a distributive share of the partnership's ordinary income or net loss on his or her personal return (Schedule E, Form 1040), regardless of whether or not the income is disbursed.

Joint Venture

A joint venture is distinguished by how the property is owned. Normally, each party in the venture holds an *undivided share* in the property. The business organization that operates the property, which may be a partnership or a corporation, holds a management agreement, but not the ownership of the property. The management company may be owned by the joint ventures, or it could be a separate company under contract.

The "joint venture" is often used to divide the ownership between a large developer and an institutional investor to build a complex development. Many joint ventures are composed of individuals, corporations, and partnerships who together can better accomplish a common purpose. Large real estate ventures can involve landowners, builders, a real estate sales or leasing firm, and several institutional lenders, each with an equity interest in the project and a strong incentive to make it succeed.

Real Estate Syndicate

The syndicate is introduced here, under "Business Organizations," because it has become a popular method of investing in real estate. It is not in itself a form of business or ownership. A syndicate can be a general partnership, a limited partnership, a corporation, or even a landholder (as a joint tenancy or a tenancy in common). In practice, the syndicate provides a way for individuals or firms to combine their investment capital to undertake a larger project than might be possible for any one of them alone. It is used as a means to raise equity cash or to sell investment property. When used for real estate investment, the term "syndicate" most often means ownership in the form of a limited partnership. But this section considers the syndicate as a method of investment, rather than as a form of ownership.

Regulations

Depending on the number of persons involved, the wording of the agreement and the manner in which it is sold, the sale of a participating interest in real property can be considered a sale of securities. Both federal and state laws control the sale of securities to the general public. These laws are designed to protect the public from fraud and misrepresentation and to require full disclosure of the facts by sellers of securities.

Insofar as real estate is concerned, regulatory authorities are concerned whenever a certificate that is sold to the public represents some *future* interest in land. It can be called an earnest money agreement, a security deposit, an advance payment, or a pre-construction sale of a right to some unit of property. The name doesn't matter. What matters is that if the sales document is a piece of paper granting some right or interest in land without a specific assignment of title, the document of sale may be held to be a security and is, therefore, subject to registration requirements. Violations of the securities laws can bring fines and felony prosecution. Charges can be brought against any or all of the parties involved in the sale of an unauthorized issue, including the original promoter, the sales personnel (who may not even be aware of the noncompliance), and the mortgage lender.

The state statutes in this area vary considerably. But registration of syndicated offerings is required by most states. And if the *offering* is made to potential buyers across state lines, or to more than 35 persons within a state, then registration is also required with the federal regulator, the Securities and Exchange Commission.

A regulatory agency's acceptance or approval of the registration to sell participating interests is no assurance of a safe or successful investment. All this approval means is that the registration laws have been complied with and all pertinent facts have been fully and accurately disclosed. The true worth of an interest in a syndicated venture is an estimate that the investor must make.

Types of Syndicates

Two basic methods are used to form a real estate investment syndicate.

1. *Sale of existing property.* Under this method, the property is identified for the investor. For example, a builder or developer (usually called the *syndicator*) owns or controls (by option or contract of sale) a suitable investment property. The syndicator then sells participating interests in the property to a group of investors.

2. *Sale of interests in property to be acquired.* The syndicator sells interests in a syndicate organized for the purpose of *acquiring* good investment properties. This procedure is also referred to, quite accurately, as a *blind pool.* Because it allows so much freedom to the syndicator in the use of other people's money, many states, including Texas, forbid sales of this type of syndicated interest.

Disadvantages and Advantages

The following discussion considers a syndication from the investor's point of view. The investor is most likely to be a limited partner in the syndicate, rather than the syndicator. As a general partner, the syndicator would have financial control and responsibility for performance.

Disadvantages. The property's description and operating figures are usually compiled by the syndicator who has a strong interest in selling the property. The result can be a biased presentation. The syndicator usually controls the management of the property, but may be a far better salesman than property manager. The division of profits can be loaded in favor of the syndicator by the use of unduly high salaries, expense accounts, unnecessary payroll additions, and other ill-advised business expenses. A *limited partnership* is broadly classified as a passive activity, meaning limited partner's losses are not deductible against other active income. The limited partner has no voice in the management. (See previous section on "Limited Partnerships.")

Advantages. The same points that represent possible weaknesses in a syndicate investment can also become advantages. Everything depends on the integrity and capability of the syndicator-operator. If the syndicator is well qualified and has a good record of accomplishment in real estate operations, the syndicate investor can enjoy the advantages of a professional management team while shouldering no direct responsibility.

There are other advantages. If the syndicate is a partnership, each member can share in the tax deductions permissible for depreciation. If the syndicate is a limited partnership, the liability of the limited partners is fixed at the amount of their investment. By participating in several syndicates, the investor may spread out the risk factor through a more diversified investment portfolio. Finally, the investor in real property should receive a higher return than is normally available from stocks, bonds, or savings accounts, as well as some protection against inflation through the appreciation potential of real estate.

Corporations

The corporation, a form of business created by state chartering laws, is an artificial "person" with rights and powers to transact business of a limited and designated nature.

The Corporate Entity

In their earliest U.S. forms, corporations were chartered by special acts of the state legislatures. As this procedure became increasingly cumbersome, the states enacted corporation statutes to provide a more expeditious method of forming a corporation. Although several model procedures have been developed, including a Model Business Corporations Act by the American Bar Association, there is still no uniform statute to guide state lawmakers.

The courts have played a considerable role in developing the law of corporations. While there are diverse opinions on the true nature of a corporation, the dominant theory conceives of the corporation as a legal entity separate and distinct from its shareholders. A corporation may enter into contracts with its shareholders, and sue and be sued by them as a separate legal entity.

A corporation is held to be a "person" under some provisions of the United States Constitution, but a corporation does not have the status of a "citizen" for all legal purposes. For example, a corporation cannot move freely into any state to conduct business, while a citizen may. On the other hand, a corporation cannot be deprived of its property without due process, which is the same protection accorded citizens.

In a landmark decision in 1819, the United States Supreme Court ruled that a charter granted by a state to a corporation is deemed to be a contract between the state and the corporation.* Thus the relationship between the state and the corporation runs through the entire field of corporation law.

The Corporate Structure

The ownership of a corporation lies with its shareholders and is evidenced by shares of stock. Stock is issued and sold by the corporation, as regulated by state laws and by the SEC if stock is sold publicly. A corporation may issue several classes of stock, including *common stock* and *preferred stock*, with each giving the holder different rights.

The shareholders elect directors who, as a group, are responsible for the

---

Dartmouth College vs. Woodward, 4 Wheat. 518, 636, 657, 4L.Ed., 629.

corporation's finances and operating policies. Corporate directors can be held personally liable for negligence in corporate matters and for any illegal actions by the corporation.

The board of directors selects the officers of the corporation, who are charged with managing the corporation's day-to-day operations. Officers may or may not be directors or shareholders of the company.

Corporations may borrow money from banks, insurance companies, or other lenders. The loans may be unsecured, or secured by a pledge of certain corporate assets. Corporations also have borrowing methods that are not generally available to others. For example, corporations can sell promissory notes (more commonly known as *commercial paper*) in the open market. And they can issue and sell bonds as a method of borrowing money. These bonds vary, depending on their purpose, collateral, and repayment commitment. One common type is a mortgage bond, which is secured by a pledge of specified real property owned by the corporation.

Regular corporations are now referred to as *C corporations* by the IRS to distinguish them from S corporations described later.

Types of Corporations

Corporations are chartered for a variety of purposes. They are considered here under three categories: (1) for profit, (2) nonprofit, and (3) government and quasi-government.

Corporations for Profit.   The corporation most commonly used for real estate investment is operated for the purpose of making a profit. It may be a "close corporation" or a "public issue corporation." Close corporations have only a few closely knit shareholders (such as a family) or even just one shareholder. Public issue corporations are authorized to sell stock and bonds to the general public and are subject to a number of state and federal regulations on such sales. States also have special rules for incorporating particular classes of business such as banks, insurance companies, and savings associations.

Nonprofit Corporations.   Certain state statutes provide for formation of corporations that are *not* established for profit. These include charitable, educational, recreational, religious, and social organizations, all of which are convenient methods of holding and operating property. Nonprofit corporations do not distribute dividends to members on their invested capital.

Government Corporations.   A government corporation is created for public purposes. It is considered an agency of whichever government forms it—federal, state, or municipal. It can be used in administering the government or providing a service such as a utility. The government corporation can be used to conduct a business operation, with the Tennessee Valley Authority, and the U.S. Postal Service being prime examples. Quasi-government corporations—those partly owned by the federal government and partly by the general public—operate businesses that are considered too large or too much in the public interest to be entrusted to private hands. Examples of the quasi-government corporation are COMSAT, which handles the communications satellites, and AMTRAK, which operates passenger railroad trains.

Disadvantages of the Corporation

For the real estate investor, the major disadvantage of the corporate form lies in the method of its taxation. There are two problems:

1. *Double taxation.* Corporate income is subject to corporate income taxes, after which the remaining income may be distributed to shareholders as dividends. Ordinary dividends received by shareholders are subject to a second taxation—they are taxed as ordinary income to the recipient.

2. *No pass-through of tax deductions.* The corporation—not the shareholder—is entitled to the normal deductions for depreciation and other losses. Corporate losses—unlike partnership losses—cannot be included in the shareholder's taxable income.

Another disadvantage of the corporate form is the investor's lack of a voice in management. From a practical standpoint, the investor will have little control over management unless he or she is a major shareholder.

Advantages of the Corporation

The advantages of the corporate form are that (1) the shareholder has limited liability, and (2) shares of stock are generally more liquid than an interest in any other form of business organization. Stockbrokers and stock exchanges promote the buying and selling of corporate stock. There is an "over-the-counter" market for stock that is not listed on the major stock exchanges. Many shares in smaller companies are traded daily in these localized markets.

Corporate Income Tax Reports

Corporations must file an annual income tax return with IRS—Form 1120—and pay the taxes due. It is beyond the scope of this text to consider the substantial body of corporate tax law, but some requirements for the individual shareholder in the reporting of dividends and other corporate distributions must be discussed.

Corporate Distributions

The four classifications of corporate distributions are (1) ordinary dividends, (2) return of capital, (3) capital gain dividends, and (4) tax-free distributions. Each class is treated differently for tax purposes.

Ordinary Dividends.   These are paid out of the earnings and profits of the corporation and are reported as ordinary income to the shareholder. Any dividend received by the shareholder, whether on common or preferred stock, is treated as an ordinary dividend unless the paying corporation indicates otherwise.

Return of Capital.   A distribution that is not made from earnings of the corporation is treated as a return of the shareholder's investment. A return of capital is not taxed until the basis in the stock is fully recovered. Any return of capital that exceeds the amount of the basis is taxable as a capital gain. Corporations usually advise their shareholders when the distribution represents a return of capital.

Capital Gain Dividends.   These are paid or allocated to shareholders' accounts by regulated investment companies, mutual funds, and real estate investment trusts. The company or fund normally indicates how much of the distribution is a capital gain dividend. These dividends must be reported if they've been *allocated* to the shareholder—even if they haven't been *received.*

Tax-Free Distributions.   A tax-free distribution is usually in the form of additional shares or rights in the corporation that do not alter the stockholder's previous proportional share in the corporation. Examples include the stock split—where the corporation distributes additional shares of its own stock to its shareholders—and a reorganization of the shares. A tax-free distribution is not reported on the shareholder's tax return.

S Corporations

A limited partnership is a hybrid between a corporation and a partnership in terms of *liability*; an S corporation is a similar hybrid, this time in terms of income taxes. Essentially, an S (Internal Revenue Code) corporation is any normally chartered corporation with no more than 35 shareholders (husband and wife treated as one shareholder) that has elected to be taxed as a partnership. The

S corporation (formerly identified as "Subchapter S Corporation) files an annual information return allocating its income among the shareholders, who must then report the income (or loss) on their personal tax return whether or not the distribution has been received. Under this procedure, the corporation does not pay corporate income taxes.

The IRS regulations covering the S corporation procedure recognize that corporate taxes can unfairly penalize the corporate form of business ownership. This is particularly true for smaller, closely held corporations whose shareholders are expected to distribute profits in a manner that is "reasonable" under IRS interpretations. Three items create difficulty with interpretation—salaries, interest paid to shareholders, and dividends.

Difficulties in Interpretation of Regulations

Salaries. The small corporation usually begins with all or most of its shareholders working full- or part-time for the company. As employees of the corporation, they are entitled to reasonable salaries, which are a normal business expense and, therefore, deductible from corporate income. If the IRS considers these salaries to be excessive, however, it can disallow the excess, then assess corporate taxes on the amount of the excess. The excess salary is then treated as a dividend to the recipient.

Interest. The capital structure of a corporation may include interest-bearing loans made by the shareholders. For example, if a corporation requires $300,000 to commence business operations, the shareholders may purchase $150,000 of stock and lend the corporation an additional $150,000 at 9% interest. The annual interest payment on the loan would amount to $13,500 and should be deductible as a normal business expense. However, the Internal Revenue Code has a rule stating that if a corporation is *undercapitalized*, interest payments made to shareholders may be disallowed as an expense and then treated as a dividend.

Dividends. To defer the effects of the "double tax" on corporate income, a corporation might delay the payment of a dividend. Accumulated earnings increase the value of the company and could lead to a higher selling price for the stock.

Under prior law, the conversion of earnings into an increase in the value of corporate stock amounted to a conversion of ordinary income into a capital gain type of income. Previously, it would result in a lower tax rate. Since the 1986 Tax Act equalized the tax rates on capital gain and ordinary income, this advantage no longer exists. What remains is a question of tax avoidance when corporate earnings are accumulated and not paid out to shareholders in the form of dividends. While the IRS may still tax *excessive accumulated earnings,* the effect has been diminished.

Qualifications for S Corporation Treatment

To overcome some of the problems that arise in corporate taxation, the shareholders of a small corporation may elect to have corporate income taxed directly to them rather than to the corporation. To qualify for this election, the corporation must:

1. Have no more than 35 shareholders, none of whom is a nonresident alien.
2. Have only one class of stock, although stock with differing voting rights is allowed and not considered a separate class.
3. Have each shareholder sign the form electing taxation as a partnership.
4. Derive no more than 25% of its income from rents, royalties, interest, and dividends, which classify as passive income.
5. Obtain IRS approval.

Advantages and Disadvantages

The S corporation has tax advantages of the partnership form and the limited liability advantage of the corporate form. If the business operates at a tax loss, the S corporation allows a pass-through of the loss as a possible offset to the taxpayer's other income. But if the business is operating at a profit and is not able to distribute that profit because of internal cash demands, a disadvantage arises in that the shareholder must pay income taxes on undistributed earnings.

Recent revisions in the tax laws have made the S corporation a more attractive option as a business organization. There has been some relaxation in rules that formerly made any violation of the fairly complex regulations cause for large, retroactive tax bills. This was true even though the violation was unintentional. There is more reason now for small corporations to examine S corporation status. This is especially true for start-up firms that expect to have losses for awhile and for profitable companies that are not capital-intensive and expect to pay big dividends.

Three pieces of recent legislation brought improvements to the tax treatment of S corporations and should be studied before undertaking this type of organization. These are:

1. The 1981 Economic Recovery Tax Act.

2. The 1982 Tax Equity and Fiscal Responsibility Act.

3. The Subchapter S Revision Act of 1982.

Major Revisions for S Corporations

The number of permissible shareholders has been increased to 35, thus allowing increased capital to be brought in. The requirement that there be only one class of common stock has been relaxed to also allow common stock *without* voting rights. This permits the donation or sale of stock to persons such as family members without a diminution of voting control. The new rules provide for a capital loss (when the S corporation's capital losses exceed its capital gain) that is passed through to the shareholders to reduce their own personal capital gains. This does reduce the shareholder's basis in the stock up to the extent of the holdings. Operating losses passed through to a shareholder in excess of the shareholder's basis (in either stock or debt) can now be carried forward indefinitely. Another change from the 1982 tax revision allows an S corporation to receive income from foreign sources.

The former rigid 20% limitation on passive income has been relaxed, making it easier for an S corporation to own real estate or other rental property, as well as stocks and bonds. In the past there was some concern that an unexpected loss of the S corporation's status would occur if the 20% limit on passive income was inadvertently exceeded. Now, passive earnings can go beyond 25% of gross earnings and are subject to taxation at corporate rates. But if they exceed 25% for each of three consecutive years, the S corporation election is revoked. Passive income generally includes gross receipts from interest, dividends, rents, royalties, annuities, and gains from sales or exchanges of stock or securities.

There are some other provisions in the Subchapter S Revision Act of 1982 that make an S corporation more nearly identical to a partnership for tax purposes. The new law requires that pro rata distribution of income and deductions based on the proportion of stock ownership be reported, just as it would be for a partnership. Further, the items of income and expense are allocated to shareholders on a per-share-of-stock-per-day-of-ownership basis. This precludes, for instance, the transfer of stock to a child in December, thus making it possible for the child to receive a full year of income from the stock.

S Corporation Tax Reports

The corporation must file a tax return on Form 1120S for each year that the election under S corporation is effective. Shareholders must include their prorated shares of the corporation's taxable income and gains in their returns, whether or

TABLE 9–1
Comparison of Business Organizations

Characteristics	Partnerships		Corporations	
	General	Limited	General	S Corporation
1. Liability of owners	Partners— unlimited	General Partners— unlimited Limited Partners— limited	Shareholders— limited	Same as General
2. Transferability of interests	Not transferable	General Partner—not transferable Limited Partner— transferable	Transferable, subject to limitations with other share- holders	Same as General
3. Management	All partners have equal voice, unless otherwise agreed	General Partners have equal voice Limited Partners have no voice	Shareholders elect directors to manage	Same as General
4. Taxation	Not a taxable entity—net income pro- rated and taxed to each partner per- sonally	Same as General	Income taxed to corporation Dividends taxed to shareholders	Net income taxed to share- holders whether dis- tributed or not
5. Method of creation	Established by agreement of the parties	Same as General, plus filing form in public office	Charter issued by State	Same as General, plus filing agree- ment with IRS
6. Duration	Termination by agreement, withdrawal, death, or bankruptcy	Term provided in the authoriz- ing certificate	May be perpetual	Same as General

not the amount is actually distributed. However, a shareholder must report in-come differently from a partner. If the shareholder's tax year is different from that of the corporation, any distribution of current taxable income must be reported in the tax year it is actually received. (For a partnership, any distributive share of partnership items is reported in the tax year in which the *last day* of the partnership year falls, regardless of the date actually received.) The S corporation reports any *undistributed* income in the personal tax year in which the tax year of the corporation ends.*

The 1986 Tax Act required all S corporations to switch to a calendar year accounting period for tax reporting purposes. However, legislation in 1987 modified the requirement allowing S corporations to retain prior fiscal year accounting periods if preferred. The change created confusion that had not been resolved at the time of this writing.

Comparison of Business Organizations

Table 9–1 provides a quick reference for comparing the general characteristics of the major forms of business organizations. An investor's selection of the best business form depends on many additional facts—goals, personal income and tax obligations, and the other people involved.

---

*Additional information may be obtained from IRS Publication 589, *Tax Information on S Corporations*.

10

Forms of Ownership

Land is everlasting, and that makes it different from everything else that can be owned. Land can be used for many purposes. The laws concerning landownership have developed in ways that recognize the many uses of land and the changing needs of the population. Landownership consists of legal rights, which can be limited in nature and duration. When a person owns all of the rights to a tract of land with no time limitation, the ownership is termed "fee simple." As the number of ownership rights diminishes, so does the quality of ownership. These are the major rights to land.

- *Possession.* The actual holding or occupancy of land.
- *Use.* The employment of the property.
- *Enjoyment.* The right to use without interference or harassment.
- *Disposition.* The right to sell, lease, mortgage, give away, or otherwise dispose of the land.

How these rights are held differentiates the various interests, or *estates*, that can be owned.

In modern law, the right of disposition, which includes the right to sell or mortgage the property, necessarily includes the right to determine the duration of the ownership term. It is this crucial right of disposition—more than mere possession or use, which can be obtained under a lease—that provides the best test of ownership.

Land rights and ownership methods are embodied in the laws of each state, and there are differences which stem from the origin of the region. The Eastern and Midwestern States normally follow English common law. The Southwestern states incorporate Spanish law, with its emphasis on community property rights. Louisiana is unique, with property rights based on French civil law.

This chapter focuses on real property law and is intended to provide the real estate investor with an overview of the law and its terminology. By understanding the major rights that are involved in landownership and the complex nature of the law, the investor can readily recognize the need for competent legal counsel when landownership rights are being determined. With a basic knowledge of the subject and its terminology, the investor can better understand the advice that a competent attorney will provide.

Trusts

One method of holding real estate is in the form of a trust. The purpose of a trust is to place assets under the absolute control of a trustee for the benefit of a designated recipient. There are tax advantages in holding assets in trusts, although taxing authorities continue to question the use of trusts. The trend of court rulings in trust ownership has been to place the burden of liability on a beneficiary if that person exercises *any* control over the trust's management. And trusts can be treated as corporations for tax purposes where the beneficial interests are transferable. There are many variations in kinds of trusts. A few of the key points are considered next.

Trust Estates

Assets may be assigned to a trustee for the benefit of a recipient by agreement or by will. The trustee has discretion over the operation and disposition of the trust assets, but must always act for the best interest of the beneficiary.

The nature of estates and trusts is another complex matter and the use of this procedure should not be undertaken without professional counsel. There can be certain tax advantages from the creation of a separate taxable entity plus the exercise of control on how one's assets are distributed. An example of a simple trust procedure is the transfer of property from A to B as trustee, with instructions to pay the income to C at periodic intervals. A is the grantor, creator, or trustor, in this action; B is the trustee, or fiduciary; and C is the beneficiary. The property transferred is the corpus, or principal, of the trust. A new taxable entity is thus created for which returns must be filed and taxes paid. *

The estate or trust—unlike a partnership—may be required to pay a federal income tax, as may the beneficiary of a share of the estate's income. There is

---

*For further information, see IRS Publication Number 448, *Estate and Gift Taxes, Federal*.

no double tax, however, as with a corporation. Some trusts require the distribution of all current income, which must be reported by the beneficiary whether or not it is actually received. Other trusts grant the trustee discretion to distribute all or part of the current income. The beneficiary must then report only the income that is required to be distributed plus any optional distribution actually made during the tax year. Any losses incurred by the estate or trust are generally not deductible by a beneficiary.

Inter Vivos Trust.   An inter vivos trust is one that takes effect during the life of the trustor or creator of the trust. One can transfer property to a trustee with instructions that income from the trust be paid to one's children, a spouse, relatives, or a charity.

Testamentary Trust.   A testamentary trust takes effect after the death of the creator. An individual can leave instructions in a will that upon death certain assets are to be placed in a trust. A bank, a trust company, or even a friend can be designated as trustee. Instructions are left to the trustee as to who the beneficiaries will be, how and when the trust income should be disbursed to them, and how the assets are to be managed. Because trusts offer property management and financial control as well as a number of tax and estate planning advantages, this form of property ownership is growing in popularity.

Land Trust

The land trust is a form of ownership permitted in Illinois, Indiana, Florida, North Dakota, and Virginia. Under the land trust procedure, a landowner conveys title to a trustee under a trust agreement that designates the beneficiary and gives the trustee full power to manage the property according to written instructions from the beneficiary. The beneficial interest is not transferable and is considered personal property (even though the asset is real estate), which simplifies the succession of ownership.

One advantage of the land trust is that it allows privacy of ownership—only the trustee's name appears on the record of title. Because this procedure can also be used to conceal conflicts of interest or withhold material information from a potential purchaser, its use has been restricted in most states.

Real Estate Investment Trust (REIT)

In passing the Real Estate Investment Trust Act in 1960, Congress intended to provide a means for the smaller investor to participate in real estate projects, as well as to increase the amount of money available for real estate financing. As an incentive, the Act permits a trust that qualifies under its requirement to pay no tax at the corporate level. Thus income is taxed only once—when it is distributed to the shareholders.

To qualify as an investment trust under the Act, each year a trust must:

1. Be beneficially owned by at least 100 persons holding transferable shares or certificates, with not more than 50% of its shares held by five or fewer individuals.

2. Earn 95% or more of its gross income from passive sources including dividends, interest, real property rents, or gains from sale of stock, securities, and real property.

3. Earn 75% or more of its gross income from real property rents, interest on real property, or gain from its sale.

4. Generally, 75% of a REIT's assets must be represented by real estate assets, cash, or government securities.

5. Requires distribution of a percentage of income to its shareholders subject to certain rules and penalties.

The 1986 Tax Act granted some relief to prior rules regarding distribution of a REIT's income. The "required distribution" is:

- 85% of ordinary income
- 95% of capital gain net income, and
- any shortfall of distribution from the prior year

There is a 4% excise tax on any excess of that amount required to be distributed over the amount actually distributed in any one calendar year.

The pooling of funds from smaller investors—thereby creating a substantial investment capacity—is the same general concept used by mutual funds (for investment in stocks and bonds), drilling funds (for oil and gas drilling prospects), and money market funds (for the purchase of treasury bills or other short-term paper). REITs have been sponsored by banks, insurance companies, and a few mortgage companies, with the management of the investments contracted to a specialized management team. The REIT investor has little voice in management and generally selects among funds by comparing their investment policies and records of accomplishment. Beneficial interests usually sell for $100 or less per unit.

In the early 1970s, REITs expanded rapidly (from roughly $1 billion in assets to $20 billion), but encountered difficulties in the declining real estate market of 1974–75. The source of difficulty was that many trusts had shifted from an emphasis on owning real estate to an emphasis on lending money for the development of real estate. As interest rates climbed to as high as 18% on construction loans, many developments fell into arrears and were unable to finish partially constructed projects. The result was damaging to the REIT as an investment form. But the basic concept is sound, and most funds have resolved their problems either through mergers or by holding on to properties taken through foreclosures that have regained value in the reviving real estate market.

Another way that the Real Estate Investment Trust concept has been utilized is in the disposition of large properties. By conveying an asset, such as Rockefeller Center, to a REIT, the former owners are able to convert their asset into cash through the sale of interests in the asset holding REIT.

Classification of Estates

The laws of real property concern the many aspects of landownership, its use, and its conveyance. Its subjects include estates, ownership, leaseholds, contracts, mortgages, deeds, land titles, recording, and more. This chapter concentrates on two of these subjects—estates and landownership. And it outlines property rights as they relate to (1) the interest in land and (2) how the land is owned.

Definition of Estate.   In real property law, an estate is an interest in land. It is the sum of property rights and/or things affixed to the land, which have a given duration of time (including infinity). An estate is concerned with the land; an ownership is concerned with people. But obviously the two concepts are not truly separable.

Historical Background

Today, every person in most free societies has the right to acquire an interest in land. We tend to overlook the fact that this was not always true. But much of our modern real property law can be directly traced to its origins in medieval Europe, where property rights were substantially less than universal.

Under the feudal system of the early Middle Ages, landownership represented far more power than it does today. Landholding provided a basis for government, as well as for military protection. It was used to determine both the social and economic status of the landowner. Land was parcelled out by the king to various lords, who might pass on a portion of their land to lesser lords in exchange for some form of service. Actual possession or use of the land was usually left to the lower classes, who worked the land for a share of its produce.

This right to work the land was essentially a lease and did not grant any continuing interest in the land or the right to dispose of it. Upon the death of a tenant, all rights returned to the landlord. Thus landownership was primarily an ownership of *present interest*. Not until after the Norman conquest of England in 1066 did the concepts of landownership that are the foundation of modern law begin. About this same time, certain other rights to land began to crystallize which we now identify as *future interests* as well as the terminology distinguishing *freehold* estates from *non-freehold* estates. Freehold came to mean the more extensive rights of ownership, while non-freehold was considered to be the "lease for years." Medieval law was essentially the law of freehold estates (since the rights of tenants in non-freehold estates were not a matter of great concern). Future interests, which are principally the reversions and remainders stemming from life estates, began when the varieties of freehold estates came to be differentiated.

The law—and subsequent court rulings—have identified a number of qualifications to the precise nature of land interests, which makes understanding difficult for the person who is not a student of the law. Further confusion results from the fact that the word "estate" has other real estate meanings, being both a large property with an elaborate house and the property of a deceased person. For the purpose of this text, the word "estate" means the degree or quantity of interest that a person has in land, the nature of the right, its duration, and its relation to the rights of others.

There is also a distinction in the law between an heir and anyone else to whom a grantor conveys property upon his death. An *heir* is the legally designated person who would be entitled to receive the deceased person's property in the absence of a will. If a grantor conveys property by will to someone other than an heir, that person is known as a *devisee*.

Outline of Major Classes of Estates

Following is an outline of the major classes of estates, which are explained in the section that follows.

1. *Present Possessory Freehold Estates of Potentially Infinite Duration.*
   a. Fee Simple Absolute.
   b. Fee Simple Conditional.
   c. Fee Simple Estates of Potentially Limited Duration.
      (1) Fee Simple Determinable.
      (2) Fee Simple Subject to Condition Subsequent.
      (3) Fee Simple Subject to an Executory Limitation.

2. *Present Possessory Freehold Estates of Limited Duration (Life Estates).*

    a. Conventional Life Estates.

        (1) Life Estate for Grantee's Life.

        (2) Life Estate Limited by Life of Someone Other than Grantee.

    b. Legal Life Estates.

        (1) Dower.

        (2) Curtesy.

        (3) Homestead Protection.

3. Future Interests.

    a. Reversion.

    b. Remainder.

    c. Executory Interests.

4. Non-Freehold Estates (Leaseholds).

    a. Tenancy for Years.

    b. Tenancy from Period to Period.

    c. Tenancy at Will.

    d. Tenancy at Sufferance.

5. Land Interests Not Deemed Estates.

    a. Easements.

    b. Licenses.

    c. Profit.

    d. Covenants.

PRESENT POSSESSORY FREEHOLD ESTATES OF POTENTIALLY INFINITE DURATION

The legal expression "present possessory" can be defined as "to own now." Possessory is to possess, or to own. And "present" means "now," not after someone has passed away or made a gift of the property. The modern definition of "freehold" is almost the same as the medieval definition—i.e., ownership of land. "Infinite duration" means that the property is inheritable by the heirs and devisees of the owner. It is not subject to "defeasance," meaning that inheritance cannot be defeated by any limiting condition in the *title* to the property.

Fee Simple Absolute.   The highest and most extensive estate in common law is called *fee simple absolute*. It is inheritable and not limited to a particular class of heirs. Termination of the estate can be accomplished only if the owner dies without a will ("intestate") *and* without heirs. If these two circumstances occur, the property passes to the state "by escheat."

The origin of the term "fee simple absolute" has an historical background. The word "fee" derives from an old Ango-Saxon word that meant cattle or property. In that time, cattle were used as a medium of exchange or payment; then property consisted chiefly of cattle. Today, fee means property, an estate, of potentially infinite duration. This means that nothing in the conveyance of title can cause its loss, such as not using the property as may be required by its title. The word "simple" passes to us from English law and means there are no limits on the inheritability of the property. Title can thus be passed to anyone, regardless of who the person is. "Absolute" means the estate is indefeasible and cannot be divested. This means that the property is under the full control of its owner who has the right to possess, use, dispose of, or pledge the property without triggering any clause in the conveyance instrument that might divest the owner of title. Thus, fee simple, or fee as it is sometimes called, is an estate in land without limitation, which is inheritable without restrictions by the heirs of the owner. A fee simple may be absolute, as described above, or it may be qualified. Qualified means there are some conditions in the conveyance of title that may restrict future use or transfer of the property. This is more fully explained next.

Fee Simple Conditional.   If the owner places a limit on which heirs are entitled to inherit the property, a conditional estate may be created. In early common law, the grantor might convey land "to grantee and the heirs of his body." This wording was interpreted to mean that the conveyance was conditional on the grantee's having a child, i.e., if no children came to the grantee, then the estate became a life estate for the grantee. Such an estate would terminate with the death of the grantee, and the estate would then revert to the original grantor and/or his other heirs. This interpretation of the conditions of inheritance was modified in 1285 to provide a life estate for the grantee and a *fee* for his heirs. Later judicial rulings limited the fee so conveyed to a life estate. If the lineal, directly descended heirs failed to produce children, the estate, as before, reverted to the original grantor and his heirs. The result of these rulings is the *fee tail*, which is a form of estate controlled by the grantor after his death through restrictions on the class of potential transferees. This kind of restriction on who might inherit land stems from medieval English law designed to protect the landowning families. If you were not a family member, it was very difficult to gain title to the land. This concept of restricting land conveyance has not been accepted in the United States.

Fee Simple Estates of Potentially Limited Duration. When the owner, or grantor, wants to control the *use* of land after his death, the wording used to convey the property expresses the intended limitation. How the conveyance is worded determines the type of estate that is granted. This method of limitation was not available under early common law, but came into existence after passage of the *Statute of Uses* in 1536. Under modern law, there are three forms of controlling land use by words of conveyance.

1. *Fee simple determinable.* The words of conveyance to the grantee can read, for example, "so long as the premises are used for a public park," or "until premises are no longer used for a public park," or "while premises are used for a public park." The conveyance may be silent as to disposition of the property if the limiting conditions are no longer met. The law holds that, in such a case, the possibility exists that the property would revert to the grantor or heirs.

2. *Fee simple subject to condition subsequent.* The words of conveyance to grantee contain a disposition clause in the event the limiting conditions are not met. These words could be "but if the property is not used for a public park, grantor may re-enter." Modern law requires court action as a prerequisite to enforcement of the grantor's right to re-enter the property.

3. *Fee simple subject to executory limitation.* This form of estate is similar to "fee simple subject to condition subsequent." The distinguishing feature is that the executory limitation causes a transfer of the interest to a third party named in the instrument of conveyance, rather than a return of the interest to the grantor. The conveyance wording might be "to grantee, but if not used for a public park, then to [a third party (not the grantor)]."

It should be noted that all three of these forms of conveyance—fee simple determinable, fee simple subject to condition subsequent, and fee simple subject to executory limitation—create a present possessory interest in the grantee, plus a future interest for the grantor in the event that the expressed condition causes a termination of the limited fee simple estate.

PRESENT POSSESSORY FREEHOLD ESTATES OF LIMITED DURATION (LIFE ESTATES)

A life estate is limited to the lifetime(s) of one or more persons. Because of its limited duration, some legal definitions class this form as a "less than freehold" interest. There are two forms of life estates: (1) the conventional form, created by an express act of the parties, and (2) legal life estates, created by operation of the law.

Conventional Life Estates.   The purpose of granting a life estate is to provide for the financial well-being of the grantee during his or her life but to deny him or her the right to pass on the property to heirs or others. The limitation can be based either on the life of the grantee or on the life of someone else.

1. *Life estate for grantee's life.* When the intention of the grantor is to limit the benefit from an estate to the grantee's life, the conveyance might be "to grantee for his life." The recipient might be, for example, an uncle faced with heavy family medical expenses. Upon his death, the property would revert to the grantor.

2. *Life estate limited by someone other than grantee.* In this form of estate, the conveyance would read "to grantee for the life of [a third party.]" The purpose might be to provide the benefit of an income property to a brother needing assistance until the death of a parent whose estate would pass in part to the brother.

Legal Life Estates.   This form of estate is created by statute (not common law). The thrust of these state laws is to protect the interests of parties to a marriage. English common law considered property acquired during marriage as belonging to the husband only. As a measure of balance, these statutes grant the wife ownership of one-third (one-half in some states) of the family's property *upon the death of the husband.* This estate owned by the wife is termed *dower right.*

1. *Dower.* To be eligible for dower rights, a wife must meet three legal requirements. These are (1) a valid marriage, (2) possession of property by the husband during marriage, and (3) the death of the husband. In those states that still recognize a wife's dower rights, a purchaser of property must obtain the wife's written consent to the sale, either through signing the deed with her husband or through a separate *quit claim deed.* Failure to obtain the wife's consent to the sale of property leaves her dower rights intact, and they may be asserted upon the husband's death at a much later date. This is one more reason for a purchaser of real property both to require a title search by a qualified attorney and to insure the title.

2. *Curtesy.* In some states a husband holds benefits in his deceased wife's property—called *curtesy*—that are similar to dower rights. These rights are not so clear as dower and may be defeated by the wife in her will. In some

states the law requires that a child be born of the marriage before a husband may qualify for curtesy.

Both the dower and curtesy rights developed from a concept of male dominance in marriage that is contrary to the modern concept of equal rights for men and women. The current trend favors a more equitable system of husband-wife property ownership, as under community property laws. The third form of legal life estate—homestead protection—is associated with marriage but provides almost equal protection for husband and wife.

3. *Homestead protection.* All but seven states* have some form of homestead protection that amounts to a life estate in the family residence. These laws are directed toward providing legal protection for a husband and wife against the forced sale of the family home as a result of debts or judgments. The laws further restrict the rights of a husband or wife to act without the other when conveying their homestead or offering it as collateral for a loan. Depending on the state, the law may require that the homestead right be indicated by a written declaration recorded in the public records. This is unlike dower and curtesy rights, which are *automatic*—not recorded—in the states that recognize them.

FUTURE INTERESTS

A future interest is a right to real property that allows possession at some future time. The term itself is somewhat imprecise since the interest must also have a present existence. There are three general classes of future interests: reversion, remainder, and executory interest.

Reversion. If a grantor conveys an interest in property to someone for that person's life (a life estate) and makes no disposition of the property upon the death of the grantee, the law presumes that the grantor intended that the interest would come back to himself (revert) or to his estate. The grantor can, of course, be more specific, stipulating in the conveyance that the property reverts to him upon the death of the grantee.

Remainder. Remainder is like reversion, except that it favors a third party, rather than the grantor. The remainder is created when a grantor conveys a life estate

---

*Connecticut, Delaware, Hawaii, Maryland, New Jersey, Pennsylvania, and Rhode Island (plus the District of Columbia).

to someone, specifying that upon that person's death the interest passes to a third party. For example, a man might convey an interest in real property to his wife for the rest of her life, and specify that upon her death the interest is to be divided equally among the surviving children. The children own a future interest in the property and are called *remaindermen*. Since remaindermen do hold an interest in the property, they have a right to require both maintenance of the premises and payment of taxes, property assessments, and any interest on debt secured by the property.

Executory Interests.   Executory interests are future interests very similar to a remainder, except that possession is not taken immediately upon the death of the person holding the life estate. These future interests follow limited interests held by others. There are two types:

1. *Springing executory interests.* The interest comes after a reversion of limited duration. A typical conveyance would read "to life tenant for life tenant's life; then, one year after life tenant's death, to [a third party] and his heirs." For the year following the death of the life tenant, the interest would revert to the grantor (or his estate). At the end of that year, the fee simple interest would automatically pass to the third party named in the conveyance.

2. *Shifting executory interests.* The future interest comes after a limited interest in persons other than the grantor. An example of the conveyance that might be used is "to life tenant for life tenant's life; but if life tenant marries outside the faith, then to [a third party] and his heirs." A marriage "outside the faith" would automatically divest the life tenant of the life estate, and simultaneously vest a fee simple estate in the third party.

NON-FREEHOLD ESTATES (LEASEHOLDS)

As developed under common law, the type of estate that conveys possession and use to the grantee—but retains ownership (with the right of disposition) in the grantor—is called a leasehold estate. It is not a freehold estate because it is not ownership of the land. The types of lease are not always clearly defined, and state laws provide some variations in interpretation. However, the following classification explains the basic kinds of tenancy under a leasehold estate.

The Tenancy for Years.   This estate is defined as any leasehold with a term that must end on or before a *specified date*. Most states limit the number of years for which a leasehold may be created. In California, for example, the maximum term is 15 years for farm property and 99 years for urban property.

The Tenancy From Period to Period. Also called a "periodic tenancy," the duration of the lease is expressed as "from [time period] to [time period]." The permissible periods may be from a day to a year in length. A term longer than one year would fall under the "for years" classification. The periodic tenancy is the leasehold found in a month-to-month apartment lease. Terminating a period-to-period lease requires some form of notification. The rule varies from state to state—generally the notification requirement is the length of the period, but no more than six months.

The Tenancy at Will. This type of leasehold estate lasts as long as both landlord and tenant wish it to last. Either party may terminate this lease at any time. Usually, however, the terminating party must satisfy a notification requirement.

The Tenancy at Sufferance. When a tenant fails to vacate the premises at the expiration of a lease, continued occupancy is termed "tenancy at sufferance." This tenancy is without right, and without the landlord's consent. However, if the landlord fails to take the necessary steps to evict the tenant, continued occupancy can be interpreted as a periodic estate. Even under tenancy at sufferance, some states require a termination notice.

LAND INTEREST NOT DEEMED ESTATES

Some *relationships* regarding land can be created between a landowner and others which fall short of being *interests* in the land. Prime examples include easements, licenses, profit, and covenants.

Easements. An easement is a right to *use* a piece of land, but carries no other rights of ownership. Under the law, the right of "use" is not the same as the right of "possession."

Licenses. A license is similar to an easement, in that it grants the right to use a portion of the land. But it differs from an easement in that it is revocable. For example, the license of a guest to use an owner's home may be revoked at any time by the owner.

Profit. The right to sever and remove certain things attached to the land, such as ore or live timber, is called in the law a "profit."

Covenants. Steps an owner takes to restrict the use of land under his control are called "covenants." A covenant can benefit the noncovenanting party, but does not entitle him or her to personal use.

Classification of Property Ownership

Ownership of land may be held by individuals in a number of ways. When two or more individuals hold a property, the manner in which they hold it determines whether or not each individual owner may dispose of his or her interest separately, and whether or not there is a right of survivorship. Following are the categories of ownership.

Sole Ownership

Property held by one person is called an *estate in severalty.* Don't let the legal terminology confuse you; think of severalty as *severed* ownership. Both single and married persons can be sole owners of property. However, state requirements concerning community property, dower, and curtesy rights must be considered when a married person is a sole owner.

Tenants in Common

When two or more persons hold undivided shares in a single property, they may do so as *tenants in common.** No owner can claim a specific portion of the property, as each has a right to possession of the entire property. Interests need not all be the same size. Each owner can sell, mortgage, or otherwise dispose of his or her individual interest. There is no right of survivorship in this form of ownership, which means that each individual's share passes to the heirs or devisees as part of his or her estate. The share does not pass automatically to any of the other owners holding shares as tenants in common.

Joint Tenancy

A joint tenancy† of two or more persons is distinguished by the following features.

1. Each owner has an undivided interest, with the right of possession to the entire property.

2. All joint tenants' ownerships must be acquired simultaneously. New joint tenants cannot be added later without creating a new joint tenancy.

3. There is only one title to the property, and each owner has a share in it. If a share is sold, the new owner must join with the remaining joint tenants

---

*Recognized by all states except Louisiana.
†Recognized by all states except Alaska, Georgia, Louisiana, Ohio, and Oregon.

to create a new joint tenancy, or else the new share owner becomes a tenant in common.

4. The interest of each joint tenant is considered equal, regardless of how much each has contributed. If there are two joint tenants, each would own one-half; if three, each would own one-third. If shares are claimed disproportionately, the law considers the owners to be tenants in common.

5. The major distinction between joint tenants and tenants in common is that joint tenancy includes the *right of survivorship*, i.e., when a joint tenant dies, his or her interest passes automatically and immediately to the remaining joint tenants. The deceased person's interest never becomes a part of the probate estate.

Tenancy by the Entirety

This form of ownership is available *only* for property owned by a *husband and wife*. It is similar to a joint tenancy in that it carries the right of survivorship. (The surviving spouse becomes the sole owner.) It is different from a joint tenancy in that—while they both live—neither husband nor wife can dispose of any interest in the property without the consent of the other. Many states do not recognize this form of ownership, while others restrict its use.

Community Property

In the Southwestern United States, Spanish law provided a basis for *community property** ownership, which is *limited to married persons*. There is some variation among the several state laws, but they are all based on the concept that a husband and wife contribute equally to a marriage and should therefore share equally any property purchased during the marriage. In contrast, English law is based on the concept that a husband and wife merge upon marriage.

Under community property ownership, both spouses must sign any conveyance or mortgage on the property. Each spouse has the right to devise his or her one-half interest to whomever he or she pleases. An interest need not go to the surviving spouse. If there is no will, however, the surviving spouse retains certain rights, which vary among the community property states.

Under community property law, both husband and wife may own *separate property*, i.e., property that is excluded from the community property estate. Separate property includes:

---

*Recognized in Arizona, California, Idaho, Louisiana, Nevada, New Mexico, Texas, and Washington. Replaces tenancy by the entirety.

1. Property owned by either husband or wife *before* marriage, the "separate" nature of which is retained after marriage.

2. Property acquired by either husband or wife after marriage through gift, devise, or inheritance.

3. Property purchased with funds which have been maintained as separate funds after marriage.

Separate property *can* be conveyed or mortgaged without the signature of the owner's spouse.

Because both parties to a marriage retain equal ownership rights to property accumulated during the marriage, community property states recognize neither dower nor curtesy rights.

11

Tools of Analysis

This chapter considers analysis procedures and ties together information covered in previous chapters. Up to this point the text has offered information on real property that is of general concern to an investor. Some has been background information on the nature of real property. Several chapters have been devoted to a study of basic property taxes and federal income tax laws. And an overview has been given on real property law and the terminology involved, plus a discussion of business organizations and the tax ramifications of each.

Real estate offers a variety of investments, and the returns derived are generally not precise in measurement. Unlike fixed income investments, such as savings certificates or annuities, real estate income can be subject to fluctuating market conditions. Nevertheless, analysis is necessary in order to make basic comparisons. It is the purpose of the next few chapters to explain the kinds of information available on real estate opportunities, some of the problems associated with the presentation of this information, and how the use of standard analysis forms can help make more accurate comparisons.

Most real property investments offer some kind of periodic income. Information on this income is usually found in a financial statement that can be a projection of what to expect (or hope for!), or it can be actual figures showing past experience. First, let's examine how financial information is offered. There are three basic financial statements: (1) balance sheet, (2) profit and loss statement, and (3) operating statement. Examples and an explanation of each follow.

Basic Financial Statements

Balance Sheet

The balance sheet details the assets and liabilities of a person or business. The difference between assets and liabilities is the *net worth*, or *equity*.

A simplified balance sheet is illustrated below.

Assets			Liabilities		
Current assets			Current liabilities		
Cash		$ 5,500	Accounts payable		$ 2,800
Rents receivable		$ 3,100	Long-term debt		
			First mortgage	$300,000	
Fixed assets			Less: Principal paid	$ 41,000	
Land		$ 78,000	Balance due		$259,000
Buildings	$385,000		Total liabilities		$261,800
Less: Depreciation:	$ 91,000		Net Worth		
Buildings (net)		$294,000	Partnership equity		$118,800
Total assets		$380,600	Liabilities plus Net Worth		$380,600

The balance sheet is a history. It shows either the results of a business operation or an individual's financial progress. The important "bottom line" is the net worth. Take a second look at the illustration above. Current assets and all liabilities are reasonably easy to verify and may be considered accurate for the purpose of a preliminary evaluation. The big question is the value of land and buildings. Are the figures in this statement the original cost of the land and buildings, usually called *book value?** Or are these *appraised values*? Or are they the owner's estimates of *market value*? A properly prepared statement uses footnotes to clarify the valuation, but many owners prefer to omit this information. To overcome this problem, a real estate investor must normally make a new appraisal of property value for use in a comparative analysis.

A balance sheet is less important to the investor buying solely an income property, i.e., *not* buying the *business* that is operating the property. Even then a balance sheet provides important information on outstanding debt and on liabilities that could become liens against the property. And a balance sheet offers any buyer some information on depreciation schedules.

Profit and Loss Statement

Like the balance sheet, a profit and loss statement is closely related to the owner's confidential financial data. The profit and loss statement lists the business income,

---

*Basis value is the asset value as determined by recent IRS rules, which may be different from book value.

all expenses, and other deductions including depreciation and allows for income tax liability. The profit and loss statement may or may not be available to a prospective buyer. The information it contains is not critical, unless the property acquisition is made through the purchase of an operating corporation. Following is an example of a P & L statement in a simplified form as it might appear at the end of the tax year:

Example

Profit and Loss Statement	
Income from Operations	$148,878
Less: Expenses Incurred	62,569
Net Operating Income	$ 86,309
Less: Interest expense	45,324
Less: Depreciation allowed	36,531
Net Income	$ 4,454
Provision for income taxes	2,048
Net Profit	$ 2,406

Operating Statement

The operating statement is generally considered the key to an evaluation of income property. It is a record of all income less all expenses, leaving the net operating income at the bottom line. It is the kind of information most likely to be found with a real estate offering.

The first problem with an operating statement is understanding the nomenclature used to identify income and expense items. The second is determining the source of the information presented. The third is making sure that no essential information has been omitted.

A simplified statement, using nomenclature suggested by the National Association of Realtors, follows.

Note first that net operating income in this example shows no deduction for either interest or depreciation. Both of these important deductions are discussed later. The purpose here is to examine the operating figures and discuss the nomenclature used to identify accounts.

The following item-by-item explanations cover the major accounts normally used in an operating statement. We begin at the first line.

Scheduled Gross Income. In a statement on income property, the first line usually represents the maximum income that the property can be expected to produce at full occupancy. It is variously called Scheduled Gross Income, Gross

Potential Income, Gross Rent Roll, Total Calculated Income, or Available Gross Income. Sometimes it even goes by the inadequate name of "Income." The first line may well show the *actual* income that has been received from the property. If so, there would be no line for vacancy and credit losses.

Example

Operating Statement

Scheduled Gross Income		$100,000
Less: Vacancy and credit losses		7,000
Gross Operating Income		$ 93,000
Less: Operating Expenses		
Taxes	$ 6,500	
Insurance	3,100	
Utilities	6,900	
Advertising licenses	1,100	
Management	5,000	
Payroll, including taxes	14,000	
Supplies	1,200	
Services	1,100	
Maintenance	1,900	
Other	500	
Total expenses		$ 41,300
Net Operating Income		$ 51,700

Vacancy and Credit Losses. If the statement shows no deduction for vacancy and credit losses, then either the first line represents actual income or it is misrepresented. The reason is that, except for very small rental properties, it is almost impossible to realize a property's full potential gross income. There will almost always be a few premature vacancies, some rental income loss while units undergo renovation, and occasional failures to collect the proper rent. The most accurate figure to use for vacancy and credit losses would be, of course, the *actual* annual amount. But if the statement is an analysis, the vacancy and credit loss figures are often based on a *percentage* loss, usually between 5% and 10% of gross potential income. The flip side of the vacancy and credit loss figure is the occupancy rate. An average 92% occupancy rate would mean an 8% vacancy and credit loss.

Gross Operating Income. This is the *actual* income received during the period covered by the statement. This figure includes not only regular rental income, but also any miscellaneous income from services sold, parking fees, or utility charges.

Operating Expenses. There are differences between fixed charges (taxes, insurance, etc.) and operating expenses, but these differences are usually not noted in an income property statement. Operating expenses include all costs except mortgage loan interest (although some accountants even include interest). The reason interest is not included as an "operating expense" is that interest is a cost of *financing*, while the purpose of the statement at this point is to learn how much income can be made from *operating* the property. Do not confuse operating expenses with the cost of financing. A property may operate at a reasonable profit, yet show a negative cash flow (loss) because it is overburdened with excessive financing costs.

Expense items in a financial statement can be "factual" and nevertheless fail to tell the full story. This problem mostly concerns the flexibility built into maintenance costs and replacement charges. If the property is new, maintenance costs can *temporarily* be held to a minimum, but restoration costs at a later date may be substantially higher. If the property contains such items as drapes, carpeting, and appliances, deterioration occurs almost daily. The cost of replacing them, however, may not crop up for three to five years. Good accounting procedure allows and allocates for these hidden expenses, thereby helping management to make informed decisions. Tax laws require that assets with a useful life of more than one year be capitalized, and only a portion of their cost is eligible for deduction from income each year.

Depreciation deduction for a building has lost much of its original meaning. This deduction was once thought of as a replacement reserve for the building itself. But depreciation is not really a "cost" by today's inflation-based standards, since buildings generally *increase* in value rather than depreciate. So depreciation is now viewed as a tax-saving device, not as an expense. The question of depreciation is examined in greater detail in Chapter 6.

Income Tax Statements

The idea of keeping two sets of books hints of chicanery. Yet it's a common practice for both individuals and businesses, and it's rarely intended to deceive anyone. The reason it's common is that federal tax laws, designed to accomplish desirable social goals as well as provide tax revenues, have built up certain requirements that tend to distort the true value of an asset.

Here are a few examples. The tax distortion can be severe for an oil operator. The reserve value of a newly discovered well is not shown on a tax return until the production has been sold. Yet this operator undoubtedly sees a substantial increase in the asset value of the property *as soon as the oil* is discovered. And this asset would represent collateral value to a lending institution. Likewise, newborn calves are assets, but are not taxable income until they are sold. A banker dealing mainly in cash and fixed-value promissory notes, on the other hand, has a minimal amount of asset distortion to reckon with. A real estate investor falls somewhere in between. Accelerated depreciation schedules, the new rules for calculating capital gains, the application of minimum taxes on tax-preference income, and the passive activity rules all have a bearing on how the real estate investor must keep records for tax purposes.

Providing a realistic statement on an operating property usually requires two sets of records—one for tax purposes, and the other for the property's owners and other interested parties. Footnotes can be used to adequately explain the major adjustments.

Does the prospective buyer of real property have a *right* to see the federal income tax statements that have been filed for the property? No. The seller has no *legal* obligation to provide this information because tax reports are considered confidential. However, the buyer *may* make the furnishing of tax reports a mandatory condition of the sale if it seems justified.

Accounting Methods

The previous section identified the basic financial statements used in business accounting. It also explained some of the distortions that can occur in both balance sheets and operating statements. To effectively use a financial statement in analysis work, a real estate investor must understand that there are differences in (1) methods of presenting financial information, and (2) the people who prepare the statements. This section discusses the principal accounting methods found in the real estate field. The next section describes the general qualifications of people who prepare financial statements.

Cash Basis Accounting

Cash basis is the simplest method of keeping financial records and is used by most individuals and smaller businesses. Essentially, this method records income only when the cash is received and an expense when it is paid. Under this system, it is possible to overlook an expense if the bill is not paid. Thus, there can be some distortion unless adjustments are made at the close of an accounting period.

The 1986 Tax Reform Act prohibited the use of the cash method of accounting for corporations (other than S corporations), partnerships with corporate partners, and tax shelters if these entities have annual gross receipts over $5 million.

Accrual Basis Accounting

As business grows, the need for more accurate and timely records becomes essential. So most businesses eventually adopt the accrual method of keeping records. Under this system, income is recorded when it is *earned* (not when payment is received), and the obligation by the customer to pay for the service is listed as an account receivable. When payment is received, it reduces (debits) the account receivable account (crediting cash). Likewise, an expense is recorded as an obligation when the debt is *incurred* (not when paid). The obligation is listed as an account payable item, which is offset when actual payment is made. With this procedure, the current status of the business operation is more accurately given without the number of adjustments necessary to correct cash basis methods.

Pro Forma Statement

A pro forma statement is an estimate. It is a projection of future earnings and asset values. For the investor, pro forma should separate what may come to pass from what has already happened. Since the analysis for undertaking an investment is based on future returns, the pro forma is an important tool. If prepared by a qualified professional, the pro forma statement can be invaluable in assessing future returns. However, because it is a projection based on estimated results, the figures can be colored to present a distorted projection.

Preparation of Statements

Lacking standards, laws, or regulatory agency guidelines for the information it contains, a financial statement can be inaccurate to the point of misrepresentation. However, there are some good restraints. The Securities and Exchange Commission (SEC) issues and enforces strict requirements for financial data presented to the general public when securities are offered for sale. Other laws govern the information that a borrower presents to a regulated lending institution in an effort to secure a loan. A misrepresentation of facts can be a felony offense. A third formal restraint are the anti-fraud laws. But for the average real estate investor, the most important assurance of complete and accurate financial information is the reputation and integrity of the person or firm preparing the statements. The following sections outline the principal sources for the preparation of financial data in the real estate market.

Certified Public Accountant

The highest designation accorded a professional in the accounting field is that of Certified Public Accountant (CPA). It is a state-defined designation. Each state has its own requirements that may vary somewhat from each other. Basically, the standards call for certain minimum education, some experience qualifications, and passing an exhaustive examination on accounting procedures. Some states award a "Public Accountant" designation to those meeting lesser standards. All states require that a CPA pass its own licensing requirements before practicing within the state. Generally, a statement prepared by a CPA can be relied upon for proper preparation and comprehensive information.

Audited Statement.   In most states, only a CPA is permitted to prepare an audited statement. *Audited* means that the information offered in the statement has undergone certain verification procedures and carries the certification of the preparer. Verification includes a careful examination of all bank statements, individual verification of each account receivable, inspection and inventory of physical assets, and certification of all accounts payable.

Generally, neither laws nor regulations require the use of professional accountants in the preparation of financial statements unless the information is used in the sale of securities to the general public. However, lenders and large investors often require that financial information submitted to them for evaluation be prepared in audited form by Certified Public Accountants.

Statements Prepared Without Audit

A statement prepared without audit is much less expensive than one prepared with full auditing procedures. "Without audit" generally means one prepared from the owner's records only. Verification procedures are reduced to a minimum, or eliminated. An unaudited statement prepared by an independent CPA has the advantage of being prepared in accordance with recognized accounting procedures, but can easily pass on to the reader the same basic errors that the property owner might have made, albeit unintentionally.

Owner-Prepared Statements

Whether or not suspicion is justified, a financial statement prepared by a property owner is *always* suspect. Owners rarely possess sufficient accounting expertise to prepare an adequate statement. Besides, it is simply human nature for a buyer to question the seller's own information. An owner's statement is often used merely as a starting point for discussion, with verification steps taken *after* a preliminary evaluation has been made and the buyer has developed some real interest in the property.

Sales Broker-Prepared Statements

A financial statement prepared by a broker trying to sell income property lacks credibility, unless the broker has a solid record of analysis expertise. Commercial brokers commonly use financial analysis sheets as a starting point in developing buyer interest. But many of these sheets are projections that mix fact with fantasy. They are seldom a sound basis for investment.

Problem Areas in Financial Statements

It must be emphasized that most problems occur when the figures are prepared by someone other than an accounting professional. Here are the most common problem areas.

Time Span Covered. One can paint an excessively rosy financial picture by selecting the time span most favorable to the property—even if that period is reported with complete accuracy. An apartment property located in a winter resort area, for example, might show marvelous operating profits from November through April. The rest of the year might not look so great. Or if property had experienced a period of very poor operations, the time span reported might be selected before or after that period. The statement could thus be perfectly accurate for the specific period covered, but still hide the full picture.

Management Costs. When a property is presented to a potential buyer, management costs might be dropped from the record. After all, the seller might say, the new owner will probably hire new management, anyway. Or the seller might rationalize that the new owner will personally run the operation, thus eliminating management costs. To many it seems absurd, but real estate professionals know that many new investors fail to place any value on the time that they'll spend managing the property. And some financial statements fail to list management as a separate cost.

Utility Costs. Utility costs have always been an important expense in real property operation, and they are becoming even more critical. At first glance, utility costs would seem to be fairly easy to ascertain. But verification is very important. In larger properties it is not unusual to have more than one meter, with each meter serving a separate building. Are all of the meters included in the total cost? If not, the figure could be too low. The inaccuracy, on the other hand, could be an overstatement of costs if utility lines are installed to serve commonly owned adjoining properties that are not all included in the proposed sale. An overstatement of costs might be used to justify an increase in rent.

Use of National Averages.   Occasionally a statement will represent the operations of a property—say, a motel—using cost figures developed from national averages for that particular type and size of property. These are an interesting study in "what might be" but of little value in the examination of a specific property.

Supplementary Reports

The detailed reports from which many financial statements are prepared can provide essential information, as well as corroboration for the formal statements. Following are the major pieces of information used for an operating business, which may also be used for an income property operation (depending on the size and the quality of its management).

Certified Rent Schedule.   This is a list of tenants and the rent paid by each, certified by a responsible official of the organization operating the property.

Inventory.   The inventory is a list of all personal property that belongs to the business and is used in its operation. The owner's depreciated basis of value does not pass to a new owner, but such valuation can be helpful in determining the amount of the purchase price that should be allocated to each depreciable asset. The inventory list should be certified by the owner. It becomes a part of the sales transaction, i.e., the transaction is closed *subject to delivery of all inventory items agreed upon at the time of closing.* An inspection of the inventory is sometimes called for as a part of the closing procedures.

Accounts Receivable.   Money owed to the seller may or may not be assigned to a new owner. Property sales are often handled as sales of the physical plant only and not of the going business. Accounts receivable are a part of the going business and are thus often retained by the seller. But if the business *is* sold as part of the property, receivables must be verified and adjusted to the closing date.

Accounts Payable.   Like accounts receivable, bills owed by the seller may or may not be assumed by the new owner as part of the transaction. A new owner must be careful not to allow an unexpected demand for payment of an old or unknown bill. The most common procedure in a sale including inventory or supplies normally purchased on open accounts is to take whatever steps and file whatever notifications are required under the state's bulk sales laws.

Cash Controls.   Operating cash is rarely transferred to the buyer in a property sale. If it is passed on to the new owner, it would be prudent for the new owner to verify the amount at the time of closing the transaction.

Escrow Accounts. An operating property may have a liability in the form of tenants' deposits held for various purposes. The principal items are:

- *Advance rentals.* Money paid for future rental when a lease is signed (usually a "last month's" rental, paid in advance) is a liability of the property and may fall to the new owner.
- *Security deposits.* Money held by a property owner as protection against loss of personal property loaned to a tenant is a liability that passes to the new property owner. A security deposit is commonly collected, for example, in exchange for keys to the leased unit. When the keys are returned, the security deposit is refunded.
- *Damage deposits.* Many landlords require a damage deposit as a part of a lease. This money is applied to repairs needed when the property is vacated. If there is no damage, it must be returned to the tenant. Damage deposits are assessed using a variety of factors, such as the amount of equipment in the rented unit, the type of business (commercial lease) that the tenant will carry on, or the number and kind of pets that the tenant will keep on the premises.

Insurance Policies. Existing hazard insurance and general liability policies may be continued after closing a sale, or the new owner may take out new coverage. It's a matter of negotiation. If the decision is to continue the existing coverage, it should be examined to make sure the coverage is adequate and that the party insured is corrected to name the new owner. If new coverage is desired, the old policy may provide helpful guidance as to the proper coverage and disclose any special risks that need insurance protection.

Ad Valorem Taxes. Tax statements from previous years should be examined for proper assessment and tax rate. Because unpaid ad valorem taxes amount to a first lien on real property, the proper payment and prorating of this tax is an integral part of the closing procedures when property is transferred.

Sales Taxes. State and municipalities have widely varying rules for sales taxes. The tax may or may not apply to rental income. If the tax *does* apply to the investment property, the investor's prime concern should be: "Has it been accurately reported and paid?" If sales taxes are assessed against the property, they could become the new owner's obligation.

Utility Charges. The investor should verify, from recent bills, the number of meters, the number of buildings connected to each meter, and the rates charged. Notifying a utility company is usually sufficient to transfer billing to the new owner and provide a final cutoff for the seller. Failure to notify the utility of an ownership change can result in erroneous billings.

Lease Agreements. An operating property may itself be leasing property from others.

- *Furniture.* Apartment operators often rent out furnished units that use furniture leased from others. Large property owners often set up a separate entity to acquire furniture and lease it directly to the tenants. Whatever the arrangement, the new owner must locate and list all furniture subject to separate leases, locate all lease agreements, and determine whether or not the seller carries a contingent liability for the furniture leased to tenants.

- *Equipment.* Certain equipment found with income property may be leased from others. Common examples are soft-drink machines and ice-makers. The investor must ask: "Can the leases be transferred to me? If so, what are the stipulations?"

- *Storage buildings.* Off-premise storage space may be leased, and it may be necessary to the continuing operation of an income property. A new owner is rarely responsible for an off-premise lease (unless a corporation is being acquired), but awareness of the property lease will help determine if continued use is essential.

- *Land leases.* The reference here is to property that's been added to the basic land area through a lease to improve or expand operations. Additional parking space, for example, is sometimes held under a lease agreement. Liability for the lease may not pass to the new owner, but the need to continue the lease must be examined.

Contracts Outstanding. Operating properties sometimes have agreements with suppliers and other vendors for continuing services. These include the following:

- *Advertising.* A contract with an advertising agency may be needed to handle publicity. Key radio and television spots may be reserved for property. There may be billboard lease agreements that should be continued.

- *Maintenance services.* Such services as pool cleaning and landscape maintenance may be handled by contract crews. These agreements are usually transferred with ease to a new owner, but doing so requires properly notifying the contractor(s).

- *Other services.* To avoid the overhead burden of a fixed payroll expense, property owners sometimes arrange for outside contractors to perform a number of other services. Laundry service is a good example, as is the servicing of heating and air conditioning equipment.

Salary and Wage Agreements.   Investment property is rarely a wage-intensive operation. However, any operating property needs personnel. How much they are paid, when they are paid, and what extra benefits are provided is essential information for the smooth transition of ownership. The following obligations are all examples of remuneration to personnel:

- *Labor contracts.* Operating personnel may be working under a labor contract that provides either for union or non-union representation. A new owner is not necessarily obligated to fulfill an existing labor contract, but an understanding must be reached with employees if the operation is to continue smoothly.

- *Health and accident insurance.* Many operating properties provide health insurance for their employees under group policies. Continuing these benefits is generally quite helpful in assuring the property's smooth operation.

- *Workmen's compensation.* Laws passed in most of the states provide for fixed awards to employees in case of industrial accidents and dispense with proof of negligence and legal actions. There is usually a minimum number of employees required before participation in the state program becomes mandatory. For a new property owner, it is best to check the local requirements for proper compliance with the law.

- *Unemployment compensation.* In every state, some form of employment commission collects assessments from employers based on their record of stability with employment and disburses these funds to employees when they lose their jobs. The rules vary among the states as to the amount of unemployment compensation that may be collected and the requirements for qualification. To insure the state funds during periods of sustained unemployment, the federal government also collects an unemployment tax from employers. This tax is *not* shared by the employees because the employer alone contributes to both the state and the federal governments.

- *Pension funds.* In general, only the relatively larger companies can support a pension plan. They are seldom found with an average-sized investment property. Recent legislation designed to protect private pension fund participants has placed certain personal liability on fund administrators and discouraged their use.

Statement Analysis

There are a number of procedures used to analyze and compare the information available from various financial statements. Some figures and ratios are more important for one kind of business than another. While all the following financial comparisons may not be used in real estate analysis, they provide some insight into the area of important ratios and what they mean.

Business analysts examine financial statements along five major lines as discussed below. These are: (1) liquidity, (2) leverage, (3) income/expense, (4) activity, and (5) profitability.

Liquidity

Is the financial condition of the property such that payment can be made on debts as they come due? This determination is made on the basis of the ratio between current assets and current liabilities. Two definitions of "current" are used. One considers all cash, accounts, and notes receivable due within one year as "current." All liabilities due and payable within one year are likewise considered "current." The other considers only cash *on hand* and liabilities *now due* as "current." Using either time frame, the prudent analyst considers "2 to 1" a safe and adequate ratio—i.e., $2.00 in current assets for each $1.00 of current liabilities.

Leverage

Leverage is the "debt to equity" ratio. It is most commonly discussed in terms of a percentage of *total invested capital*. For example, if a business property has a total asset value of $1,000,000 with an indebtedness of $650,000, the debt ratio would be 65% ($650,000 ÷ 1,000,000 = .65). Or, conversely, the equity ratio would be 35%. Large, publicly held corporations strive for a ratio of about 50%—half debt and half equity. Real estate investments lean to higher leverage ratios, with 70% to 80% debt fairly common.

Income/Expense

Another financial statement ratio (which some analysts also classify as "leverage") is the multiple of net income in relation to all fixed expenses. The ratio may be expressed:

$$\frac{\text{Net Operating Income}}{\text{Fixed Expenses}} = \text{Multiplier}$$

The use of this ratio will show how low the income can fall before the property is unable to meet the fixed expenses. It is one determination of a break-even point. For this particular analysis, the break-even point would be when the multiplier equals 1.0—when the net operating income just equals the fixed expenses. The larger the multiplier, the stronger the operation. An example of this determination follows:

Example

Scheduled Gross Income	$49,350	
Less: Vacancy and credit loss	2,640	
Gross Operating Income		$46,710
Less: Expenses:		
Fixed expenses		
Taxes	$8,200	
Insurance	2,100	
Total fixed expenses	$10,300	
Operating expenses		
Utilities	$ 1,820	
Payroll	3,400	
Supplies	1,340	
Repairs	1,925	
Total operating expenses	8,485	
Total Expenses	18,785	
Replacement reserves	2,745	
Total expenses and reserves		21,530
NET OPERATING INCOME		$25,180

Using the above figures in the income/expense formula:

$$\frac{25,180}{10,300} = 2.44 \text{ (multiplier)}$$

To determine the break-even point more accurately, it would be necessary to add certain *minimal operating* expenses to the fixed expenses for use in the formula. However, income/expense ratios provide solid guidelines for analysis regardless of where the lines are drawn between the fixed and operating expenses. The important point is to be consistent, i.e., compare the same basic set of figures each time an analysis is made.

Activity

Activity tests reveal how effectively assets are being used. This ratio compares the *gross operating income* to total assets. To determine the ratio, divide the gross income from the property by the total asset value. Let's take an example of an apartment project worth $1 million producing gross annual income of $185,000:

$$\frac{185,000}{1,000,000} = .185 \text{ or } 18.5\% \text{ (activity ratio)}$$

The same basic ratio, when applied in a reverse method, is often used to provide a rule of thumb evaluation of operating properties. For example, an apartment project with a gross operating income of $185,000 would be valued somewhere between 5 and 8 times that income. The multiplier used depends on the condition of the property and the judgment of the investor. A multiplier of 5.4 × $185,000 gives a value of $999,000.

Profitability

The success of an investment is determined by its *profitability*. For a real estate investment, a key element of profitability does not appear in a normal operating statement, and that is appreciation. However, if we consider that one of the purposes of an analysis is to provide a basis of comparison for similar investments, two additional ratios should be explored. These are profitability ratios on the following two bases:

- *Return on the net worth.* The ratio of after-tax (net) profit to the net worth of the investment.

- *Cash return.* The ratio of cash returned to the equity invested (in jargon— cash on cash).

Amortization Tables

Amortization tables identify the periodic payment necessary to pay off principal and interest during the term of a loan. They are indexed by the amount of the loan, the interest rate required, and the payment period for each installment. For residential loans, the tables most commonly used are indexed by the amount of the loan and the term of the loan; the applicable interest rate is the heading for each table. A monthly payment is standard.

For the investor considering a larger loan than would normally be needed for a residential property, or a loan that is to be repaid on a schedule other than monthly, another form of table is more convenient to use. This is a table of the payments necessary to amortize $1,000. To determine payments for large loans, multiply the listed payment by the number of thousand-dollar units in the loan. The two indices are the term of the loan and the interest rate. The heading of each table is the payment schedule—monthly, quarterly, semiannually, or annually. (See the Appendix for an example.)

Loan Constant

A loan constant is the annual (or monthly) debt service expressed as a percentage of the loan amount. There are several reference tables published* which provide loan constants for a broad range of interest rates and loan terms. Loan constants are most effective when used to calculate payments for fixed interest, constant-level payment mortgages.

To understand how a loan constant is computed, study the following example. For this purpose, let's use a $1,000 loan, a 25-year term, and a 9% interest rate. By referring to a standard amortization table, we find the monthly payment for this $1,000 loan is $8.39. Multiply this figure by 12 to convert it to an annual amount and it equals $100.68. The annual debt service of $100.68 amounts to 10.068% of $1,000, which is the loan constant. The equation for the above calculation reads as follows:

$$\frac{\text{Monthly Payment} \times 12}{\text{Loan Amount}} = \text{Annual Constant \%}$$

$$\frac{\$8.39 \times 12}{\$1,000} = .10068, \text{ rounded to } 10.07\%$$

Using a loan constant in the preliminary analysis stage provides a solid basis to compare the required debt services of several loan possibilities offering various terms and interest rates. Assume, for example, that the investor is offered a choice between a 25-year loan at 8.5% and a 30-year loan at 8.75%. Which offers the more favorable repayment schedule? Reference to the Loan Constant Table shows that the 25-year loan at 8.5% interest has a constant annual percentage rate of 9.66%, whereas 8.75% interest paid over 30 years produces a constant annual percentage of 9.44%. If the loan amount is $1 million, the 8.5% rate gives a debt service of $96,600 per year, while the 8.75% rate calls for a payment of $94,400 per year. The loan constant clearly shows which interest rate and term to choose. In practice, loan applicants commonly ask the mortgage lender to include loan constants in any loan offer. (See the Appendix for an example.)

*Loan constant tables and amortization tables are available from Financial Publishing Co., 82 Brookline Ave., Boston, MA 02215, or Professional Publishing Corp., 122 Paul Drive, San Rafael, CA 94903.

12

Comparison Screening

The previous chapter emphasized financial statements—how they are prepared, what information they should contain, where the problem areas lie. It is important to know how such information is presented, since much of it is useful. However, the experienced real estate investor usually relies on an analysis prepared from the investor's own knowledge of property management and his or her own investigation of the property's operating figures.

Any analysis takes time and money. How much an investor should *spend* on analysis depends on the intensity of interest in a property. The type of property, its location, and timing are all important investment analysis considerations, but these depend more on the investor's personal interests and personal financial considerations. Later chapters examine these considerations in detail. For now, let us consider solely the financial aspects of a preliminary property evaluation.

For an initial screening procedure, most investors use general guidelines developed from years of experience—either their own or others' experience. Some guidelines are strictly personal methods of determining the most suitable investment property and may be considered confidential information by the investor. Other methods are so widely used that they are almost "rules of thumb," although they are generally overly simplified methods of establishing acceptability for undertaking further analysis work.

Popular Guidelines

Income Multipliers

One of the easiest and most common preliminary screening indicators for income property is the ratio between a property's annual gross operating income and its price. This ratio—or *multiplier*—varies slightly with the location and age of the property. But essentially it denotes the fact that the value of an income property relates directly to the property's income. Following are examples of multipliers for various types of property:

Gross Income Multipliers

Type of Property	Low	High	Average
Office buildings	5.25	8.7	7.02
Commercial buildings	4.0	9.0	7.1
Industrial buildings	8.33	10.07	9.47
Apartments	7.7	10.05	8.47

Source: Richard N. Ratcliff, Professor of Land Economics, University of Wisconsin.

This list of multipliers was developed from market studies and appraisals of a substantial number of properties nationwide. However, a multiplier is of greatest value to an investor only when it has been calculated for properties in the investor's local area of interest. In some areas of the country, the multiplier for a good apartment investment is as low as five to seven. Motel values are sometimes estimated at three to four times the gross annual room rental. (The motel estimate uses income from room rentals only, excluding restaurant, lounge, and other income.)

Cash on Cash

A common sense form of value estimate strips away many of the variables and considers only the equity portion of an investment. The procedure is variously called "dollars out for dollars in," "valuing the cash flow," or "cash on cash."

This method determines (1) the amount of cash required to purchase the equity interest in a property (i.e., the difference between the sales price and the mortgage loan), and (2) the cash remaining from income after all expenses and debt service have been paid. The expenses for this method of valuation include all fixed and variable operating expenses, but no depreciation. Debt service includes both principal and interest. Potential income tax effects are ignored. Whatever cash remains—after expenses and debt service are subtracted from income—is then capitalized. If a rate of return at 10% is selected, then the value of the equity interest equals 10 times the remaining cash. Following is a simplified example of the elements used in this method:

Example

Gross operating income	$100,000
Less: Operating expenses	43,600
Less: Principal & interest	44,444
CASH REMAINING	$ 11,956

By capitalizing cash remaining to determine equity value:

$$\frac{\$11,956}{.10} = \$119,560 \text{ is the equity value}$$

Or, by using the reciprocal:

$$10 \times \$11,956 = \$119,560$$

"Per Unit" Value

Certain types of property—such as apartments and motels—lend themselves to using a "per unit" value as a guide to the property's total value. While the size of the units in an apartment may vary considerably, investors commonly place a value on the property according to the number of units it contains. In evaluating a motel, they consider the number of rentable rooms. Two different methods are used:

1. *Market value.* By collecting recent sales data for the area, the prices paid for apartments can easily be converted to a price per unit. Appraisers routinely collect such data to guide their own evaluations. Under this approach to value, land costs are included in the per-unit price.

2. *Construction cost.* Any experienced builder of apartments or motels can quote a reasonably accurate figure on construction cost per unit. Remember that the builder will *not* include the cost of land, sales costs, or start-up costs in this figure. The construction cost of a new building provides an upper-limit guide for an investor's preliminary evaluation.

The "per unit" method of valuation is not so accurate as the "square foot" method described below, but it can be quite helpful whenever detailed information or building plans are not immediately available.

"Square Foot" Valuation

A value per square foot can be determined for any kind of building. An investor can determine this figure using either market values or construction costs. Commonly evaluated by this method are office buildings, shopping centers, and warehouses, because none of these have standard rental units to measure. Many investors reduce all figures to a cost per square foot basis during a preliminary evaluation. Both rental income and operating expenses are readily reduced to an amount per square foot of space to provide reasonably accurate information for comparisons.

The square foot method of valuation is a standard used by appraisers, the FHA, the VA, lenders, and investors.

Property Income and Expense Analysis

Once an investor has determined from preliminary (and relatively inexpensive) evaluation that additional investigation is justified, the next step would involve a more detailed financial study. Financial data should be assembled, verified, and summarized in a standard format to assure easy comparison later in the game. Income figures must be examined in relation to financing and the investor's projected income tax liability. First, let's review the analysis form.

Standard Analysis Form

Owners and builders do not use a consistent format or nomenclature to present financial information. As a result, a potential investor can easily overlook important information. The investor should select a comprehensive form, either a good one already on the market or one that the investor designs for his or her own purposes. The same form should then be used for all analyses of similar properties. A suggested form—listing all major account headings for income and expenses, and using nomenclature recommended by the National Association of Realtors—is reproduced as Figure 12–1. The form suggested can be used for either a preliminary comparison of properties, or as a basis for studying operating problems.

FOR COMPARISON PURPOSES

As a comparative statement, the standard format clarifies the income figures and operating costs by using the same account nomenclature. The accounts that are not so obvious but that require special attention are management, replacement allowance, and repairs. For instance, should the free use of an apartment for the resident manager count as an operating cost, or should it be a reduction in Gross Operating Income as a part of the Vacancy & Credit Loss item? The answer is the analyst's choice as it makes no difference in the "bottom line" of Net Operating

FIGURE 12–1 A Standard Form for Comparison Analysis

STANDARD ANALYSIS STATEMENT

Property _Skyline Apartments_   Date _3/1/89_

Location _____   Price _$975,000_

Loan data:

Priority	Initial Amount	Rate	Term	Balance Due	Annual Payment
1st 2nd	560,000	14%	20 yr.	511,851	83,563.20

Account	Percent of GOI	
GROSS SCHEDULED RENTAL INCOME		188,200
Plus: Other Income	_____	4,520
TOTAL GROSS INCOME	_____	192,720
Less: Vacancy & Credit Losses	_____	10,921
GROSS OPERATING INCOME	100	181,799
Less: Operating Expenses		
Accounting & Legal	_____	900
Advt'g., Licenses, & Permits	_____	1,180
Property Insurance	3.67	6,670
Property Management	3.14	5,700
Payroll Resident Management	3.30	6,000
Other	4.82	8,762
Taxes—Work. Comp.	_____	1,838
Personal Property Taxes	.80	1,450
Real Estate Taxes	4.35	7,900
Replacement Allowance	1.32	2,400
Repairs & Maintenance	3.56	6,470
Services Janitorial	_____	1,260
Lawn	_____	2,430
Pool	_____	2,020
Rubbish	_____	840
Other	_____	
Supplies		
Utilities Electricity	4.62	8,400
Gas & Oil	2.33	4,230
Sewer & Water	.76	1,380
Telephone	_____	290
Other	_____	
Miscellaneous	_____	

TOTAL OPERATING EXPENSES   70,820

NET OPERATING INCOME   110,979
Less: Total Annual Debt Service   83,563
CASH FLOW BEFORE TAXES   27,416

PROFITABILITY RATIO (NOI to total investment)   11.38%

CASH FLOW TO EQUITY RATIO   5.92%

Income. But it becomes a critical item when a comparison of different properties is being made. So whatever practices are selected, they must be consistently applied to each analysis.

Always a key figure for comparison purposes is an operating property's profitability. The use of *ratios* simplifies this comparison. While there are a number of interesting ratios that might be applied, Figure 12–1 offers two that are important. These are the *profitability ratio* and a *cash flow to equity* ratio. The profitability ratio compares the total investment in the property with the net operating income. In this example (Figure 12–1), the total investment is considered to be the purchase price ($975,00) and the net operating income is $110,979. The ratio is derived as follows:

$$\frac{110,979}{975,000} = .1138 \text{ or } 11.38\%$$

The cash flow to equity ratio narrows the measure to a comparison between the cash flow and the equity amount. Cash flow is identified here as the cash remaining after payment of debt service (both principal and interest) and before payment of income taxes, amounting to $27,416 in the example. The equity amount is the difference between the total investment ($975,000) and the balance due on the mortgage loan, shown in the example as $511,851, which amounts to $463,149. Thus, the cash flow to equity ratio calculates as follows:

$$\frac{27,416}{463,149} = .0592 \text{ or } 5.92\%$$

There are other numbers that can be compared with ratios depending on the investor's special interests. The cash flow may be defined as that cash remaining after payment of interest only (not including principal portion as identified above), or the preference may be to include an income tax payment as a reduction in the cash flow. Whatever election is made, it must be followed consistently for accurate comparisons.

FOR STUDYING OPERATING PROBLEMS

The same standard analysis form used for comparison purposes may easily be used to study existing operating problems. As a historical record of income and expense, the standard format ensures uniform handling of each item. If a substantial record of the previous year's operations is available, a good study can be made by comparing the actual figures. For instance, if electricity cost three years ago was $10,945 and last year was $8,400, obviously there is some kind of an improvement. But has the improvement resulted from lower electrical rates, more efficient use of the facilities, or simply a drop in occupancy? The only realistic improvement in an expense item is measured in the *percent of GOI* column. Theoretically, if the gross operating income declines, so should the expenses. But, of course, it doesn't always work out that way! Nevertheless, by using a percentage measure, the investor/owner may find good clues as to precisely where the expense disparities are. If income declines, and an expense item shows an excessive increase, it is quickly highlighted in the percentage column.

Another good use of the standard analysis form for examining operating problems is in comparison with other similar operating properties. Here again, it is the percentage column that is most illuminating. For example, if rubbish disposal costs show at 3% of gross operating income for the subject property and are 1% for a competing similar property, there must be a serious problem. Professional property managers are often so familiar with their particular kind of property that they can simply scan a percentage column and point out the problem items of excessive expenses. The dollar amounts themselves are important, but not as easy to compare as when they are reduced to a percentage figure.

Some Analysis Problems

In preparing an operating statement, there are questions that need further discussion, such as what costs should be assigned to which accounts, and what basis should be used in calculating a percentage column. Also, what steps might be taken to verify operating figures? First, a look at several of the more difficult accounts.

Management Account. Operating properties often utilize the services of a management company, or general supervisor, in addition to resident personnel. Also, certain perks might be available to this group, such as free housing, use of company cars, and sometimes club privileges. The standard analysis statement suggested (Figure 12–1) separates only "Property Management" from "Resident Management," which may be inadequate for larger operations. It could be helpful to identify the various costs of management with additional sub-accounts. Detailed cost accounting can be interesting but must be maintained in a consistent manner. Also, accumulating detailed information costs money and must be weighed against its value in making informed decisions.

Replacement Allowance. Certain rental properties contain substantial personal property that is consumed with its use. Foremost in this group are apartments containing appliances, carpets, and drapes. Since these items classify as capital assets and are normally depreciated over a cost recovery period, the cost is not always included in an operating statement. Nevertheless, it is a cost of doing business and should be identified as such. It may be necessary to estimate the cost each year as replacements may not be necessary for three or four years, or longer. It is for this reason that the item is listed in the statement as an "allowance" as it is not necessarily a cash expenditure every year. Some managers include this cost in the "Repairs and Maintenance" account, which recognizes the expense but is not so clearly identified as with a separate account.

Percent of GOI Column.   Advantages of using percentage ratios were discussed earlier in this chapter. There are several additional questions that should be considered. First, what figure should be used as a basis for the ratio? It is an option of the analyst as to whether or not the expense should be measured against the Gross Scheduled Rental Income, the Gross Operating Income, or an income amount that eliminates "Other Income." The use of Gross Operating Income is favored because that is really what the property produces in total earned income each year, and it is from that cash flow that expenses are paid.

Another question is which accounts should be calculated as a percentage of Gross Operating Income? Again, it is the analyst's option, but seldom are all accounts so measured. Selection of accounts is based on such points as which are the larger accounts, which are more flexible, and which are most subject to management abuses. The answers vary with different properties.

VERIFICATION OF DATA

Information for the investor's analysis form should be verified wherever possible. An examination of bank statements, phone calls to utility companies and insurance agents, and discussions with the manager or management firm can clear up a number of questions.

The need to verify information at an early stage of interest in the property is not so great as in later acquisition steps. A property owner usually must *authorize* inquiries into his financial situation; most are reluctant to do so until a potential investor exhibits solid evidence of willingness to buy. An option agreement or earnest money contract to buy property can also be made subject to the purchaser's verification of certain financial data submitted by the seller.

Net Operating Income

One of the most important figures in an operating statement is the Net Operating Income. Referring back to Figure 12–1, net operating income is that amount remaining from gross operating income after all expenses are paid. Note that in the expenses listed there is no deduction taken for interest or depreciation. Does this mean they are not important to an investor? Not at all. But it is also important to distinguish the operation of a property from its financing costs and its tax consequences. That is the purpose of the net operating income. Neither the debt burden of a property nor tax consequences for the owner are reflections of property operation. In another sense, if a property is overburdened with debt, firing the manager is not the answer!

Net operating income serves some other functions. It is the true measure of profitability on total capital invested, and it is considered by lenders as the cash available to service debt payments. It is this figure that is used in the application of coverage ratios to measure acceptable loan payment amounts.

Equity Growth Rate

For measurement purposes, and as a sales tool, investors sometimes calculate an *equity growth rate*, expressed as a percentage rather than in dollars. Properly used, the growth rate adds (or subtracts) the change in total property value to (or from) the equity share. The percentage addition reflects any appreciation in total property value (usually, although not always, caused by inflation). Following is an example:

Assume: Property value	$900,000
Less: Mortgage loan	575,000
Value of equity	$325,000

The above property produces:

Net operating income	$100,000
Less: Interest on loans	45,818
Less: Income taxes	5,670
NET EQUITY INCOME	$ 48,512

To compute equity growth rate:

		Percent of Equity ($325,000)
Net equity income	$48,512	15
Appreciation (at 5% per year on total value)	45,000	14
TOTAL EQUITY INCREASE	$93,512	—
TOTAL EQUITY GROWTH RATE PER YEAR		29%

Property Appraisals

The appraisal is the most common tool of professional real property analysts. It's designed to *estimate* value. An investor should be aware of the process used in determining an estimate because the process itself provides important information on the property and several approaches to its value. This section briefly explains (1) how an appraiser examines property, and (2) the essential elements of the three basic approaches to value that are used in making final estimates of value.

An appraisal always estimates value *as of a specific time.* That time is usually the present but need not be. Retroactive appraisals are sometimes made, as in the case of settling an estate. Sometimes appraisals are made for some future date. At the beginning, therefore, an appraiser defines the time period that the evaluation covers.

Second, the appraiser must define the type of property holding that is being evaluated. Appraisals of real property are made for whole interests, partial interests, leasehold estates, mineral interests, air rights, frontage rights, and all other types of holding.

Third, the purpose of an appraisal must be clearly defined. A professional appraisal can reach only one final estimate of value for any one interest in a property. It never shows a "buyer's price vs. seller's price." But the purpose of an appraisal can indicate which approach to value should be emphasized in reaching a final estimate. For example, if the appraisal is conducted to aid in settling an insurance claim for fire loss, the cost approach to value is the best way to establish replacement value. If the purpose is to determine land value of undeveloped land, the estimate must consider the lack of attributable income. If, on the other hand, undeveloped land is appraised for its value as an apartment site, a proportionate share of the apartment's projected income is attributed to the land, thus enhancing its estimated value. An appraisal of land in the process of condemnation to widen an existing highway may not reflect the property's frontage value. The reason is that value is based on the *use* of the land; the remaining land would retain the frontage value of the original property. As you can see, an appraisal's stated purpose *does* affect its final estimate.

The integrity of appraisals is protected by a number of professional societies which require their members to meet exhaustive testing and experience requirements. Two of these organizations of peer groups are older and probably better known within the industry. The Society of Real Estate Appraisers is an outgrowth of the staff appraisers employed by savings and loan associations. The Society grants three professional designations: Senior Residential Appraiser (SRA); Senior Real Property Appraiser (SRPA), for commercial properties; and the highest designation, Senior Real Estate Analyst (SREA), which qualifies the holder to appraise *any* type of property. The American Institute of Real Estate Appraisers is organized under the National Association of Realtors and requires all applicants to be NAR members. The Institute awards two designations: Residential Member (RM) and Member Appraisal Institute (MAI).

All of these designations are important for real estate investors. The higher the appraiser's professional designation, the more respect the appraisals receive. In fact, lenders often base their minimum standards for an acceptable appraisal on these professional designations.

Appraisers and their qualifications came into question as a result of substantial property foreclosures during the mid-1980s. Defaulted real estate loans were one of the principal causes of failure in some lending institutions. Whether or not faulty appraisals were involved, many states began examining the need for better practices. As a result, some states have established state licensing boards authorized to qualify appraisers. In addition, the federal government is considering legislation to correct appraisal fraud and inconsistency. In an effort to avoid further legislation and correct matters themselves, eight appraiser organizations joined together to establish a self-regulatory system. In the fall of 1987, this group established the Appraisal Foundation to promote uniform standards for appraisals and to establish qualification criteria for professional certification.

Appraisal Approaches to Value

When evaluating a property, the professional appraiser relies on basic economic principles—supply-and-demand, conformity, highest and best use of the land, anticipation, and others. Estimates of value are made in accordance with three different "approaches to value." These are (1) cost, (2) market, and (3) income. All three are explained below.

Cost Approach

The only approach to value suitable for *any* type of building is the *cost approach*. It calculates the cost of replacing a building at the time of appraisal, subtracts accumulated depreciation, then adds the value of the land.

Replacement Cost. The cost of duplicating an existing structure at the time of appraisal is its *replacement cost*. Labor and material cost increases are fully included in this calculation. The computation may be made on a "per unit" basis, as a contractor would do in preparing a construction bid. Or, if current cost figures are available for similar structures, a cost "per square foot" or "per cubic foot" may be used.

Depreciation.   Day-to-day deterioration of a building decreases its value and must be deducted from replacement cost for the purpose of this calculation. Depreciation can be found in three categories.

1. *Physical deterioration.* The normal wear, rust, and rot that occurs in building materials. This deterioration may be classed as "curable," (as with a coat of paint) or "incurable" (not economically feasible to repair).

2. *Functional obsolescence.* Any loss of value in a building resulting from poor design, inadequate facilities, or outdated equipment. These factors, too, can be classified as "curable" or "incurable," with proper adjustments made to the valuation.

3. *Economic obsolescence.* Any loss in a building's value resulting from factors outside the property. A new freeway's bypassing a service station, for example, lowers the station's value. Outside factors can also increase the value of a neighboring property. A new bridge across a stream, for example, may allow development of land that was previously inaccessible.

Land Value.   The value of land is determined separately from the value of the buildings on it. Appraisers generally use the market value of the land, determined by studying recent sales of similar land in the vicinity. When conducting this study, an investor must remember that land can reflect an increase in value, usually—though not always—from inflationary pressures.

Even though the economy is adjusting to continuous inflation, not all land increases in value, and very few tracts increase at a constant rate.

Market Approach

Appraisal by the market approach concentrates on the sales prices of similar properties. Since no two properties are exactly alike, this approach compares the subject property with three to six similar, recently sold properties. The appraiser determines the "plus" or "minus" value factor of each major difference between the subject property and each similar property. For example, if a similar property had been sold two years earlier, it would be reasonable to assume that the subject property would reflect an inflation-caused increase in value (a "plus") because of the two-year time differential. A fireplace in the subject property would give it a "plus" factor in any comparison with a similar property lacking a fireplace. Comparisons are comprehensive, covering such points as location, size, physical condition, and amenities.

Remember that only *actual* sales prices reflect *actual* market values. Thus, asking prices for similar properties are not an acceptable basis for comparison.

Neither are forced sales comparable (unless, of course, you're appraising a property subject to forced sale). The "willing buyer and willing seller" standard of a free market sale is lacking in a forced sale. A sale by an estate or within a family can give a distorted impression of a property's actual value in the free market.

A reexamination of a "sales price" as a sound basis for comparing market values of property developed in the mid-1980s. During the early 1980s, it had become common for home sellers, particularly home builders, to offer attractive financing plans as a sales tool. By offering lower than market interest rates during the early years of a mortgage, sellers were able to attract more buyers. The cost of the "buy-down" of the mortgage loan was usually added into the price of the house. Since the sales price then reflected a finance cost, it was not an accurate indication of the actual market value of the property. Most lenders have since added a requirement that any "market value" used as a basis for property comparison be adjusted downward to reflect any excessive finance costs. FNMA and FHLMC have revised their definition of market value to "the most probable price which a property should bring."

The market approach to value is the one most commonly used to appraise residential property. The market for houses is large and continuing, so that good comparisons are usually possible. In larger cities, commercial properties such as apartment projects often sell frequently enough to allow accurate use of the market approach. The accuracy of the market approach, of course, *always* depends on the availability of sales figures for similar nearby properties.

Income Approach

The income approach estimates a property value based on the income derived from it. The income considered is generally that obtained from the property's operations each year, plus any profit that is gained from the sale of the property at the end of its ownership period. The income approach is the most important analysis for a commercial property. For many investors, it is the *only* acceptable approach because it bases value strictly on the profitability of the property.

The first step in this approach is to calculate the property's net operating income. This is the income remaining after payment of all operating expenses. The payment of debt service is not a consideration in the calculation of property value for this purpose. The way a property is financed can be critical for an investor; however, to include the cost of financing in an income approach to value can introduce a distortion. The successful operation of a property should not be confused with a possible overload of debt.

The second step in an income approach calculation is to select a rate of return that's acceptable for use in capitalizing the income stream. The rate of return for this purpose is not so much a mathematical calculation as it is a matter of individual judgment. An appraiser would most likely use a rate commensurate with current market rates adjusted to compensate for the risk involved.

The third step in the calculation is to convert the annual net operating income into a value for the property. There are several methods of accomplishing this goal, two of which are described next: (1) capitalization and (2) discount analysis.

CAPITALIZATION

Capitalizing the cash flow that is the net operating income is accomplished with the following formula:

$$\frac{\text{Income}}{\text{Rate of return}} = \text{Value}$$

Example

An income property is producing an $18,000 net operating income each year. The appraiser selects a 12% rate of return as appropriate. The capitalized value of the income stream is:

$$\frac{18,000}{.12} = \$150,000$$

At the end of the ownership period the appraiser estimates the property can be sold at a price that allows a profit of $80,000. Add this "residual value" to the value of the income stream as follows:

$150,000 + 80,000 = $230,000 (property value)

DISCOUNT ANALYSIS

The above calculation ignores the *time value of money*. While there is justification for the "capitalization" approach, many appraisers believe a more accurate valuation can be made by discounting the future cash flows to a present value. The purpose is to recognize that money in hand today can be put to work earning interest. The cash flows from an income property become available in future years in exchange for a purchase price that must be delivered at the time of acquisition. Thus, a more accurate valuation is to reduce the value of future cash flows to their present worth. Add to this figure the present worth of the profit that may be realized when the property is disposed of at the end of its holding period and the sum of the two is the actual value of the property. Further consideration of discount analysis is offered in the next chapter.

Appraisal Conclusion

An appraiser uses all three approaches to value whenever possible. Some properties, however, do not provide sufficient data to allow all three methods. For example, a city hall appraised for insurance coverage would probably forbid both the market approach and the income approach. And a major office building in a small city won't usually be amenable to market comparisons.

Using all three approaches for the same property generally produces three different estimates of value. The appraiser's job is to select the appraisal method most appropriate for a specific property, make an estimate of final value, and then provide reasoning that justifies the final value that has been estimated.

Feasibility Report

To assist in an investment decision, particularly when a large property is involved, the investor may commission a *feasibility study*. This study is more than an appraisal. By skillful use of market data, it attempts to determine the proposed investment's prospects for success. The study can be made for either existing property or proposed construction.

Like an appraisal, a feasibility report uses background information to arrive at value estimates. But a feasibility report focuses more on market evaluation than on property evaluation. A feasibility study surveys the market area, charts population and business growth, analyzes present and future traffic patterns, and researches occupancy and income levels for comparable properties in the neighborhood.

Feasibility reports are prepared by marketing analysts, appraisers, property managers, and real estate brokers. Unfortunately, the integrity of some feasibility studies is suspect, since no professional society or state agency regulates this field. An investor must therefore exercise considerable care in selecting an individual or firm to prepare this report. The reputation of the preparer is crucial.

Feasibility reports follow no standard pattern. The information presented varies, as does its sequence. However, the following outline represents a good and widely followed procedure.

1. *Conclusions.* Unlike an appraisal, conclusions are often presented first, since this is the purpose of a feasibility report.
2. *Property.* An adequate description of the property is presented.

3. *Market evaluation*. This is a detailed study of the market in the neighborhood, including any laws, regulations, and other restrictions that might affect future operations of the property.

4. *Environmental effect*. As environmental requirements continue to expand, separate reports are becoming standard practice for all large projects. A feasibility report may only detail the requirements, leaving it to other specialists to determine their impact.

5. *Income and expenses*. The profit potential of the project is studied in depth. One purpose is to determine the break-even point, which is used along with the market study of occupancy in the area to show when positive cash flows can be expected.

Physical Inspection

Real property is tangible and should be inspected before an investment is undertaken. Many investors consider this so important that it is a part of the *preliminary* study. If an inspection is made in the early screening process, it may consist of only a drive-by, or, if appropriate, a fly-over of the property. Some of the important points that can be found in a simple inspection are as follows:

1. The general appearance of the property.
2. The nature of the surrounding area, neighboring buildings, and use of the land in that area.
3. The general traffic patterns in the vicinity of the subject property.
4. Land drainage around the property—a visit during or shortly after a rain storm can be illuminating.

During such an inspection, questions should be noted that are not immediately important but call for additional study should the property be given serious consideration later. An example might be some nearby construction work, or a close-in stream or drainage channel, or perhaps a difficult traffic pattern that could be improved with street signs. If other information justifies further examination, a much closer physical inspection would be necessary.

13

Discount Analysis

The preliminary screening and analysis procedures outlined in Chapter 12 show the potential investor (1) a few simple guidelines for evaluation, (2) the advantages of a standard form for financial analysis, and (3) an initial basis for comparing real estate properties. As shown in that chapter, the investor who uses net operating income to determine value has a sound basis for investment analysis and comparison. That method reduces the many variables of investment to a simple standard of present profitability. By capitalizing present profitability, the investor can determine a reasonable price for a property, which can also be used for comparison with other possible property investments.

When a property value is calculated by capitalizing a present income stream (the net operating income), it is assumed that the income will continue indefinitely at the same level. Obviously, such a calculation allows no measurement of possible fluctuations in future income. While there is no known way to predict the future, there can be changes in future income levels that will be known in advance. This would include rent increases that may be included in lease agreements and possibly a factor to recognize inflationary pressures. Along with the question of determining future income more accurately is another major concern. And that is the fact that the income used to establish a property's value is not going to be received at once, but over an extended period of time in the future. How to cope with the element of income received over an extended time period is the subject of this chapter. The next chapter takes a look at the problems involved with measuring the future cash flows.

Real estate and many other investments produce income at periodic intervals over a lengthy time period. The idea behind the discount analysis approach is to determine what that future income is worth today—that is, to reduce each future receipt of income to its present value. In other words, if you had the money today, instead of some future time, this money could be put to work earning interest. Therefore, money promised in the future is not worth as much as money in hand today. This is what is meant by the *time value* of money. It is the purpose of discount analysis calculations to determine just how much money would be needed in hand today, earning interest, that would achieve the same value as a given amount promised at some future point in time.

Analysts for major investors compare all available types of investment in an effort to determine the most effective placement of investment funds. Economists, analysts, consultants, and investment advisors employ a number of techniques to measure the anticipated yield from a proposed investment. No single procedure gives an absolute answer, particularly when the proposed investments are in real estate. Recently, discounted cash flow analysis and present value approaches have been accepted as theoretically correct methods of measuring expected profitability under conditions of certainty. Unfortunately, the real estate field seldom presents the "conditions of certainty" needed for accurate projections. With the exception of mortgage loans and high-grade leases, projections of future income and future value in real estate property are subject to considerable conjecture. Nevertheless, values determined by discounted cash flow approaches are being applied to real estate for comparative evaluation. This chapter examines the essential elements involved in these calculations.

The Time Value of Money

Chapter 12 explained that "capitalization" is a means of determining property value as a direct function of income. Income-producing property is valued by its anticipated profit. The simplified equation is:

$$\text{Value} = \frac{\text{Income}}{\text{Rate of Return}}$$

This equation represents capitalization in perpetuity. The important element of time, or *time value*, is not included.

To understand time value, consider the difference in the value of $1,000 delivered today and $1,000 delivered one year from today. Today's $1,000 invested at 7% simple interest, for example, would be worth $1,070 at the end of one year. So $1,000 delivered today would actually be worth $1,070 at the end of one year. The comparison can be stated as follows:

$$\frac{\$1,000}{\$1,070} = .9346, \text{ or } 93.46\%$$

Using the percentage so derived, you can see that the value of $1,000 delivered one year from today would be only 93.46% as much as $1,000 delivered today because of the interest that could be earned. Stated another way, the *present value* of $1,000, if delivered one year from today and figuring the money could earn a 7% return, would be 93.46%. Or the discounted value of the $1,000 would be $934.60 as calculated below:

$$\begin{array}{ll} \$\ 1,000 & \text{Amount to be received in one year} \\ \underline{\times .9346} & \text{Discount at 7\% annual interest} \\ \$934.60 & \text{Present value} \end{array}$$

To prove this present value, take the $934.60 sum today and invest it at 7% interest for one year.

$$\begin{array}{ll} \$934.60 & \text{Amount invested} \\ \underline{\times\ \ \ \ .07} & \text{Annual interest rate} \\ \$\ 65.40 & \text{Amount earned in one year} \end{array}$$

Clearly, $934.60 invested at 7% interest would equal $1,000 at the end of the year ($934.60 + $65.40 = $1,000).

Compound Interest

The time value of money illustrated above is based on *simple interest*, since interest is earned only once—at the end of the year in this example—and thus is earned only on the original investment.

In a number of investments, however, periodic interest earnings are retained and reinvested, thereby supplementing the original capital. These reinvested interest earnings then earn interest themselves. Thus, earned interest is periodically combined—or *compounded*—with the principal investment to increase the total investment.

Here is an example of interest compounding on $1,000 at 7% interest per year over five years:

Year	Investment at Beginning of the Year	Interest Rate	Interest Earned for the Year
1	$1,000.00	.07	$70.00
2	$1,070.00	.07	$74.90
3	$1,144.90	.07	$80.14
4	$1,225.04	.07	$85.75
5	$1,310.79	.07	$91.76

Interest can be compounded at time periods other than one year, such as semiannually, quarterly, monthly, or even daily. The following table illustrates the effect of semiannual compounding, using the same $1,000 initial investment and the same 7% annual interest rate:

Year	Six-Month Period	Investment at Beginning of Six-Month Period	Annual Interest Rate	Interest Earned Each Six Months
1	1	$1,000.00	.07	$35.00
	2	$1,035.00	.07	$36.23
2	3	$1,071.23	.07	$37.49
	4	$1,108.72	.07	$38.81
3	5	$1,147.53	.07	$40.16
	6	$1,187.69	.07	$41.57
4	7	$1,229.26	.07	$43.02
	8	$1,272.28	.07	$44.53
5	9	$1,316.81	.07	$46.09
	10	$1,362.90	.07	$47.70

Following are three mathematical steps to help clarify how the basic equation used to calculate compound interest is developed. The example considers $1,000 earning 7% for one year, payable annually:

$$\$1,000 + (\$1,000 \times .07) = \$1,070$$
$$\text{or } \$1,000 (1 + .07) = \$1,070$$
$$\text{or } \$1,000 (1.07) = \$1,070$$

Or, in algebraic symbol form:

$$P(1 + i) = S$$

where: P = principal amount invested
1 = one
i = annual interest rate
S = sum to which P has grown

The most basic expression in the study of compound interest is the function of $(1 + i)^n$. The "n" represents the total number of years, or periods, during which interest is paid. In the equation just discussed—$1,000 $\times$ 1.07 = $1,070—the interest is computed for a single period of time. When compounding is more frequent than once a year, both the "i" and "n" must be changed to reflect this fact. If, for example, compounding takes place semiannually for a two-year period, the equation would be modified as follows:

$$\$1,000 \left(1 + \frac{.07}{2} \right)^4 = \$1,147.53$$

As shown, the "i" becomes one-half of the .07 annual interest (to reflect the semiannual payment), and the "n" becomes 4 to reflect the four semiannual periods in a two-year term.

Discounting Cash Flows

If given a choice between $950 delivered today and $1,000 delivered one year from today, most of us would opt for the $950. But why? For an investor, the $950 could be put to work earning interest and be worth more than the $1,000 delivered one year from now. Obviously, money in hand today can generate a return over a period of time. The purpose of the discount calculation is to determine just how much money in hand today, earning interest over a given period of time, will equal a cash amount promised at some future point in time. Say, if money can earn 12% in the present market, how much is needed today earning interest to equal $1,000 in one year? The answer lies in the discount equation explained in this chapter.

But why be concerned about the present worth of any sum delivered in a future time period? Because income property investments offer returns in future years, and the investor is expected to pay for that future income at the time of purchase. It is important to know what the future cash flows are worth if a return on the investment is expected.

Cash Flows Described

Three identifiable sources of cash can be measured by a discount calculation. These are:

1. After-tax cash flow from operations.
2. Gain on the sale of property after deducting applicable capital gain taxes.
3. Cash obtained through additional financing or refinancing of the property. If a larger loan can be obtained, even at a different interest rate, it can produce spendable cash, which may be desirable to consider in the com-

putation of present value. From a practical standpoint, cash obtained from a loan that must be repaid with interest quickly loses its value if the ownership period is extended. Additional financing is most effective if it can be used to induce a favorable sale of the property. The examples and equations illustrated in this text do not include additional financing as a cash flow item.

It is obviously difficult to make an accurate projection of future income from a real estate investment, or of its future resale value. But it should be pointed out that the uncertainties of future returns, characteristic of real estate invest-ments, present precisely the same problems for analysis whatever method is used. The discounting technique works best, as mentioned earlier, under more certain conditions, e.g., on a fixed-interest bond or mortgage loan. But discounting *can* be used as one measure of analysis for real estate property. It's examined here within the following limited framework:

1. *Present value approach*. Used to determine the value of future cash flows if a given rate of return is expected.

2. *Internal rate of return*. That rate, determined by trial-and-error methods, which makes the present worth of future cash flows equal to the initial investment.

Before examining the various formulas used in discounting cash flows, two of its components need further discussion. One is the *capitalization rate*, which is the rate of return used in making the discount calculations; the other is the *mathematics of discounting*.

Capitalization Rates

A capitalization rate is the annual return that an investor expects to receive, expressed as a percentage of the investment amount. The terminology is syn-onymous with rate of return. When an income stream is "capitalized," it is meant to express the value of that income based on a given rate of return. For example, if an income of $1,000 per year is converted to a value based on a 10% rate of return, the value becomes $10,000 ($1,000 divided by .10 = $10,000). Or if the investor requires a 12% rate of return, the $1,000 annual income converts to a value of $8,333. ($1,000 divided by .12 = $8,333.) The rate used is a matter of judgment—whatever rate is considered reasonable to the investor in the present market. In a very real sense, this rate measures the quantity, quality, and probable duration of the income stream.

A perfect investment, if it could be found, would have a minimum required rate of return. As the property recedes from perfection, the required rate of return must be increased to compensate for the increased risk involved. The ideal investment would contain the following features:

1. Absolute security of the principal.
2. Adequacy and certainty of return.
3. Ready marketability.
4. Tax-free income.
5. Good financing.
6. Probability of capital appreciation.

In addition to evaluating the risk features of the property under study, a required rate of return also reflects market conditions for other capital investments. A further consideration would be whether the investor's own portfolio requirements dictate diversification into alternative investments.

While a capitalization rate cannot be based on pure mathematics, it must realistically measure risk. One way to simplify this determination is to dissect the risk into its separate components. The summation approach is a four-part accumulation method, as follows:

1. *Safe rate.* The rate of return that can be expected from a risk-free investment. Government bonds are considered risk-free as an investment. Almost as safe are savings accounts with insured institutions such as savings associations and banks. Assume a present risk-free rate of 10%.

2. *Hazard rate.* The increase in return (over the safe rate) needed for the increased risk of the investment. The real estate investment hazard ranges from 1% to 3%.

3. *Non-liquidity rate.* The percentage of increase in return needed to offset the lag time during which no cash may be realized from the investment. The usual range is from ½% to 2%.

4. *Management rate.* Compensation for the owner's time spent in managing the property investment. This rate averages about 1%.

To accumulate these four components, using some typical rates of return:

Component	Return Required
Safe rate	10.00%
Hazard rate	2.50%
Non-liquidity rate	1.50%
Management rate	1.00%
Capitalization rate	15.00%

The Mathematics of Discounting

The concept of a discount as it relates to the time value of money was illustrated earlier in this chapter. The example compared the value of $1,000 delivered today with $1,000 delivered one year from today, applying a 7% interest rate and using simple arithmetic. The same figures as used in the earlier example are used again in the following series of equations to illustrate how the discounting factor is obtained. The same basic element used to compute compound interest—$(1 + i)^n$—is used as a *divisor* to obtain the discount factor:

$$\frac{P}{P(1 + i)^n} = \text{Discount Factor}$$

The following equations show several ways to express the mathematics of discount calculations, all of which reach the same conclusion.

$$\frac{\$1,000}{\$1,070} = \text{Discount Factor}$$

$$\text{or} \quad \frac{\$1,000}{\$1,000 + (\$1,000 \times .07)} = .9346$$

$$\text{or} \quad \frac{\$1,000}{\$1,000(1 + .07)} = .9346$$

$$\text{or} \quad \frac{\$1,000}{\$1,000(1.07)} = .9346$$

If the comparison is made after the second year, the equation is as follows (note that the interest factor is multiplied by itself once for each time period involved in the discount calculation).

$$\frac{\$1,000}{\$1,000(1.07)^2} = .87344$$

or $\dfrac{\$1,000}{\$1,000(1.07)(\ 1.07)} = .87344$

or $\dfrac{\$1,000}{\$1,144.9} = .87344$

To prove the compounding effect of this calculation, using the interest factor to the second power:

	$1,000	
	×.87344	Discount factor
Present worth	$873.44	×.07 = $61.14
	+61.14	1st year's interest added
Value, end of 1st year	$934.58	×.07 = $65.42
	+65.42	2nd year's interest added
Value, end of 2nd year	$1,000.00	

The use of $(1 + \text{annual interest rate})^n$, or $(1 + i)^n$, is the most basic element in the calculation of present worth. This factor is used as a multiplier to calculate the growth of invested capital at compound interest. And used as a divisor, this same factor reduces a future cash flow to a present value at a compound rate. The factor can be expressed as $(1 + .07)^n$, or $(1.07)^n$. The "n," you remember, indicates the number of years (or compounding periods) to be entered in the actual calculation. This is called an "exponent" in mathematical language, meaning that whatever number is given, the number within the parentheses must be multiplied by itself that number of times. For example, if the $1,000 cash flow is delivered after five years, instead of two years, the equation would read:

$\dfrac{\$1,000}{\$1,000(1.07)^5} = \text{Present Worth Factor}$

or $\dfrac{1,000}{1.4026} = .71296$

The calculation of $(1.07)^5$ is figured:

$1.07 \times 1.07 \times 1.07 \times 1.07 \times 1.07 = 1.4026$

Present Value Approach

Applying the Discount Calculation

The calculation of a discounted amount as explained in the above section results in a "present value" for the amount discounted. ("Present value" and "present worth" have the same meaning and can be used interchangeably.) The purpose is to figure exactly how much money would be needed today, earning interest, to result in an amount equal to the cash flows offered by the investment in each of the future years of ownership.

The discounted value, or present worth, of any sum can be determined by reference to a financial table. The one most easily used is identified as the "Present Worth of $1.00."* The table gives a decimal factor (such as .89286) for each rate of return for future years which, when multiplied times the future cash flow, will give the value of that amount today. That is, it shows the amount needed to be put to work today to earn interest that will compound into the same sum as the future cash offered by the investment.

To illustrate how the present worth factor can be applied, consider the following example. The present worth factors are used to reduce future cash flows to their value today. The sum of the discounted cash flows gives a present worth for the property, i.e., a value today of the future cash flows if the investor anticipates a 12% rate of return on the cash invested.

Example

The cash flows that can be earned from an investment property amount to $10,000 after taxes the first full year and are expected to increase each year by 10%. At the end of a 3-year holding period, the property will be sold for an expected net profit of $85,000 after payment of capital gain taxes. The investor requires a 12% rate of return. To achieve this rate of return, how much could he pay for the property today?

The following example uses a "Present Worth of $1.00" factor for a 12% rate of return.

End of Year	Income	×	12% P.W. Factor	=	Present Worth	
1	10,000	×	.89286	=	8,929	
2	11,000	×	.79719	=	8,769	
3	12,100	×	.71178	=	8,612	
			Present worth of income stream			$26,310
Cash flow from sale after 3 years:						
3	85,000	×	.71178	=		60,501
			Present Worth of Property			$86,811

The above example illustrates the calculation of present worth using factors offered by a financial table. If such tables are not available, the factors needed can be readily figured with a hand calculator by dividing "1" by the appropriate $(1 + i)^n$ number. Following is an example of how the present worth factors used in the above table for a 12% rate of return can be calculated.

*See Appendix for an example of a "Present Worth" Table, or as may be found in other source books of financial tables.

Example

In order to calculate the present worth factor when tables are not available, use the following procedure:

12% P. W. Factor for end of the first year:

$$\frac{1}{1.12} = .89286$$

12% P.W. Factor for end of second year:

$$\frac{1}{(1.12)^2} = \text{P.W. Factor}$$

$$\frac{1}{1.2544} = .79719$$

12% P.W. Factor for end of third year:

$$\frac{1}{(1.12)^3} = \text{P.W. Factor}$$

$$\frac{1}{1.4049} = .71178$$

Note that in the above example, the mathematical calculation of the present worth factor, i.e., 1 divided by $(1 + i)^n$, results in the identical present worth decimal numbers given in the Present Worth column used in the first calculation above. Also, present worth calculations are programmed in many financial analyst hand calculators on the market today. With these calculators, the need to know mathematics is minimized, as long as you know the right sequence of buttons to push!

What has been determined from this calculation is that a property with income as shown in the example and a net sales profit after three years of $85,000 is not worth more than $86,811 today. This is based on an expected rate of return of 12%. Expressed another way, $86,811 placed in some other investment, say a certificate of deposit paying 12% for three years, would produce just as much income as the investment illustrated in the example. Thus, a present value approach is an important method of judging the value of future income as measured in a cash amount today. If the investor expects to make 12%, he should not pay more than $86,811 for the property illustrated. As a practical comparison, if the property is offered for sale at *less than* $86,811, it would bear further examination. If the price is more than that, eliminate it from serious consideration.

It should be pointed out that the discount analysis approach to value necessarily introduces a "holding period" that is the number of years the property will be owned. This time period is necessary in order to calculate, or (more accurately) to estimate, the profit, or cash flows earned each year plus that earned when the property is sold. The concept actually stems from financial analysts who use this approach with securities, some of which have fixed maturities. For example, a $1,000 bond may offer 12% annual interest and mature in 10 years. Each year the investor would earn $120, plus repayment of the $1,000 when the bond matures in 10 years.

This limited-holding period concept differs somewhat from that applied to the capitalization of an income stream (described earlier) which regards income as perpetual and considers value of the property at time of disposition as a residual value.

Present Value of Total Capital Invested

The present value calculation as explained above is a method of *discounting* future cash flows. As shown earlier in this chapter, there are several different kinds of cash flows found in income properties. Let's distinguish between the two major ones: (1) cash flow on total capital invested, and (2) cash flow on the equity invested. Because terminology is not always precise in these matters, what is meant here by "total capital invested" is the total value of the property. For instance, if a property is purchased for $1 million with $800,000 borrowed and $200,000 paid for the equity, the total capital investment amounts to $1 million. The equity investment is $200,000. For an investor, such as a pension fund manager who is able to acquire property without borrowing money, the important return is what can be realized on total capital invested.

Since the total capital invested represents an all cash amount, i.e., no borrowed money, the cash flows earned from the operation and ultimate sale of the property are not reduced by any mortgage payment or pay-off of a mortgage loan. As a matter of fact, with some computerized analysis programs, the numbers applying to total capital are simply identified as "no debt" figures. However, it is necessary to reduce the cash flows by the amount of applicable income taxes. The investor is interested only in the after-tax returns on an investment.

Present Value of Equity Invested

Since the equity amounts to a portion of the total capital invested, the cash flows attributed to the equity investment are a portion of the total cash flows or earnings. The difference is the borrowed money. Hence, repayment of the borrowed money reduces the cash flows for the equity investment. For example, if a property is showing an annual after-tax cash flow on total capital invested in the amount of $75,000 with a mortgage payment (principal and interest) of $55,000, then the cash flow for the equity amounts to $20,000 ($75,000 minus $55,000 equals $20,000).

To calculate the present value of the equity investment, the analyst simply uses the after-tax cash flows reduced by the mortgage payment. The cash flow realized upon sale of the property has to be reduced by the pay-off of the mortgage loan. Once the cash flows attributable to the equity portion of the investment are determined, the same present worth factors used before can be applied to calculate the present value of the equity.

It is easy for the student at this point to confuse the repayment of principal on a mortgage loan as an improper deduction from the cash flow or earnings. If we were calculating income taxes, this would be true. But here we are looking at the cash recovered, or profit, for the equity investor. If the money to purchase has been borrowed, it must be repaid with interest and the repayment reduces the cash flowing back to the equity investor. Likewise, any payment of income taxes reduces the cash flowing back to the investor, hence all calculations for this purpose are *after-tax* cash flows.

Example

Assume an investment property with an income (cash flow) on total capital invested of $80,000 the first year, increasing at the rate of 10% per year. As an older property with less favorable tax deductions, say there are some income taxes due, shown as rounded off amounts in the example. Then the mortgage payment is deducted, leaving the cash flow attributable to the equity portion of the investment. At the end of three years, the property is sold and a gross profit of $600,000 is realized. After payment of capital gain tax and payoff of the mortgage loan, $160,000 is left for the equity investor.

Problem: What is the present worth of cash flows for the equity investment at a 12% rate of return?

End of Year	Income on Total Capital	−	LESS Income Taxes	−	LESS Mortgage Payment	=	Cash Flow Equity	×	12% P.W. Factor	=	PRESENT WORTH
1	$80,000		$5,000		$55,000		$ 20,000		.89286		$ 17,857
2	$88,000		$7,000		$55,000		$ 26,000		.79719		$ 20,727
3	$96,800		$9,000		$55,000		$ 32,800		.71178		$ 23,346

Present worth of income stream $ 61,930

Cash flow from sale after 3 years holding:

Gross profit from sale	$600,000
LESS: Capital gain tax	$100,000
LESS: Pay-off of mortgage loan	$340,000

$160,000   ×   .71178   = $113,885

Cash flow to equity owner

$175,815

PRESENT WORTH: ALL FUTURE CASH FLOWS

In the above example, mortgage financing is assumed and the equity portion of the investment shows a value of $175,815 *if the investor expects a 12% return on the equity.*

Internal Rate of Return (IRR)

The internal rate of return is used to make comparisons among investment opportunities. The IRR produces a number, a rate of return, that reflects the value of future cash flows as a measure of the asking price for a property. It also serves as a benchmark for screening investments before more time and money are spent on in-depth studies. For instance, if an IRR exceeds, say 9%, the investment is worth further consideration.

The calculations needed to determine an internal rate of return are quite similar to those used in the present value methods explained previously. Only the purpose is different. Both the present value method and the internal rate of return calculations begin with a known sequence of cash flows from the subject property. The present value approach assigns the investor's required rate of return to the calculation to answer the question: "What can be paid for this property (its present worth) in order to achieve the required rate of return?" In contrast, for an internal rate of return, the same cash flows are known, *plus the present worth* of the property. Now the question becomes: "What rate of return reduces (discounts) the cash flows so as to *equal the present worth?*" For an IRR calculation, present worth is the asking, or purchase, price of the property.

IRR Calculation

The calculations used to determine an IRR may best be described as "trial and error." This may sound unorthodox for mathematics, but the numbers involved contain too many variables to do otherwise. In fact, hand calculators programmed to deliver IRR calculations actually use a trial and error matching procedure. Only they do it so fast it is hard to distinguish. Remember, the goal is to produce a rate of return that discounts future cash flows to a sum that exactly equals the present worth (purchase price) of the subject property. The correct rate is obtained by testing different rates to see which one actually discounts the future cash flows to a sum that matches the asking price of the property.

To recall an earlier point, a change in the required rate of return produces an inverse result in present worth. That is, an increase in the rate of return results in a lower present worth amount. So if the first rate of return selected produces too high a present worth, then a higher rate must be used to reduce the present worth. To better illustrate the results, the following chart uses Present Worth of

$1.00 factors for the fifth year to show the reductions in present worth that occur when the required rate is increased from 9% to 12%.

Rate Required	P.W. Factor	Income	Present Worth
9%	.64993 × $25,000		$16,248
10%	.62092 × $25,000		$15,523
11%	.59345 × $25,000		$14,836
12%	.56743 × $25,000		$14,186

Now apply the above information to another example. If the first rate selected reduces the future cash flows to an amount less than the asking price (present worth of the property), then the rate must be *decreased* for another trial. Say the second calculation at a lesser rate results in a present worth greater than the asking price. With one rate producing a present worth less than the asking price and a second rate producing a present worth greater than the asking price, the result is a "straddle." The goal, which is to produce a present worth exactly equal to the asking price, can then be achieved through an interpolation between the high and low rates.

Example

Use the same income stream, 3-year-holding period, and selling price from the previous example given on page 228, i.e., $10,000 annual income increasing by 10% each year and a net return from the sale after three years of $85,000. Say the asking price for this property is $95,000. What is the internal rate of return? (What rate of return will produce a present value of exactly $95,000?)

First, we know from the previous example that a 12% rate of return produces a present worth of $86,811—and that is too low. The target is the asking price of $95,000. Remember, increasing the rate of return decreases the present worth—so it will be necessary to try a lesser rate of return in order to show an increase in the present worth. Try the calculation at an 8% rate of return.

End of Year	Income	8% P.W. Factor	Present Worth
1	$10,000 ×	.92593 =	9,259
2	$11,000 ×	.85734 =	9,431
3	$12,100 ×	.79383 =	9,605
Present worth of income stream			$28,295
Value of resale:			
3	85,000 ×	.79383 =	$67,475
Present worth at 8% rate			$95,770

The result, $95,770, is higher than the target amount of $95,000. Therefore a higher rate must be tried to lower the present worth a bit. Try an 8½% rate:

End of Year	Income	8½% P.W. Factor		Present Worth
1	$10,000 ×	.92166	=	9,217
2	$11,000 ×	.84945	=	9,344
3	$12,000 ×	.78291	=	9,473
	Present worth of income stream			$28,034
Value of resale:				
3	85,000 ×	.78291	=	$66,547
	Present worth at 8% rate			$94,581

The results of the two trial calculations produce a straddle of the $95,000 purchase price target amount. An 8% rate of return shows a present worth of the cash flows in the amount of $95,770, while an 8½% rate results in a present worth of $94,581. The true internal rate of return falls in between—closer to the 8½% rate than the 8%. There are mathematical procedures to interpolate the precise rate between the two but these go beyond the scope of this text. Suffice it to say at this point that a $95,000 asking price for a property with the income stream given in this example produces an internal rate of return slightly less than 8½%. You might try 8.32%!!!

In a reversal of the normal sequence of information, now take a look at the definition of an internal rate of return. It is the rate of return at which the present worth of future cash flows exactly equals the initial investment.*

What is the purpose of an internal rate of return? Keep in mind that one of the purposes of an analysis is to provide a means of comparing one investment with another, the return from one property with that of another. The best comparisons are made when standards of measurement are available. The internal rate of return provides one standard of measurement: one that considers the time value of money in expressing a yield from an investment.

Problem Areas in Computations

Two problems occasionally arise in the computation of discounted cash flows. The first is that income properties can produce *multiple rates* of return. For calculation purposes, the rates can be averaged to produce reasonable accuracy. Or separate projections can be made for each rate of return, and the results added together.

*Stephen D. Messner, Irving Schreiber, and Victor L. Lyon, *Marketing Investment Real Estate*, Realtors National Marketing Institute, 1975.

The second problem has to do with the handling of projected *negative* cash flows. One solution to this problem is to subtract the negative flows from the positive flows and delay any discounting until the property achieves a positive flow. Another method is to assume that the property owner will borrow the deficit amount each year, and project a zero cash flow for each deficit year. Remaining deficits and interest costs can be deducted from the proceeds of the final sale.

Listing Properties with DCF Techniques

Knowledge of compound interest and discounting techniques is essential to understand investment. And it is most important for a broker offering income-producing properties for sale to understand how investments are analyzed. The basic building block of calculation—$(1 + i)^n$—is used by financial analysts to evaluate all types of investment. Since real estate should be able to withstand the scrutiny of comparison with alternative investments, the techniques of discounting future cash flows as an analysis procedure need to be understood.

One cannot ignore the difficulty of comparing relatively uncertain income property investments with more reliable investments such as bonds and mortgage loans. The point, however, is that major investors *do* apply discounting techniques to the real estate field. And some mortgage lenders use discount analysis, usually prepared by in-house economists, when considering a large commercial loan application. The analysis gives insight into the potential for the property under consideration and provides the lender with a solid basis for comparison with other investments.

The discount technique is still not widely used as a sales tool, in part because it isn't very well understood within the industry. It *can*, however, give a sales presentation a powerful factual argument. Consider, for example, the competition for a listing on a commercial property that is coming up for sale. The owner wants "top dollar" for the property, sometimes to the point of overreaching the market. By projecting the known return from the property over a reasonable period of future ownership, and then discounting that return to its present value, the broker may be able to convince the owner—through a simple comparison with the same money invested in, say, a good bond—that the asking price is not competitive with alternative investments and, is therefore, unreasonable. The same kind of careful analytical presentation might convince a prospective buyer that an asking price is quite reasonable when compared with other uses of an investment dollar.

For the average investor, the most important thing is to *understand* the methods of calculating compound interest and discounts. The investor need not wade through all the calculations. The factors used to compute compound interest, discount, present value, and a number of other common real estate measurements have been put together in tables, which chart these factors for various holding periods and interest rates. The most commonly used series is the *Ellwood Tables for Real Estate Appraising and Financing*.* To gain greater confidence in these analysis procedures, either for oneself or to explain to others, it is helpful to practice with the figures and problems. A review of the examples in this chapter using a calculator can be beneficial.

*L. W. Ellwood, *Ellwood Tables for Real Estate Appraising and Financing*, published for the American Institute of Real Estate Appraisers by Ballinger Publishing Co., Cambridge, Mass.

14

Cash Flow Projections

Prior chapters examine certain existing records, such as balance sheets and operating statements, that report what has happened to a real estate investment in previous years. The information is factual and very important in the analysis of an investment. It is an excellent way to make investment comparisons. The historic record is also the best way to pinpoint operating deficiencies.

However, new investment is generally made in anticipation of *future* returns. So a further purpose of the historic record is that it can be used as a basis for projecting what might be expected in future years. How such figures may be used and how the many variables that affect future returns may be applied is the subject of this chapter.

The variables are many, including what historic data is selected for a projection, how much increase or decrease might be expected in future income and expenses, and simply how long a period the property is to be held. In addition to these questions, there are many tax requirements that affect future returns. Trying to estimate future tax liabilities under the present system of continuous revision cannot be done realistically. Nevertheless, projections must be made as accurately as possible to cope with the very important tax obligations.

Crucial to any calculation of an investment return is the measurement of cash flows. It is the projection of cash flows that underlies all future return analysis. The purpose of such projections is to provide information that will assist an investor or analyst in reaching a more accurate decision.

Understanding Cash Flows

Cash flow has many meanings. To some it is the total amount of cash passing through a business entity, like its gross income. To others it can mean that cash remaining after all expenses and all debt service (including principal) has been paid. A third use of the expression is to indicate the monthly principal and interest payments generated by an underlying block of loans, such as found with a mortgage-backed security. In many kinds of investment, cash flow is totally predictable. Unfortunately, such is not true of most income property investments.

The standard used for real estate has to be a reasoned estimate of future cash flows. What is important is how the gross income of a business is disbursed so as to figure *how much remains for the owner/investor*. Thus for the purpose of analyzing future returns, cash flow means those cash items that can be projected, both income and expense, in a manner that allows a determination of future profitability.

Cash Flow From Real Estate

The above definition of cash flow is a broad one. But it points out the need for further definition of its components. What should be classed as income? Is interest on mortgage debt an operating expense or is it a cost of financing? Should profitability be determined before or after the deduction of income taxes? These questions, and many more, illustrate variables that may be involved with analyzing something as complex as a real estate investment. Many of the answers depend on judgment calls—what is right for one analyst may not be treated the same by another. If there is one constant, it is to *be consistent* in applying whatever analysis is used. For instance, changing the projection from a before-tax figure as applied to one property, to an after-tax figure for another property will obviously result in a serious distortion when comparing the two properties.

As discussed earlier, another difficulty with understanding analysis procedures is the lack of uniform terminology with which to communicate information. The names used to identify various income and expense accounts are not always the same. Such variation is not as important in a projection as it is with historical information. A projection is focused more on future profitability rather than on pinpointing operating problems. Nevertheless, comparisons are easier if the measures are uniformly identified.

Analyzing Cash Flow Variables

Following is a discussion of the major questions in determining cash flows. It does not attempt to give a "right or wrong" answer, but to point out the options available and the reasoning that may be needed in selecting the most suitable procedure.

Gross Income. In previous chapters, a distinction was made between "gross potential income" and "gross operating income." The difference between the two is the deduction of vacancy and credit loss items from the gross potential figure. For analysis of a past record of performance, the distinction has considerable meaning. For a projection of future income, the distinction is not so important. What is meaningful in the projection is the actual cash income—the amount that is deposited in the bank each day. Since it is at best an estimate, the detail is less important.

What can be important in the gross income projection is to distinguish between the different kinds of income that may be available. Income properties can produce miscellaneous income in addition to lease income. This includes such sources as income from vending machines, a laundromat, or the rental of public rooms for meetings or receptions. The reason this distinction is important is that the different sources of revenue can produce different growth rates. For instance, the income from a battery of pay phones might flatten or decline due to changing technologies.

Thus, for a projection of income, it would be simpler and just as accurate to list the various kinds and amount of income and to consider growth rates, or declines, for each separately.

Operating Expense. Operating expenses are seldom considered individually when a projection is made. If the projection is accomplished with a manually prepared spread sheet, certain expense items can be separated to show greater accuracy in estimating changes for each. However, with most computer programs all expenses are simply lumped together and given a composite growth rate.

The operating expenses of income properties should include property taxes and insurance costs. In business accounting, these items should not be considered a cost of financing as is implied in residential loans. With residential loans it is standard procedure to identify a "mortgage payment" as the sum of principal, interest, taxes, and insurance (the jargon expression PITI or "pity"). This combination-type mortgage payment does not apply to commercial property analysis. While both property taxes and insurance costs could easily have different growth rates projected, for estimating purposes, a composite rate is generally used.

Two other "expenses" that should be mentioned are depreciation and interest on mortgage debt. Neither are treated as operating expenses. Depreciation is a non-cash type of deduction that is considered more as a tax benefit than a cost of doing business. This should not be confused with *replacement costs*. Replacement costs incurred in the usage of such tangible assets as appliances, draperies, furniture, and rugs are definitely part of the operating expense if applicable.

Interest on mortgage debt is a cost of financing and distinguishable from operating expenses. The distinction is important for a historical analysis as well as a projection. So depreciation and interest on mortgage debt are discussed later in connection with tax considerations, rather than as operating expenses.

Net Operating Income.   Gross income less operating expenses equals net operating income. The importance of this figure was emphasized in an earlier chapter as the key to a property's operating success. The suggested caution then was to judge operations at this point, not after a financing burden has been added. And the same thing applies to a projection. Net operating income is that money available to pay debt service. It is the key to figuring return on total capital invested.

How to Use Net Operating Income

Although a projected net operating income is still basically an estimate, it is the crucial number used to figure the impact of three very important variables. These variables are: (1) depreciation deductions, (2) the impact of debt service at different interest rates and loan terms, and (3) income tax liability and the possible effect of other income or losses.

Depreciation Deductions

Depreciation as a tax deduction (also called "cost recovery") is based on the time an asset is placed in service. Prior to 1981, there were almost no changes in how this tax benefit was calculated. Since then there have been four significant changes. To estimate future deductions, a taxpayer must apply whatever the current depreciation procedures may be, assuming the property is placed in service currently.

The 1986 Tax Reform Act offers no taxpayer elections in the depreciation of real property assets—if the property is residential, it must be depreciated over 27½ years; if nonresidential, the recovery period is 31½ years, all straight line.

However, if the property is tangible personal property, there are some options. And since many real property investments include some personal property, the options are important. There are six cost recovery classes for personal property and a choice between straight line or accelerated deductions. Since an important purpose for making a projection is to select the most beneficial among options that are available, it could be helpful to see whether or not accelerated deductions are cost savings in the long run.

Debt Service

One of the key questions that can be illuminated by a projection analysis is the impact of debt service. Debt service is defined as the periodic payment of principal and interest on mortgage loans. The interest cost of any other borrowing should be categorized as an operating expense.

Financing is a critical part of real estate investment and its cost can make or break a property's ultimate value. Since long-term loans are still available at fixed interest rates, loan repayment is one of the few costs that can be projected with some degree of accuracy. Even though repayment of a loan must be measured against estimated income, the calculation helps determine whether or not cash flows will justify a particular mortgage loan.

With a projection, it is possible to examine the effect of several different kinds of loans: different loan terms, different interest rates, and even different repayment schedules.

Income Tax Liabilities

One of the important questions for investment analysis is whether the return should be figured before or after the deduction of income taxes. There are sound arguments for both positions.

Since the true return on an investment is that remaining after all costs have been paid, there is good reason to figure the cash flow *after* taxes have been deducted. Because it makes good sense, the after-tax return has long been used as a solid analysis procedure.

Nonetheless, as tax liabilities have become more complex, and individual taxpayers may face obligations that differ for the same amounts of income, there is a growing need for "before-tax" analysis. The 1986 Tax Reform Act consigns *all* real estate investment to the category of passive activity income. Since passive activity income is limited to offset by *only* passive activity losses, an investor's "after-tax" position becomes even more personalized.

Thus, to properly recognize the effect of taxes on an investment, it becomes necessary to make two projections. A before-tax projection is necessary to develop adequate comparisons between properties. And an after tax projection is needed for each investor to reflect the effect of additional income, or losses, as applied to each individual's tax return.

Holding Period

The older concept of capitalizing an income stream to estimate property value assumed a perpetual life for the asset. Now, more accurate measures to estimate property value apply a limit on the time span for holding an asset. The concept stems from financial markets where bonds offer a limited life. For instance, within a time span of 5, 10, or more years a bond *matures*. At best, a holding period for real estate assets must be an estimate. A real estate investment does not "mature," and is not easily sold at the end of a holding period. But for estimating future values, it is an important measure.

Manual Spread Sheet Analysis

To make use of the information discussed in the previous sections, consider a case study. Assume an operating statement that gives certain figures for an existing property that will be used for projections. First, several variations can be made on the cash flows that result in a projected *net operating income*. Then, the net operating income can be further analysed to illustrate the effects of variables such as depreciation deductions, the impact of various debt loads, and an examination of returns before taxes.

Since a projection is an estimate and its purpose is to predict certain final results, it can be less detailed than an operating statement like the one described in Chapter 12. Because of this, a cash flow projection can identify income as actual income—no real need exists to refine the estimate as to possible potential income, then deduct vacancy and credit loss. Expenses could be reduced to a single figure as is most common with a computer investment analysis projection. However, a manually prepared statement as illustrated in Figure 14–1 offers an opportunity to more accurately project various costs. Sometimes advance information is available on what future costs might be for such items as property insurance and taxes, maintenance expenses, and the kind of services that will be under contract. If such figures are used, the projection will be far more accurate than a sweeping percentage rate of increase applied to the basic costs.

Another difference between an operating statement that presents historic information and a projection that attempts to look at the future is far less need for a percentage column. These are the percentages that show a ratio between a cost item, such as electricity, and the gross operating income. As pointed out in an earlier chapter, the percentage column provides an excellent basis for comparison with similar properties as well as to identify problem areas in the operation. However, when future costs are estimated, there is minimal value in comparing one detailed guess with another.

In the example of a projection that follows (Figure 14–1), the same basic income and expense figures shown in Figure 12–1 (Chapter 12) are used, although with some consolidation of accounts. Several of the accounts are projected as if the numbers are known in advance, and some are simply projected with a percentage rate as shown in the "Rate of Increase" column. Of course, if future costs are known, or fixed by a long-term contract, those should be used in a projection. The rate of increase percentage is an alternative that is, at best, an estimate. To save space and time, the projection is made for only three years. For longer projections, a computer program might be a better choice.

Following is a hypothetical example of a cash flow projection covering only three years.

FIGURE 14–1 Example of a Manual Cash Flow Projection

	Rate of Increase	1989	1990	1991
Gross Rental Income	n/a	175,000	188,000	210,000
Other Income	n/a	4,500	6,000	6,000
Gross Operating Income		179,500	194,000	217,000
LESS: Operating Expenses				
Acct. Legal, Advt.	n/a	2,080	1,500	2,100
Property insurance	6%	6,670	7,070	7,494
Management	4%	11,700	12,168	12,655
Operating personnel	6%	10,600	11,236	11,910
Real and personal taxes	10%	9,350	10,285	11,313
Repairs & maintenance	n/a	8,870	10,580	8,350
Service & supplies	6%	6,550	6,943	7,360
Utilities	8%	14,300	15,444	16,680
Miscellaneous	n/a	700	800	900
Total Operating Expenses		70,820	76,026	78,762
NET OPERATING INCOME =		108,680	117,974	138,238
Debt Service:				
560,000 @ 14% 20 yr.		83,563	83,563	83,563
NET CASH FLOW =		25,117	34,411	54,675
Income Subject to Tax:				
Add payment on principal		5,509	6,332	7,278
Deduct depreciation		41,100	51,300	41,700
TAXABLE INCOME =		(10,474)	(10,557)	20,253

Projections by Computer Program

A number of excellent computer programs on the market allow an investor to generate substantial information for analysis. Where the computer excels is in the high-speed sorting of information that affects an investment over future years. Unfortunately, the computer has the same limitations as humans in the ability to foresee future events. The same uncertainty that causes problems for a manual projection also creates difficulty for the computer; that is, the accurate projection of future income and expenses. In fact, the manual method might be more accurate in that it allows greater flexibility in determining what changes might occur in future income and which of the various expense items might or might not increase in future years.

To achieve its goal of analyzing the effect of debt payments and income tax liabilities on an investor's future income, the computer treats income and expense items as if they increase at a consistent rate each year. Some programs consider both income and expenses as lump sum amounts. Each increases (or decreases in some cases) by a consistent percentage amount each year. While this consistency may not be realistic in a real estate investment, it is what must be used to arrive at a cash flow projection.

The purpose of the computer projection is not simply a comparison of future cash flows. Rather, the point is to use a reasonable estimate of what should be the correct cash flows, then examine the effects of various mortgage payment plans and various depreciation schedules on the same cash flows. While the cash flows cannot be totally accurate, they do provide a consistent basis for the measurement of the other variables, one being the tax consequences. In this way, an end result can be foreseen and decisions on mortgage plans and depreciation schedules can be made with better informed judgment.

It is not within the scope of this text to examine and explain computer programs used for investment analysis. Nevertheless, their purpose and an example of the kind of result that can be obtained with several different methods is helpful. By knowing what might be expected, it is easier to know if the information will be useful.

Spreadsheet Calculations

A spreadsheet calculation is one that can accept an input column of numbers, then mathematically extend each number to additional columns with constant level increases for each. Examples of this type of program are offered by Lotus 1-2-3 and Microsoft Excel. The difference between the spreadsheet and a manually prepared form is that each line must be numbered and each column lettered for proper guidance of the computer calculation. Further, the key demands for results are identified in the bottom lines. The bottom lines also show the projected increases in both income items and expense items as constant percentages. What the computer does is project the percentage increases to the future years, calculate the net results for each year, then convert the results to a profitability ratio.

An illustration of how the information appears in a typical spreadsheet form is shown in Figure 14–2. To achieve this result, the program disk is placed in position in the computer. Then the information is inserted in columnar form. Because of space limitations, only four years of information is shown. For easier comparison, the same basic numbers are used as were offered in the manual projection (Figure 14–1).

In the example given in Figure 14–2, the cost figures are increased at a compound rate of 5% and the income at 7%. The result, of course, is not the same as the manual projection of Figure 14–1 although both began with the

FIGURE 14-2 Example of Spreadsheet Projection

A	B	C	D	E	F
1	Skyline Apartments				
2	Price	975,000			
3	1st Mtge Ann pmt	83,563			
4					
5		1989	1990	1991	1992
6					
7	Gross Sched. Inc.	188,200	201,374	215,470	230,553
8	Plus: Other income	4,500	4,815	5,152	5,513
9	Total Gross income	192,700	206,189	220,622	236,066
10	Less: Vac. & loss	13,200	14,124	15,113	16,171
11	Gross Operating Inc.	179,500	192,065	205,510	219,895
12	Less: Operating Exp.				
13	Acct. Legal Advt.	2,080	2,184	2,293	2,408
14	Property Insurance	6,670	7,004	7,354	7,721
15	Management	11,700	12,285	12,899	13,544
16	Operating personnel	10,600	11,130	11,687	12,271
17	Real & pers. taxes	9,350	9,818	10,308	10,824
18	Repairs & maint.	8,870	9,313	9,779	10,268
19	Service & supplies	6,550	6,877	7,221	7,583
20	Utilities	14,300	15,015	15,766	16,554
21	Miscellaneous	700	735	772	810
22	Total operating exp.	70,820	74,361	78,079	81,983
23	Net Operating Income	108,680	117,704	127,431	137,912
24	Less: Ann. debt serv.	83,563	83,563	83,563	83,563
25	Cash flow before tax	25,117	34,141	43,868	54,349
26	Profitability ratio	.1115	.1207	.1307	.1414
27	Rate of cost increase	1.05			
28	Rate of income increase	1.07			

same set of numbers. The manual projection uses a selective increase in both costs and income while the spreadsheet uses a constant percentage increase. The two examples should illustrate a basic difference in projection results.

Investment Analysis by Computer

A more advanced type of computer program offers much greater depth of analysis information than can be found in the simple spreadsheet. In such programs, the input information is generally reduced to lump sum amounts for income and expense. A growth rate is applied to each. With the information inserted, the program calculations produce not only the basic income and expense projections found in spreadsheets, but also amortization numbers, taxable income and after-tax data, plus overall rates of return and internal rates of return.

One of the carefully researched investment analysis programs available is prepared by The Real Estate Center, Texas A & M University.* It is designed to accept fairly simple input data and then calculate over 30 columns of information, projecting it for up to 20 years. The input information from the manually prepared projection statement (Figure 14–1) has been inserted into this program in the following manner.

Skyline Apartments

Holding period for property	10 years
Resale expense rate	6%
Annual gross income	$188,200
Gross income annual growth rate	6%
Vacancy rate	7%
Annual miscellaneous income	$4,500
Miscellaneous income growth rate	7%
Annual operating expenses	$70,820
Operating expenses annual growth rate	5%
Investor's first year tax rate	28%
Investor's last year tax rate	28%

List of Assets

Building basis (Residential)	$750,000
Personal property (5 yr class)	$75,000
Land cost	$150,000
Total assets (Purchase price)	$975,000
Annual growth rate for assets	3%
Total debt (20 yr. 14%)	$560,000
Initial equity (Down payment)	$415,000

*Program: "Investment Analysis" by Jack Friedman, PhD, and Gary Earle, The Real Estate Center, Texas A & M University, College Station, Texas 77843-2115. Dr. Richard L. Floyd, Director.

Income tax liabilities are based on the 1986 Tax Reform Act's requirements with an option to claim up to $25,000 of passive losses against other active income as a small property owner. Based on the above listed data, the computer printout of selected information for a 10-year holding period follows:

Year	Potential Gross Income	Vacancy Allowance	Misc Income	Operating Expenses
1	188,200	13,174	4,500	70,820
2	199,492	13,964	4,815	74,361
3	211,462	14,802	5,152	78,079
4	224,149	15,690	5,513	81,983
5	237,598	16,632	5,899	86,082
6	251,854	17,630	6,311	90,386
7	266,965	18,688	6,753	94,906
8	282,983	19,809	7,226	99,651
9	299,962	20,997	7,732	104,633
10	317,960	22,257	8,273	109,865

Year	Net Operating Income	Interest Expense	Principal Amortization	Before-tax Cash Flow
1	108,706	78,055	5,509	25,141
2	115,982	77,233	6,332	32,417
3	123,732	76,287	7,278	40,168
4	131,988	75,200	8,364	48,424
5	140,783	73,951	9,614	57,218
6	150,149	72,515	11,049	66,585
7	160,125	70,865	12,700	76,561
8	170,749	68,968	14,596	87,185
9	182,063	66,789	16,776	98,499
10	194,111	64,283	19,281	110,546

Year	Depreciation Expense	Taxable Income	After-tax Cash Flow	Adjusted Tax Basis
1	41,100	− 10,449	28,067	933,900
2	51,300	− 12,551	35,931	882,600
3	41,700	5,745	38,559	840,900
4	35,940	20,848	42,586	804,960
5	35,940	30,892	48,568	769,020
6	31,620	46,014	53,701	737,400
7	27,300	61,960	59,212	710,100
8	27,300	74,481	66,330	682,800
9	27,300	87,974	73,886	655,500
10	27,300	102,527	81,838	628,200

Year	Internal Rate of Return on Initial Equity	Overall Rate of Return	Break -even Ratio	Present Value of Equity at Discount 10%
1	−0.06%	11.149%	82.032%	−37,959
2	5.82%	11.549%	79.164%	−30,007
3	8.22%	11.962%	76.441%	−18,543
4	9.69%	12.389%	73.856%	−4,230
5	10.75%	12.829%	71.401%	12,437
6	11.59%	13.284%	69.068%	31,124
7	12.28%	13.754%	66.851%	51,471
8	12.88%	14.239%	64.744%	73,166
9	13.39%	14.741%	62.741%	95,992
10	13.83%	15.258%	60.835%	119,753

Sensitivity Analysis

Experience with computer programs allows an investor to more easily explore another facet of business operations. This is the determination of how sensitive future cash flows are to unexpected changes in operating figures. For instance, how are cash flows affected by a sudden increase in property taxes? Or what is the result of eliminating charges for the private use of a public room by tenants?

One way to answer this question is to take a specific cost item and select what might be a high, a low, and a medium level of increase in its cost. Then, using the three different levels of increase, run the entire cash flow projection as described earlier in this chapter to see what the end result may be for each level of increase. This should illustrate the impact of change in that specific cost item on the final result. If a large increase in the cost creates only a minor change in the end cash flows, then that particular cost is not as important. This would mean the result is not so "sensitive" to that particular item.

The same kind of projection can be made with specific income items to determine the effect of a sudden increase or decrease in a particular income item.

Negative Cash Flows (NCF)

Not all real property investments produce positive cash flows each year. Properties can have a negative cash flow for tax purposes, yet produce a positive cash flow to the investor. This, of course, is because of the deduction for depreciation as a non-cash item. Some properties require an input of cash each year to cover operating costs; after several years they produce a profit upon disposition due to an escalation in value.

Counting on inflation in property value to produce a profit amounts to speculation, but it has proven successful in many areas of the country. If one applies an average inflation rate to the value of a specific property on a compound basis for the next five years, a substantial increase in value results. When measured against the amount of initial equity cash required, the value increase can be most impressive.

The following example illustrates the impact of property appreciation as it offsets negative cash flows.

Example

Assume the following conditions:

Property value: $80,000   Loan: $60,000   Equity: $20,000
Annual income: $5,500   Annual Expenses: $8,700
Negative cash flow: $3,200

Assume the owner is eligible for the $25,000 exclusion of passive income and can claim the loss against other income

Annual operating loss	$3,200	
Income tax savings 28% bracket)	895	
Annual loss	$2,305	
Loss over 5 years (5 × 2,305)		11,520

After 5 years, assume the $80,000 property has increased in value at a 7% annual rate to a sales value of $112,200.

Sales value after 5 years	$112,200	
Less: Mortgage loan payoff	52,600	
Value of equity	$ 59,600	
Less: Capital gain tax		
(32,200 × .28) =	9,016	
Value of equity after taxes		50,584
NET GAIN OVER 5-YEAR PERIOD		$39,064

To figure return on original equity invested:

Gain per year ($39,064 divided by 5) = $7,812
Return per year on original equity:

$$\frac{7,812}{20,0000} = .39 \text{ or 39 percent}$$

The figures above do not take into consideration the time value of money and make no effort to discount the cash flows. The illustration shows that an investment of $20,000 in equity might produce an average increase in value of $7,812 per year, for a 39% annual return on investment.

The key questions, of course, are these: "How certain is the inflation rate that's estimated for a particular property over the next five years?" and "Is the investor prepared to increase the investment each year to cover deficits?"

NCF *for Commercial Properties*

If the location is sound, and financing is assured or can be assumed, there is some merit to an investment based on a likelihood of continuous inflation.

But new financing is very difficult to obtain for a property that's losing money, i.e., a property with a negative cash flow. This is not because lenders believe inflation will decline. Lenders, like most other business people, see little change in the economic and political policies underlying *general* inflationary pressures. The reason for lenders' reluctance is that the amount of inflation that can be anticipated for a *specific* property is still a matter of considerable speculation. In short, properties are not uniformly affected.

A second major question for the lender is the valuation of the property. How does an appraiser impute income value to a loss? The result is that conservative lenders refuse to make loans on commercial properties that are losing money.

NCF *for Residential Properties*

Negative cash flow is often heralded as a "smart" procedure when it's applied to single family rental houses. Escalation in property values has generally been greater for houses than for commercial properties, and residential operating losses are more easily outweighed by the gains from a sale. Also, it is normally the residential borrower's *personal* income—rather than the *property's* income—that provides the basis for a loan.

Nevertheless, rental housing poses some problems for an investor. One is the growing concern exhibited by the various government housing agencies and private residential lenders that speculative home buying causes a "spiral effect" in home prices. Many lenders will not initiate loans (or permit the assumption of existing loans) for anyone who isn't planning to live in the house to be bought. Few lenders consider home loans as "commercial loans," but they *can* easily apply the stiffer requirements and higher interest rates normally applicable to commercial loans for investor-owned housing.

Another problem for a rental house investor may be the neighborhood where the property is located. Even in times of general inflation, properties in some urban areas decline in value because of changing living patterns. Careful selection of location is always important, but even more so when the anticipated return is based not on operating income but on a speculative increase in property value.

Conclusion

The computer programs offer very interesting looks into the future—as long as all factors remain constant. The information should be used as one element in reaching an investment decision. But numbers alone are not the complete answer. Consideration must be given to many other influences on future values such as the economy, the available management, the nature of the property, and the possibility of laws imposing additional costs in taxes and restraints on property usage. In the last two chapter those influences that depend on judgment calls, rather than mathematical solutions, are examined.

15

Examining Real Property Risk

An investor can acquire an interest in real property in several different ways. The investment can be a beneficial interest in a real estate trust. It can be as an inactive participant in a real estate syndicate. Or the investment can be as an active owner. Whatever the investment method may be, risk evaluation is important to all.

From an income producing standpoint, as well as for income tax purposes, there are several different categories of real property investment. Following are the principal distinctions:

1. *Income property* produces a return from leases spanning a month or longer, such as an apartment or office building. The IRS also identifies this kind as "trade or business" property to separate it from investment property.

2. *Investment property* is the same as income property except that the investor retains minimal management responsibility and is subject to special tax limitations.

3. *Inventory property* derives its income from a sale or exchange, such as with vacant land or building lots.

4. *Business-type real estate* produces income from the day-to-day sale of services, such as a restaurant, or day-to-day rental such as a hotel. In both cases, specialized management produces income from a business operation that is separate from the rental of space alone.

The distinction between income property, investment property, and inventory property is concerned with tax law. Prior rules denied capital gain treatment in the sale of inventory property. This is no longer relevant because capital gain is taxed the same as ordinary income. However, investment property is still distinguished from income property in the tax code. Interest deductions for investment property are limited to the net income from that property (subject to a phase-out provision in the 1986 Tax Act). (See Chapter 5.)

This chapter examines income property from the standpoint of risk evaluation and common concerns affecting all properties. These are principally leasing methods and the general operation of properties. This is followed by a study of raw land, its risk as an investment, and its development for further construction purposes. The next chapter reviews major questions involved with the operation and marketing of the principal classes of income property and business-type property. First, a look at the special risks involved with assessing the reliability of an income stream.

Risk Associated with Income Stream

As previously discussed in this book, investment analysis of any kind is a study of risk. As an investment's risk increases, so must its expected return. Otherwise, investors will not be attracted. When an investment is expected to yield a return from a continuing income stream, the character of that income must be carefully considered. Three traits of the income stream must be examined in terms of risk: (1) quantity, (2) quality, and (3) durability.

Quantity

The more income a property produces, the more that property is worth. A property that produces $50,000 per year in net income is worth five times as much as a property that produces $10,000 in annual income. This is the most obvious component of risk, and by far the most amenable to comparison. The difficult aspect of measuring the quantity of income comes in determining the probability of its attainment. Is the expected income a realistic projection? Does the income figure include any non-cash returns that would create a distorted comparison with another property's income? And is the quantity of income being compared produced over a like period of time?

Quality

The quality of income refers primarily to the nature of the source of that income. A rental property consisting of rooms and small apartments that cater to transients is almost certainly worth less to an investor than a small, well-leased industrial warehouse—even if the properties produce the same quantity of net income. The *quality* of the two income streams makes the difference. The assurance represented by the well-leased industrial warehouse tips the balance, when compared with the uncertainties of a transient clientele. Yet present income and future projections may indicate an indentical return to the investor. The quality of the income indicates the reliability of that income.

Durability

Two main factors constitute the durability of income. One is the term of the assured income, and the other is the useful life of the property. A property with 15 years left on its lease has a more durable income than one with only three years to run. This is not to say that there are not potential advantages in a lease expiration—indeed, expiration can permit a new lease on better terms. But these possibilities must be weighed in light of the quantity and quality of the expected income. The expected useful life of a property is always a limit factor for the investor, especially when the analysis concerns an older property. As a property grows older, the costs of maintenance and repairs can absorb more and more of its expected income. Durability of income indicates the expected life of that income.

Leases

The types of leasehold estate have already been discussed in Chapter 10. That chapter examined the limited rights of ownership conveyed with a lease and gave a general outline of the laws that apply to leases. This section considers the types of lease and rental payment provisions most commonly used with income property. Based on how rentals are paid, leases for commercial properties fall into three categories (with combinations in between). These are term leases, net leases, and percentage leases.

Term Leases

The term lease is also called a *gross lease* or a *flat sum* lease. In legal terminology, it is a less-than-freehold estate in which the property is leased for a definite, fixed period of time and is identified as a *tenancy for years*. In most states, such a lease must be in writing if it extends beyond one year. Unless a statute, or an agreement, states otherwise, the tenancy is considered to be personal property and passes to the tenant's heirs upon death.

In most commercial leases of this type, the term is short, from one month to five years. The rent is negotiable depending on the size of the space and its location within the building and the neighborhood. With short-term leases it is fairly common for the agreement to include annual rent increases in anticipation of higher costs. With longer-term leases, escalation clauses are generally used to offset increased costs, and these depend on the type and amount of services rendered for the tenant.

The services provided for tenants by the landlord vary with the lease conditions but commonly include the exterior maintenance of the building and parking lots, furnishing of all or a part of the utilities, trash disposal, and payment of all taxes and insurance for the building (but not its contents). It is these services that have shown erratic cost increases and have popularized the use of general escalation clauses in all kinds of leases, particularly for term leases at otherwise fixed rentals.

Escalation Clauses. In more stable, less inflationary periods (generally prior to 1970), the use of escalation clauses in lease agreements was confined to covering an increase in taxes and insurance. Now there are almost no limits to the types of cost that may be included under escalation clauses. Landlords are wary of long-term commitments to furnish space and services to tenants because future costs are not determinable. As a result, the term lease often allows for annual adjustment in rent to compensate for increases in taxes, insurance, utilities, maintenance, and management. To provide a measure of protection for the tenant, the escalation provision usually requires the landlord to produce (1) some form of documentation of increases in operating costs, and (2) details on how these costs are being allocated to each tenant. This allocation can be done on a basis of the square footage under lease, or as a percentage of the space actually occupied in the building.

To attract tenants, an escalation clause may contain a "cap"—a limitation on the amount of increase that can be charged in any one year. If there is an advantage for a tenant leasing under an escalation clause, it stems from permitting a lower initial rental rate. Otherwise, the landlord would have to estimate future costs and base the rent on speculative cost increases.

Net Leases

A net lease is one in which the tenant not only pays rent for the occupancy, but also pays for maintenance and operating expenses of the premises. This kind of lease is favored by investors who want a steady income without having to handle the problems associated with management and maintenance. Buildings offered for lease in this manner are generally free-standing facilities used by grocery chains, oil company service stations, and fast food franchises.

While there is a broad range of such leases, the tenant is generally responsible for expenses relating to the premises as if the tenant were the owner. These expenses include such costs as real estate taxes; special assessments; insurance premiums; all maintenance charges, including labor and materials; cost of compliance with governmental health and safety regulations; payment of claims for personal injury or property damage; and even costs of structural, interior, roof, and other repairs.

With risk minimized, the rental charged is figured as a fair return on the invested capital only. The landlord retains such tax benefits as are available to real estate investment. However, a lease for longer than 30 years is subject to an IRS interpretation as "ownership" for the tenant. If so construed, the lease payments are treated as mortgage payments, and the tax benefits of ownership are passed to the tenant for the purpose of calculating tax liabilities.

There is some variation among real estate professionals in the way they use the word "net" when talking of a lease. One interpretation is that the single word "net" means that the tenant pays all expenses *except* taxes and insurance. The term "net, net" means the tenant pays all expenses *and* the insurance. "Net, net, net"—or "triple net"—means what has been described above as a net lease, i.e., the tenant pays all costs, including taxes and insurance.

Escalation clauses are generally included in those net leases that require the landlord to pay for either taxes or insurance. Otherwise, the lease is generally written to provide a fixed return for the investor over the term of the lease.

Percentage Leases

The most common lease form for stores and shopping centers is the percentage lease. Rental payments are based on gross sales figures, not on any computation of profit. The use of sales figures to determine rental charges is most common for stores where products are sold, rather than where services are rendered (which occurs most often in office buildings). Sales figures can be easily verified through (1) a lease clause that permits the landlord to audit the tenant's records, or (2) a certified copy of the tenant's sales tax reports.

There are three ways that rental can be computed in a percentage lease:

1. Straight percentage of gross sales.
2. Minimum base rental *plus* a percentage of gross sales.
3. Minimum base rental *or* a percentage of gross sales, whichever is larger.

Also, sometimes a ceiling, or cap, is included in the percentage rental. Also, minimum rental is desirable because it provides the landlord with the protection of an assured income to cover mortgage payments and operating costs. Without a minimum, it is possible for a tenant to achieve a volume of sales that gives an

TABLE 15–1
Examples of Lease Percentage Ranges

Business	Percent	Business	Percent
Auto supplies	3–5	Gift shops	7–10
Barber & beauty shops	7–10	Groceries (large)	1–2
Books & stationery	5–7	Hardware stores	4–6
Bowling lanes	8–9	Motion picture theaters	10–11
Cocktail lounge	8	Office supplies	4–6
Convenience store	4–6	Parking lot/attendant	40–60
Department store	2–4	Restaurant & fast foods	5–7
Discount houses	1–2	Shoe stores	5–6
Drug stores	2–6	Sporting goods	5–7
Furniture	5–8	Toy stores	4–5
Gas stations (cents per gallon)	1½–8	Women's dress shops	6–7

adequate profit but does not provide the landlord with sufficient rental to cover the costs of leasing the space.

An escalation clause appears in most percentage leases, but it's usually more flexible than a term lease's escalation clause. After all, under a percentage lease any increase in sales prices due to inflation (or any other cause) should result in an increased rental payment. Most commonly, the escalation provision adds to the minimum rent requirement all or part of any increases in taxes, insurance, or other agreed upon expenses. The escalation clause may permit the tenant to *recapture* an increase in the minimum rent (if due to escalation of costs) when the percentage rent exceeds certain specified levels.

Percentage leases give the shopping center owner a good incentive to cooperate with the tenants in advertising and promoting the center. Careful tenant selection and judicious placement of the stores within the center can achieve maximum benefit of the shopping traffic; greater sales can thus be realized.

Rental Percentages. Several real estate organizations such as The Institute of Real Estate Management and the International Council of Shopping Centers publish percentage lease tables that can be used as general guidelines for lease negotiation. Some examples of percentage ranges as applied to various classes of merchants is shown in Table 15–1.

Lease Covenants

Lease conditions determine *who* pays for *what*. Following is a point-by-point consideration of the relevant expense allocations.

Taxes. Except under a net lease with special terms, property taxes are paid by the owner. Some leases call for an escalation in the rental structure if taxes increase. The exact responsibility for payment should be spelled out in each lease, including (1) whether the tenant pays all, some, or none of the base year's taxes, (2) when taxes are paid, and (3) how taxes are paid. If the tenant's operations create an increase in the tax assessment, this should also be anticipated by the lease. (Any taxes due on the tenant's property may become a claim against the landlord if protection is not provided.)

Insurance. The landlord usually pays for hazard insurance for the premises. A tenant *does* have the right to know how the leasehold interest is being protected against loss, and may require the landlord to provide a copy of the insurance policy. If the cost of insurance increases, the increase may be prorated to the tenant in accordance with an escalation clause. If the activities of the tenant create an increased risk for the property, the resulting increase in insurance cost may be passed on to the tenant.

Other types of coverage must be considered in lease agreements. The landlord may require that the tenant maintain liability insurance with a protective clause in favor of the landlord. If plate glass is a part of the premises, a separate insurance policy may be required (it can be the responsibility of either the landlord or the tenant). Any other special risk of exposure that must be covered should be spelled out in the lease agreement.

Maintenance. Under the normal division of costs between a landlord and tenant in rental property, the landlord pays for exterior maintenance and the tenant pays for interior maintenance. But the line between "exterior" and "interior" is not always easy to define; it needs to be defined in the lease. Such things as electric-eye-operated doors, exterior lighting for the special use of the tenant, trash and garbage areas, and exterior protective screens or walls used only by the tenant are all subject to dispute if maintenance requirements are not clearly detailed in the lease.

Parking. The lease agreement should detail the tenant's rights to parking facilities, both for employees and for customers. Furthermore, the lease should allocate the costs of lighting and upkeep for the parking area (in whatever shares may be agreed upon by the parties). Additional charges on a "per car" basis are sometimes written in lease agreements, especially for office buildings. Or employees may be offered parking privileges in exchange for a pay reduction, the amount depending on the accessibility of the space. At large shopping centers, the common practice is to set aside a specific area—away from major customer traffic patterns—which is reserved for employee parking.

Improvements and Trade Fixtures. A lease should specify who pays for improvements and who pays for trade fixtures. Normally, improvements are made by the landlord and added to the rental price. Improvements remain the property of the landlord. Trade fixtures usually belong to the tenant, are paid for by the tenant, and may be removed by the tenant at the termination of the lease. Trade fixtures installed by the landlord may become a part of the leased premises as a sales inducement for the tenant. If so, the landlord's ownership should be clearly determined in advance. Structural changes in the building may be agreed upon, but are generally not a part of the tenant's leasehold rights.

Terms, Payments, and Conditions. The term of the lease should be clearly stated, as should the date or time that rental payments become due. Different payment times may apply to a base rent and to a percentage (or gallonage, in the case of a service station), so as to allow time for computation or verification. If the lease permits any adjustments in rental payments (such as the recapture of tax and insurance payments against a percentage over base rent), *when* these adjustments are allowed should be clarified in the lease. And it should specify the time that any escalation payments become due.

Many other conditions that limit leasehold rights may be included in the lease. The lease may or may not be *assignable.* If it is assignable, what are the continuing obligations of the original tenant? The lease should say. Limitations are usually placed on how the property may be used as a protection to other tenants and to the landlord's continuing property value. Further, the right to *sublet* all or part of the leasehold interest may or may not be granted under the original lease.

Leasing New Properties

Most problems that must be resolved in a lease agreement occur whether the property has been previously occupied or is a new building awaiting its first tenant. For new properties, however, some additional questions—involving the final steps of construction and finishing out the premises to be leased—must be considered. Initial lease-up requires that both the investor-owner (landlord-to-be) and the leasing agent have a good knowledge of construction procedures and current costs. For instance, the leasing agent's promise to add an interior wall or alter a plumbing installation may appear inconsequential and, thus, inexpensive. But the addition or alteration may require changes in other areas of the building that substantially increase the cost. The following discussion focuses on the principal areas of concern in completing a new building to suit a tenant's special requirements. The general guidelines offered here apply to all newly constructed income properties, with one exception. Apartments are almost always finished (carpeted, painted, wallpapered, fixtures installed) *before* leasing unless the tenant is permitted to select the color of walls and carpeting.

Planning

If a building is pre-leased, the future tenant normally is deeply involved in the planning details. Any plan changes can be made before construction is completed, and any resulting addition or reduction in costs can be built into the rental structure. A common alternative procedure is for the landlord to agree with the tenant on a basic plan for the building, and then charge the costs of any alterations directly to the tenant. A cost overrun on a pre-leased building is almost impossible for the landlord to recover and must be prevented if at all possible. The best preventive medicine is planning carefully and requiring that tenant-created alterations be paid for by the tenant.

For buildings that are constructed on a speculative basis (i.e., without pre-leasing), planning should proceed only to the extent of providing basic minimum requirements. This is termed a "shell" because the building at this point has exterior walls and a roof, but no ceiling, perhaps no floor, no interior finishing, no utility outlets, and no interior walls. Leasing a shell to a new tenant requires detailed planning of exactly what the tenant requires and of how the costs of installation will be allocated. Two basic procedures are used to assess completion costs to the new tenant. One is to pass the full cost directly to the tenant (who may even handle the subcontracting for the work); the other, to allocate costs on a "per unit" basis, i.e., so much for each additional running foot of wall, so much for each new electrical outlet, etc. The following sections discuss the components that are most commonly furnished by the tenant on newly constructed buildings.

Interior Walls. The design of office, shop, or warehouse space is best handled by the tenant who will be using the space. The building design, of course, limits the location of interior walls that will conform with the load-bearing columns or walls which support the roof. Within these limits, non-bearing walls and dividers may be located in the way that best serves the tenant's requirements. In office buildings, the most common method of passing on this cost to the tenant is to charge for each running foot of wall. The lease agreement may, for each running foot of wall. The lease agreement may, for example, permit the tenant to install 200 feet of non-bearing wall under the basic rental price. Any additional wall might be charged to the tenant at $30.00 per lineal foot. (Actual prices vary substantially.) Shopping centers and warehouse buildings are more apt to make a flat charge for additional walls, based on the contractors' construction bids.

Ceilings.   Ceilings are not enclosed in new construction until the property is leased because of the need to locate lighting and air conditioning outlets at required positions (which in turn depend upon the interior wall arrangement). The cost of the ceiling is generally not a separate charge in office buildings because the owner knows that the amount of the ceiling will be the same as the square footage to be leased. In shopping centers, it is not unusual to ask tenants to furnish their own ceilings (with appropriate adjustments in rent) so that they may tailor the design of ceiling, lighting, and air ducts to best suit their marketing needs. Warehouses and industrial buildings normally do not require ceilings.

Concrete Floors.   With the exception of large shopping centers and some warehouse space, floors are completed prior to leasing. The reason these exceptions wait until a tenant is obtained is to permit the installation of underground plumbing, electrical outlets, and any special piping or wiring needed by the tenant. If the floor is for warehouse use, the tenant may require a stronger than normal floor to support unusually heavy loads. When flooring is constructed to meet a tenant's special requirements, the cost is usually assumed by the tenant.

Utility Outlets.   Most tenants have special requirements for the location of each utility service outlet, including electricity, water and water drainage, natural gas (if needed and available), and telephone outlets. In an office building, the normal procedure is to charge a flat fee for each outlet, based on the cost of installation. The flexibility that a new tenant has to lay out space in the most effective manner is a major advantage of the newly constructed building.

Doors.   The location of interior doors for a newly constructed building can usually be determined by the tenant. If a tenant requires special doors, or more doors than are anticipated by the initial plans, an additional charge can be made.

Interior Finishing.   Painting or wallpapering interior walls, the installation of lighting, and any other required finishing are normally the responsibility of the tenant in commercial leases. The landlord may insist on having approval of any plans for finishing to be undertaken by the tenant. Most new office buildings and a few new apartments have some finishing requirements that will provide a uniform exterior appearance. The office building owner may supply drapes, or require a certain pattern for window shades or blinds. For carpeting, wall coverings, and paint, the building may offer a selection of several basic color combinations that can be installed at the landlord's expense; variations may be charged to the tenant.

Operation of Income Properties

All types of income property have substantial similarity in basic areas of operation. These are its management, including the handling of utilities and other services.

Management

All income properties require management—some more, some less. An operating property is a form of business that requires the collection of rents, the keeping of records, and the protection and maintenance of the property itself. The investor must either hire outside management or be willing to spend time handling the management responsibilities. These responsibilities are (1) maintenance of the premises, which includes both repairs and capital improvements; (2) securing, screening, and locating tenants in the most effective way; (3) supervising all operating personnel; and (4) controlling the use of the premises by tenants and their customers.

Maintenance of the Premises.   Income properties are usually maintained, at least in part, by the landlord or owner. Even though tenants may be responsible for maintaining interior walls and some of the heating or air conditioning equipment, the landlord should specify minimum maintenance standards. Various levels of maintenance are required, depending on the type of property and the conditions of the lease. Because of this flexibility, maintenance duties should be detailed in the lease agreement, e.g., how often the tenant can require exterior painting, etc.

    As for capital improvements, such as the replacement of an air conditioning unit or the addition of a new sales area, the management must have written guidelines in the lease (or drawn from the leases) in order to make a fair allocation of costs to the tenants. An addition to the premises of one tenant may conflict with the premises of another, so the rights of the tenants need to be settled in advance.

Securing and Screening Tenants.   Securing occupancy of a building may be done through leasing agents or through the owner's advertising and sales representation. The quality of tenants is always a major problem for the landlord and can easily determine an operation's success or failure. The quality of tenants must fit the use intended for the building, i.e., the type of work and services they perform should be compatible, and the customer groups they serve must be similar. An office building catering to the medical profession is not a suitable location for a nightclub. A shopping center with predominantly low prices and discount stores is not attractive to an exclusive dress shop.

Tenants of all types must be screened for financial responsibility. Major companies are often the preferred risk, of course. But in fact most tenants are small—as well as new to the area when the initial lease is consummated—and they should be investigated for their previous records of operations and credit-worthiness. Evicting an undesirable tenant can be expensive and can be avoided by careful advance screening.

Both tenant and landlord have an interest in where an office, shop, or storage facility is located within a building complex. The choice of location can be based on (1) the flow of customer traffic (most important for a shopping center), (2) the availability of required utilities, or (3) the ease of access to transportation or to the handling of materials. Naturally the choice of locations is more flexible in a new building than in an existing building, and immediate optimum use of the space is easier to accomplish. With an existing property that has tenants, it may be desirable to reject even a highly qualified prospective tenant if locating that tenant in the only space available could jeopardize future operations and leasing.

Supervision of Operating Personnel.   Property owners often try to avoid becoming burdened with personnel problems—payroll records, personal problems, the complex set of equal employment and labor relations laws, and the need for constant supervision. Larger income properties can afford to employ highly competent, professional managers to handle personnel responsibilities. Medium-sized and smaller operations may prefer to use contract management companies, which are growing rapidly all over the country and provide much-needed expertise. And smaller property owners may simply serve as their own managers, aided by one or two maintenance and service employees.

Using service contractors is another growing method of avoiding the problems of directly employing people. Many services can be furnished by contractors, including janitorial service, maintenance of heating and air conditioning equipment, periodic and minor plumbing repairs, painting, and window washing. Many larger cities have contracting companies that provide all-inclusive services for operating properties.

Control Over the Use of Premises.   One of the most difficult management responsibilities is that of controlling how the premises are used after leases have been signed. A loosely drawn lease may leave a tenant free to operate a shop or office any way he or she sees fit. A leasehold does grant the rights of possession and use, but the landlord retains the right to protect the property against loss of value that may result from misuse. Limits on use may be (1) spelled out in the lease, (2) based on customary use, or (3) negotiated between the building management and the tenant. Careful advance planning is the best procedure to prevent conflicts in this area. Unfortunately, even careful planning isn't fail-safe—businesses change, and sometimes their products or services are changed by market requirements. When things do change, the interpretation and settlement of conflicting situations becomes a management responsibility. For example, a tenant restaurant that replaces its piano bar with pornographic entertainment can diminish the value of the property for other tenants—and for the management. But "pornography" has proven difficult to define, even by the courts. So management must walk a thin line in dealing with the change. Consider one more example. The introduction of a new chemical process or electronic testing procedure—which may later prove hazardous to occupants, customers, or the building itself—is always of concern to an alert management.

The tenants' customers are even more difficult to control, and sometimes necessitate security agreements in the lease. This is especially true for large shopping centers, which can become "hangouts" for undesirable characters. This problem must also be considered as the landlord examines prospective tenants and the types of automobile and pedestrian traffic they are likely to attract to the premises.

Utilities and Other Services

Utilities and various other services are still very much an accepted part of the covenants found in an income property lease. But increasingly they are excluded from the obligations of the landlord. Landlords once paid for almost all utilites, arguing that utilities could be furnished to tenants most cheaply through the use of a single master meter. Today that practice has given way to separate meters for each tenant, or to a strict allocation to each tenant of the month-to-month costs. Rapidly rising utility costs are, of course, the reason.

Landlords are also attempting to shed their obligations for as many non-utility services as possible.

Utilities. Included in the category of "utilities" are electricity, natural gas, water, and sewer facilities. The trend among landlords is to pass on these expenses to their tenants.

Electricity is most easily separated from the landlord's responsibility through the use of a separate meter, very much as telephone service is separated. Industrial properties, warehouses, and other free-standing, single-tenant rental properties have long used separate meters to allow the tenant to pay electric charges. Apartment owners tried for a while to use a single meter, furnishing electricity to tenants as a part of the services provided under their basic rental payment—but abuse and escalating costs have changed all that. New apartment houses are including separate meters for each apartment, and older units are converting to separate meters where possible. When conversion is not practical, landlords usually allocate the single-meter costs so that each tenant pays a proportionate part of the total cost. Office buildings generally have not moved to the use of separate meters but most do include escalation clauses in leases so that cost increases are allocated among the tenants.

Natural gas is not always a necessity for apartments and office buildings. But when gas is used, it is generally handled in much the same way as electricity, i.e., separate meters for new buildings, and allocation of cost increases for older buildings with single meters. Industrial and commercial use of natural gas is almost always measured through separate meters, since it is more often a processing component than a landlord-provided service.

Usable *water* is far more precious today than it was only a few years ago. Yet even now few lease agreements for apartments, office buildings, or smaller commercial buildings call for separate metering of water. Rental increases in term leases and escalation clauses in commercial leases generally have been sufficient protection for the landlord to justify continuing this service as part of the leasehold rights. Larger commercial properties and industrial buildings are more easily adapted to separate water metering, and they usually do provide this separation.

Sewer facilities are usually provided (and charged for) by the same entity that furnishes water, often a municipally owned utility plant. Not too many years ago, sanitary sewer lines and storm sewers were an accepted part of a community's service to the taxpayer. Sewage itself was often dumped into waterways without much treatment. The need to build adequate waste treatment plants has escalated the cost of such utilities. It is this cost that has multiplied user's bills in recent years.

Janitorial Services. Sweeping, cleaning, and polishing public areas are services found in shopping centers, apartments, and office buildings. In addition, office buildings often provide the same service for tenants' office space. Older lease forms usually included this kind of maintenance as a part of the building services covered by the basic rental fee. Now some landlords are assessing these costs as a separate monthly maintenance charge that is determined by the costs incurred. Office buildings that provide cleaning services for the tenants' offices include this cost in escalation clauses.

Maintenance Service. Plumbing and electrical repairs, painting, and other building repairs are normally the responsibility of the landlord. Lease provisions define the tenant's area of responsibility (usually interior maintenance) *and* the landlord's. As maintenance costs increase, the landlord may want to include repairs in the escalation clause, thereby permitting an increase in rent to cover the added costs. The need for repairs is unpredictable—unlike cleaning services—so they are not as easily translated into a monthly service charge. However, some leases allow for an all-inclusive service charge that includes repairs as they become necessary.

Heating and Air Conditioning. With some forms of income property—such as warehouses, shopping centers, and other commercial buildings—it has long been possible for the landlord to require that the tenant furnish, install, and maintain the heating and air conditioning equipment. Naturally the rental structure in these cases reflects the landlord's lower investment, but the tenant is responsible for the maintenance expense and the potential of lost sales (as would occur if a store's air conditioning failed for an extended period of high summertime temperatures). In an office building with multiple occupancy, heating and air conditioning are considered part of the services offered to the tenant. The general practice is to include maintenance of this equipment in escalation clauses, allowing for annual increases.

Trash Disposal. This is an optional service that may be assigned to either the landlord or the tenant, depending on the terms of the lease. The disposition of trash has become a more and more difficult problem—suitable dumping grounds are becoming scarcer and farther removed from the source of the trash. However, there has been some recognition of the salvage value in trash, and a few companies have devised their own procedures for separating usable materials from waste. Office buildings that contain large accounting operations—and, thus, large quantities of waste paper—may recover marketable materials through a simple sorting of the trash. Printing shops produce high-quality waste paper. Restaurants and bars may have a sales potential for old cans and even glass bottles. While trash disposal is still commonly seen as an expensive nuisance, there is a growing trend for both landlord and tenant to take a closer look at what trash is being produced and to investigate the potential for selling the material.

Security Systems. Alarmed by the increasing incidence of vandalism, assaults, and robbery, all forms of business activity have sought better methods to protect their investments. This is another service that may be the responsibility of either the tenant or the landlord. In practice, only larger office buildings consider security to be the landlord's responsibility; even then, the landlord accepts no liability. Shopping centers often provide for security through a merchants' association where each contributes a portion of the cost of maintaining a security system. Buildings with a single tenant or a small number of tenants have considered security wholly the responsibility of the tenant(s) and usually do not refer to the subject in leases. However, security is a matter of growing concern, and one that should be defined in all lease convenants.

While landlords have preferred a "hands off" approach to security, a property owner is well-advised to cooperate with the tenant in furnishing property protection. Fire warning systems can reduce both insurance premiums and the potential for loss. Sonic monitors detect sound and movement in or on the premises under the scanning instrument, and then sound an alarm. Electric eyes and laser-beam-type instruments can detect break-ins, and possibly prevent or reduce property damage from vandalism or robbery. Centrally located control monitors manned by computers have reduced the costs of surveillance to the point where even small companies (and homeowners) may find the service attractive.

Land as an Investment

Undeveloped land may be acquired for a number of purposes. However, the interest here is in the use of its surface rights only. Such land may be held for appreciation and resale to others for their use and development. Or the land may be developed into lots for sale to home builders or industrial parks for commercial developments. Land held for resale to others is deemed *inventory property* by the IRS.

Inventory Property

"Property held for inventory" is a term used by the IRS to distinguish undeveloped land or other property held for appreciation and future sale. The risk associated with this kind of property is very difficult to measure because the property lacks an existing or projected income stream that can be evaluated. Because of this problem, many analysts prefer to classify such acquisitions as "speculation," rather than "investment." Regardless of the terminology, there are some guidelines that are helpful even though they do not lend themselves to statistical analysis. In Chapter 1 of this text, the types of return that may be realized from real estate were identified as (1) income, (2) appreciation, and (3) value gain. It is appreciation (the passive form of increase in investment value) and value gain (the active input of expertise by the owner or management, resulting in an increase in property value) that provide the guidelines for examination of inventory-type property.

Land Selection

Population growth patterns and the restrictions on land use directly affect future land value. Care must be taken in the selection of a tract of undeveloped land to be held for appreciation to ensure that it lies in the general path of population growth, the potential zoning problems will not grossly inhibit future use, and that utility systems and transportation patterns will support future use. The key word is "use"—basic land value is increased in direct relation to its growth in usefulness. It is the change in the land's usage capability that causes value to increase (or decrease).

Financing Land Acquisition

Loans to finance the acquisition of undeveloped land are not generally favored by lenders. Repayment of the loan is tied in some measure to the ability of the borrower to sell the land. And *when* this objective might be accomplished is an uncertainty that bankers do not like to contend with. However, the landowner can realize a much better profit margin from the leverage offered by borrowed money. For these reasons, the *seller* of undeveloped land is often the lender, providing financing in the form of a relatively small required down payment and low amortization payments for a limited span of time. To understand the value of leverage in land acquisition intended for resale, take an example of a tract costing $5,000 per acre. Assume that after three years the land can be sold for $7,500 per acre, giving a $2,500 per acre gross profit.*

Selling price	$7,500
Less: Acquisition cost	5,000
Gross profit	$2,500
Less: Selling expenses	450
Less: Three years' taxes and insurance	500
Net profit	$1,550

To compute return on investment

$$\frac{\$1,550}{3 \text{ years}} = \$516.67 \text{ per year}$$

$$\frac{516.67}{5,000} = 10.33\% \text{ return per year}$$

*For simplification, the time value of money is not considered in this example.

If the acquisition is made with $1,000 equity cash and $4,000 in borrowed funds, the return is calculated as follows:

Selling price	$7,500
Less: Loan principal repaid	4,000
Less: Equity cash used	1,000
Gross profit	$2,500
Less: Selling expenses	450
Less: Three years' taxes and insurance	500
Less: Three years' interest ($4,000 @ 9%)	1,080
Net profit	$ 470

To compute return on investment:

$$\frac{\$470}{3 \text{ years}} = \$156.67 \text{ per year}$$

$$\frac{156.67}{1,000} = 15.67\% \text{ return per year}$$

The result of the borrowed money is a 50% increase in the return on the equity capital invested. However, borrowed money sharply curtails the time frame within which a profit may be realized in the example above. Assume that the selling price of $7,500 is not realized within the projected three-year span. The buyer for cash must continue to pay taxes and insurance at the rate of $166.67 per year, which would take another nine years to reduce the return on the investment to zero. But the buyer using $4,000 in borrowed money is converted into a loss position in the fourth year of the holding period if the $7,500 selling price has not been realized. Thus borrowed money increases the return for the equity owner if a sale can be made within a reasonably short time span, but it also limits the length of the holding period within which a profitable sale can be made.

In the example above, the increase in land value from $5,000 per acre to $7,500 over three years represents slightly less than a 15% per year appreciation rate. The returns shown in the example are hardly adequate to justify the substantial risk involved. There is little assurance that a favorable sale can be consummated within the time span to achieve optimum profits. Some investors feel that land values must *double* every three years to justify the risk. While the risk is quite high for an investment in undeveloped land, the right combination of growth factors can provide higher profit margins than from any other kind of real estate venture.

Timing

Timing is the key to success in holding land for profitable resale. The longer land is held, the greater the holding costs. Appreciation does not increase land values at a steady rate. Rather, increases come in spurts as potential use changes. Over a period of years, a tract of land may proceed through a whole litany of potential uses. It may first be suitable for single family residences, then for higher-density housing, then for light commercial use, then for a high-traffic shopping center or office building, and finally for high-rise structures. With each change in potential use, the land value jumps upward. So the basic question is: "At what point can a specific piece of land be sold with a maximum differential between its cost (plus holding charges) and its selling price?" The answer depends on the local situation. Astute landowners try to project the length of time until the next change in usage may occur, then decide if the costs of holding will be justified by the resulting increase in value.

The appreciation described above should be distinguished from the appreciation in value that is more and more being created by inflation. There is little real gain to an investor from inflation. The rise in land value attributable to inflation is offset by the loss in purchasing power of the dollars realized at the time of sale. To create profit, land values must increase at a greater rate than that induced by inflation.

Holding Land

There is no requirement that a land investor—or "speculator," if you prefer—must stand idly by and wait for the land to increase in value. On the contrary, many dealers in land find it advantageous to make some use of the land during the holding period. There are a number of ways for the landowner to recover at least some income from the property to help pay the taxes. The problem is to find a use for the land that neither encumbers it with a long-term lease commitment, nor alters the land itself in a way that could discourage a higher use later on.

Following are some suggestions for interim land use, which have general application in all regions. Note, however, that what is practical for a particular tract of land depends on its location and nearby population density.

1. *Recreational facilities*—pitch-and-putt golf courses, playing fields for rent, kiddie land parks, or small race tracks.
2. *Parking lots*—a standard holding procedure for high-value downtown land.
3. *Carnivals, rodeos, and other special shows* may rent land for short-term periods.

4. *Mobile home parks* in some areas have been used as a good way to "ware-house" land. Utilities can be designed for higher land use at a later time.

5. *Golf courses*—used by some large developers to hold land for later development.

6. *Farming partnerships* for crop production, with season-to-season leases.

7. *Timber* can be harvested and logs sold for firewood from forested tracts.

8. *Sod or turf production* for replanting can be developed on land that is not intended for further use as farm land.

It is the local demand for usable land that best determines what interim use is most practical. In some cases, the temporary use has developed sufficient profit to justify continuing its operation. There is always the possibility that the higher use for the property may not materialize, and the interim use may be the only viable alternative. So even if the landowner must make a sacrifice to accomodate an interim use, it is a good hedge against the future if the cost is not too great.

Land Development

Land may be acquired for holding; it also may be acquired for development. For the purpose of this discussion, "development" includes building streets and installing utility systems to service houses or commercial buildings that may be constructed at a separate time. Land development is an integral part of the design and construction work involved in most large apartment complexes and many commercial projects. Smaller builders, however, depend on developers to do the land planning, construct the service facilities, and then sell the finished lots to others.

Financing land development is an easier procedure than financing the acquisition of raw land. Savings associations, which must classify a loan for undeveloped land as "commercial" (i.e., non-residential) in their loan portfolios, can consider a development loan as "residential" if that is the obvious plan for the land's development. As indicated in Chapter 4, the savings association's charter requirements and tax advantages strongly favor residential-type loans. Savings associations have an additional incentive to finance development projects for houses: their initial financing puts them in a "first refusal" position to supply the financing for construction loans to the builders and permanent loans to the home buyers. The advantages that accrue to a savings association from maintaining a close relationship to a development project apply equally to all lenders. However, commercial banks and some insurance companies—which *will* make land development loans and building construction loans because they are short-term (less than three years)—are not so interested in making longer-term loans to the home buyers.

Another relationship that has developed between large institutional lenders and land developers is the joint venture. The lender makes a sound loan for the development and acquires a continuing market for its financial services. The developer has access to capital resources that might not otherwise be available to handle a large development project.

An interesting angle on land development can be seen by looking at the permissible loan limits. Depending on the lender, the maximum loan may range from 60% to 80% of the unimproved land's value. When acquiring undeveloped land, these loan limits mean that the buyer must put up 20% to 40% of the *acquisition* cost. In a development loan, the lender will generally accept an appraised value of the *finished* lots as the land value. The cost of the land, plus the cost of development of that land, should not exceed 75% of the finished lot price. Therefore, an 80% loan based on a finished lot price could provide a loan in excess of the acquisition cash expended by the developer. In practice, however, most lenders prefer to limit the loan amount to the actual cash needed to pay for the land and to build the streets and utilities. For experienced and reputable developers, the loan limits can amount to a 100% loan!

Mortgage Clauses

A land development loan is usually made with a mortgage lien in favor of the lender covering the entire tract of land. Two covenants that have special application to a development loan are involved. These are the plan used for development and the requirements for partial release of the completed lots.

The Development Plan.   In some cases, the lender specifies the order in which the mortgaged property can be developed. The purpose is to assure the continuing value of the entire tract during the development period. The plan must be agreeable to the borrower-developer and is generally a logical procedure to encourage a complete development.

The Release Clause.   The initial mortgage on the entire development tract must provide a mechanism to permit the sale of lots to others as the *lots are developed*. This is most commonly accomplished by requiring a minimum payment of cash to the lender for each lot released. The minimum required payment, for example, may be 85% of the initial price of the finished lots, plus 50% of any amount realized in excess of the original price. The lender's purpose is to obtain full repayment of the loan before the last—perhaps marginal—lots can be sold. Thus, much of the developer's profit can be tied up until the entire project is sold out.

Lots

The above discussion of finished lots applied to land that is developed for the purpose of constructing buildings. Not all "lots" offered for sale are developed, i.e., suitable for building. In some states—primarily Florida, Arizona, and California—developers have acquired large tracts of land in relatively remote areas and divided them into lots of from one to 10 acres each. These lots are then offered for sale through mass advertising programs, with small down payments and the balance in monthly payments over five to ten years. Many of these tracts are years away from practical development and have disappointed many buyers.

To prevent misrepresentation and outright fraud in this type of land sale, Congress created the Office of Interstate Land Sales Registration (OILSR) in 1968 to operate under the Department of Housing and Urban Development (HUD). The OILSR has since established specific rules and requirements under which land developers may offer their lots for sale. Severe penalties can be assessed against developers for failure to comply with the requirements. Essentially, the requirements call for full disclosure of information regarding the landownership, tax rates, proximity of schools, available utilities, and plans for future development. The development plans become a part of the sales package; if promised, completion is mandatory. However, the OILSR requires only that the facts be presented to the buyer; it is then up to the buyer to appraise the value offered. If the entire development tract is tied up in a master mortgage lien that cannot be released for, say, another 10 years, the sale of an individual lot is permissible so long as that fact (and all others) is disclosed.

Government regulations of this type are not directed towards the prudent investor, who examines in detail all aspects of a property and always inspects the property before signing a contract to buy. The purpose of these regulations is to protect the general public from unscrupulous promoters.

16

Marketing Investment Property

Whatever kind of property an investor is interested in, there is a need to study the market for its product. Successful investment is that which can market its product. If the product or services offered by the property are not marketable, the property itself suffers the same fate. Each kind of property is analysed from a slightly different approach to the marketing question. For instance, an apartment developer studies local area occupancy rates and competing rental rates; for office buildings, the focus is more on potential business growth and the ability of an area to absorb additional space; and for shopping centers, the analysis is based on population in the area, traffic patterns, and income levels.

It is the purpose of this chapter to examine the special problems associated with major classes of investment property. This includes (1) apartments, (2) office buildings, (3) retail store centers, (4) warehouse buildings, (5) special purpose buildings, and (6) business properties.

Apartments

Of the major forms of income property investment, an apartment offers the most transient—and therefore most unstable—form of occupancy. Leases are often on a month-to-month basis, and termination by the tenant is seldom difficult. The *continued* high occupancy rate of an apartment is more dependent on its competitive location, management, and operating policies than are income properties held for longer-term business leases. The unique problems associated with apartment properties can be summarized under the following headings:

1. Location.
2. The building and amenities.

3. Optimum mix of apartment units.

4. Rules and regulations.

5. Furnished vs. unfurnished apartments.

6. "Adults only" or "children accepted."

7. Tenants and lease agreements.

Location

An apartment is, of course, a residence. Tenants expect a reasonable proximity to schools, shopping facilities, churches, and recreational areas. In addition, the apartment dweller wants easy access to transportation (freeways, buses, etc.) and to places of employment. Some successful apartment operators consider location the most important factor in maintaining a good occupancy rate. Others consider a good location of equal importance to sound management and an attractive building.

The Building and Amenities

An attractive, well-maintained building is obviously more desirable than a run-down property. Probably more than any other factor, the physical condition of the building and the amenities (pool, tennis courts, clubhouse, etc.) govern an apartment's rental value as it competes with other apartments in the same area. Higher rentals generally can be sustained by the apartment that offers better physical facilities, so long as the overall charges are reasonably competitive for the neighborhood.

Optimum Mix of Apartment Units

An essential element of continued good occupancy is the ability to offer the types of apartment that meet local market requirements. In larger cities, where apartment dwellers are a growing segment of total housing, the older "shotgun" approach to variations in the units offered has given way to careful research designed to determine precisely what the market requires. In smaller cities, it is common to mix the number of one-, two-, and three-bedroom apartments in an arbitrary manner that should offer "something for everyone." In areas of increasing competition among apartment owners, the effort is directed along the guidelines furnished by market analysis. In an area catering to young couples and singles, the demand may be for one-bedroom or studio-type apartments, with the larger units holding low occupancy. Where the market is dominated by older couples and retirees, the best occupancy can be achieved in one- and two-bedroom units that emphasize ground floor units and few stairs. There is a growing apartment market for larger families that can no longer afford to purchase or rent suitable single family housing. Families with growing children need easy access to schools, as well as three- and four-bedroom units.

When an investor uses apartment occupancy rates as a guide for additional construction, it should be noted that a distortion can occur during periods of high occupancy (generally in excess of 95%). Under these conditions, tenants will live in a larger, or smaller, unit than is desired, until suitable accommodations become available.

Rules and Regulations

One of the most difficult problems facing apartment management is to establish and enforce equitable rules. People object to being told that their particular life-style is disturbing to a neighbor. Yet rules are very important and are primarily for the benefit of all tenants.

All rules should be clearly explained to the prospective tenants *before* a rental agreement is concluded. The tenant has the right to know what is expected. Besides that, an understanding of the rules and the reasons for them is the first step toward good enforcement. The rules should cover how and when the public areas (such as a pool) may be used, the hours within which noise levels are restricted, the proper disposition of trash and garbage, the parking requirements, any limitations on improvements and decorating within the rented unit, restrictions applicable to pets, and any limits on the activities of children. The apartment owner should keep in mind that a major cause of moveouts is incompatibility with a neighbor. Rules can help avoid potential conflicts.

Furnished vs. Unfurnished Apartments

A choice facing all apartment owners is whether to offer furnished or unfurnished units. There are three factors involved in making this decision:

A *Requirement of the Particular Market.* In some neighborhoods, essentially the only way an apartment may be rented is to offer it furnished. If a survey of the market shows generally that furnished apartments are well-rented while un-furnished units are standing vacant, the apartment owner has little choice but to furnish.

To Stabilize Occupancy. Again, the market in the area controls whether or not a furnished apartment prolongs average tenancy. Generally, tenants with their own furniture will remain longer than those without. However, many tenants see the question of "furnished or unfurnished units" as a minor consideration in the length of occupancy. More important concerns for them are (1) compatibility with their neighbors, and (2) their personal situations, such as their progressing income level. With a furnished apartment, tenants tend to judge the unit by the quality of the furniture, rather than by the quality of the unit itself; an exchange of furniture can thus provide a reason for continued occupancy. Another consideration in the furniture question is that unfurnished apartments can require more decorating because of damage to walls and doors as furniture is moved in and out. Also, the unfurnished apartment presents a "bare look" to the prospective tenant, which may make it more difficult to rent.

For Additional Income. The rental of furniture to apartment dwellers is a big business in most major cities. Many apartment owners rent furniture as a "sideline" business. Larger operators can buy furniture at wholesale, then offer it for rent at the capitalized value of the retail price. Furniture is "personal property" for tax purposes, and its cost recovered over the applicable cost recovery period. Furniture is generally rented at a price that will pay for the furniture in about one-half of its useful life. And there is often a residual value in the repair and resale of the used furniture. The return on the investment in furniture often proves to be greater than the return on the real property.

"Adults Only" or "Children Accepted"

Most apartment owners consider that children of tenants necessitate an increase in general maintenance costs for the property. Therefore, there has been a tendency to offer apartments for "adults only" when the market will permit. Tenants have successfully fought discrimination suits in some areas of the country to overcome this form of restriction. But the results of these suits have not yet dictated a uniform pattern, and the choice remains mostly in the hands of the landlord. As with most other criteria for successful apartment operations, the choice between "adults only" and "children accepted" is determined by the market, except where restricted by state or local laws.

Tenants and Lease Agreements

One of the many important advantages that come from experience in apartment management is the ability to screen prospective tenants in a fair and reasonable manner. The problem of screening has become more difficult because of the need to be nondiscriminatory. The landlord's desire to obtain immediate full occupancy must be tempered by the longer-range goal of maintaining that occupancy. Noise, objectionable use of the premises, and a tendency to vandalism are all qualities that can be detrimental to an apartment owner, who has an implied obligation to maintain a reasonable living standard for all tenants. One first-time apartment owner recently bemoaned the fact that he never realized a tenant would consider the living room carpet a suitable place to change the oil in his motorcycle!

Office Buildings

The investor in an office building may acquire property that is pre-leased (prior to construction) or already existing under lease. Or the building may be built or purchased with the *expectation* of leasing it to others, i.e., for speculative leasing. (Owner-occupied office buildings are not considered in this text because they are a limited form of investment and more closely related to a business analysis than to analysis as an income property investment.)

Pre-Leased Buildings

Pre-leasing is generally restricted to single-tenant office buildings (built to tenant's requirements), the ground floor space in high-rise office buildings, and larger users of upstairs space. A pre-lease arrangement offers substantial advantages for both the landlord and the tenant. The landlord can use the leases to support applications for financing, and the assurance of one or more major tenants helps to lease the balance of the space. An important reason for the success of several major office building developers is their ability to pre-lease a large portion of a new building to a major company, and then name the building after that company. The business operations of the major tenant attract supporting supply and service businesses to the same location.

For tenants, a major advantage of pre-leasing is in the planning of their own floor space, creating the optimum layout for their individual operations.

Speculative Office Space

Those who build office space for speculative leasing must have some assurance that a market will exist for that space. The best first step is a market analysis, prepared by a person or firm with adequate experience in the office building field. The necessary information can be listed as follows:

1. Amount of competing space in the area.
2. Quality of competing buildings (an opinion).

3. Current rental and escalation requirements.

4. Vacancies, and reasons for vacancies.

5. Record of absoption rate in the area.

6. That portion of the market the builder may expect to capture.

From this information, a realistic projection of rental income may be made for the speculative space. It is important to remember that rental rates depend more on the market for office space in the geographic area than on the construction costs incurred. Therefore, the market analysis must precede the final construction budget. The maximum investment in the office building should be based on the projected income.

Location

One service provided by a modern office building to its tenants is access to supporting service industries. Attorneys favor locations near courthouses or major clients. Doctors locate near hospitals or other medical facilities. Main offices for banks locate near legal and accounting services. Hotels locate near good transportation systems. All of these advantages—and many more—occur in the downtown areas of major cities. "Downtown" is still the primary location for major office buildings. But since World War II, a trend away from the downtown areas has developed due to new freeway patterns and the growth of suburban areas and regional shopping centers. There are now four prime areas for office buildings:

1. *Downtown areas of major cities* (which still command the highest rentals).

2. *Airport locations.* Passenger and freight traffic generated by major air terminals have brought a need for supporting office space to service airlines and their customers.

3. *Regional shopping centers.* These are not always ideal locations, but can be good if a full complement of supplemental services (bank, restaurants, apartments, etc.) are available to tenants. An office building is best located on the periphery of a shopping center, with easy access for non-shoppers.

4. *Along freeways or heavily traveled main roads.* Urban freeways have sprouted rows of new office buildings catering to the easy access provided by freeways (although congestion in some "growth areas" is negating this ease of access). The majority of office workers depend on cars for transportation, and many favor locations away from the more inaccessible downtown sites. In most major cities, freeway patterns have brought large developments that integrate

office buildings with shopping centers and apartment complexes, thereby catering to suburban neighborhoods.

Parking

The automobile created the need for freeways. With freeways came the growth of outlying areas, to the detriment of downtown growth. The problem has not been accessibility so much as it has been parking. Most downtown areas, locked into high-cost land use patterns, have not managed to keep pace with the growth in demand for parking space—and loss of occupancy for office buildings has been the result. Most building codes for new buildings now require certain minimum parking space for each square foot of rentable office space, which has further encouraged development in outlying areas where land costs are lower.

Most outlying office buildings and those in shopping centers offer free parking for tenants and customers. Buildings along freeways closer to the downtown area and those in the downtown area itself usually make an additional charge for parking space to both tenants and their customers or clients.

Use of Available Space

Office buildings are most commonly leased on a "per square foot" basis. However, there are two methods of calculating the square footage that is being leased. One is the *net* leasable area, which comprises the amount of square footage within the actual perimeter of the office space being leased. The other is a calculation of the *gross* leasable area, which allocates to each space actually rented a proportionate share of the corridors, wash rooms, elevator space, and maintenance areas. This latter method is also called the "New York Plan." The normal ratio between net and gross leasable area holds that 80% of the total area is usable for tenants' offices, with 20% allotted to corridors and service areas.

Service features in office buildings—a rooftop restaurant, health club, lounges, meeting rooms, and the like—are "plus" factors in leasing space. But they are often costly to maintain and may necessitate additional rent. Some major office buildings offer a subsidy payment for a good restaurant operator to provide quality service for the tenants.

Leasing Conditions

Office space is leased to major tenants for as long as 25 years. Smaller tenants often use a five- to 10-year term. Seldom does a term last less than three years. An excessively short lease term does not allow time to amortize the cost of standard tenant improvement allowances. Time extension options should be avoided, if at all possible. They make future leasing plans uncertain and should therefore be granted only if an option is required by a major tenant and the building owner has some protection on future rent.

Expansion options should also be discouraged, as they may also conflict with future leasing plans. Some tenants who anticipate expansion are willing to pay a premium to hold adjoining space for future growth. However, it is proper to advise any tenant who is occupying space under option to another individual or group that there is a commitment outstanding for that space.

Escalation clauses for the landlord are especially important here. More than other forms of income property, office buildings have a special vulnerability to rising costs because they customarily provide all utilities, heating and air conditioning, and janitorial services for the tenant as part of the lease agreement.

Lease agreements should provide a convenant covering rules and regulations for the tenants' proper use of the building. These rules are for the benefit of all tenants, and building management must be able to enforce them. When the office building is a part of a larger shopping center or other multi-building complex, rules may be drawn up and enforced by a tenants' association or a merchants' association.

Tenants

Experienced management is needed to screen prospective tenants and assign to each the most suitable space in an office building. The local market is controlling, but there are a few general guidelines.

It is difficult to mix medical and general office tenants. General office tenants usually object both to the overloading of elevators and passageways by incapacitated persons and to the odors common in medical facilities.

Professional people, such as lawyers and accountants, prefer that a certain prestige be associated with their location. They do not favor noisy and unorthodox neighbors, such as discos and nightclubs.

Businesses that attract large numbers of the general public can create parking problems and congestion within a building if these businesses are not located for easy access.

Companies that take multi-floor occupancy and require frequent elevator travel between upper floors should be located so as to cause minimum delays for the other tenants.

Shopping Centers

The market analysis for a successful shopping center must look to the market that is reasonably available for the goods and services offered by the merchant tenants. The question here is not one of finding tenants, as it is in an apartment or office building analysis. The question is: "Will the tenants have a market for their wares?" Market analysts know statistical buying patterns—how much various kinds of people spend on food, on clothes, on eating out, on entertainment, and on all the other things they buy. What is needed are figures on the population in the market area (especially income levels), the area's growth pattern, and freeway and street patterns. With these figures, an estimate can be made of the potential sales volume for each class of store, which in turn determines the gross income that may be achieved from the leases.

The following discussion considers how the trade area is determined, the population of the market, and its income and spending patterns.

Trade Area

Trade areas are *not* determined by drawing a circle around an existing or proposed location, and then counting the people within that boundary. A careful examination must be made of the forces that can direct people to the specific location in question. These forces may be identified as traffic patterns, proximity of other competitive facilities, and limiting geographical features.

Traffic Patterns.   Regional shopping centers are a creation of the freeway system; to a lesser degree, all other shopping centers also develop from traffic patterns. The ease with which a shopper can enter a store or service facility has long controlled both store location and the resulting land value. (Note the growth of smaller communities whose service stations and "fast food" stores are concentrated on the right-hand side of the entering highway.) To assess the trade area available for a particular location, it is first necessary to examine all streets, highways, and freeways that carry traffic to or through the subject location. Then, study the areas that access routes lead *from.*

What is the land use of the areas along the access routes? If one of the major highways leads from a large steel fabricating plant employing mostly male workers who live on the far side of town, the market potential from that area would be minimal. If another boulevard leads directly from undeveloped land that has been purchased primarily by home builders, the market potential is good, but not immediate. If a major highway or freeway leads from several small communities with limited shopping facilities, that population could be considered market potential. If the subject location sits along a thoroughfare that simply connects several densely populated areas or business districts, the high volume of passing traffic is a substantial market "plus." Of course, a major resource for any shopping center is an established and growing series of residential subdivisions surrounding the proposed location. However, the proximity of a good subdivision is of no benefit to the shopping center if there is limited access between them. Utility line easements or rights-of-way, streams, and political boundaries can separate entire subdivisions, encouraging traffic patterns to develop in directions other than what would appear to be normal.

City planning commissions and highway departments develop master plans for street and freeway development; these are important guides to future population trends. Zoning restrictions for surrounding areas must be charted to provide an indication of how growth patterns might develop. Undeveloped land within a 10-minute drive of the subject location should not be overlooked. A major shopping center itself encourages development of more houses in the area.

Competing Facilities. The trade area for a shopping center is restricted by existing competition. Furthermore, the nature of that competition is a factor in determining the types of goods and services that may be offered for sale. People will travel greater distances to purchase major "hard goods" than they will travel to purchase necessities, conveniences, and services. A nearby major regional center usually restricts a new development to a "neighborhood convenience center" type of outlet. The important considerations are to (1) weigh the market that is served by existing facilities, and (2) define the subject location's trade area outside the competitive sphere. A new center always has an initial impact from curiosity seekers, but the trade flow soon returns to that of greatest convenience for shoppers. Attracting traffic from a competing facility is always possible through promotions and special inducements for shoppers—but there is no monopoly on sales promotion ideas, and the traffic can flow both ways. The prudent analyst bases market size on proven statistical values, rather than on transient promotional techniques.

Limiting Geographic Features. The concern for geographical limitations is not for obvious features like a shoreline or mountain range; it is for the lesser features, such as an unbridged stream. Population trends often follow the line of lowest-cost development, and this can mean avoiding expensive stream crossings, rough terrain, and areas of potential hazard such as flooding or sliding land. These limitations are, of course, reflected in street and highway patterns. However, it is an area that a shopping center analyst should consider as a means of increasing the trade area, i.e., would an offsite improvement, such as a bridge or connective street, justify the cost? Most communities welcome private support in the construction of new streets or bridges; if a new trade area can be opened, the cost may be justified.

Population of the Market

Once the limits of the trade area have been defined, it is easy to determine the population within that area. The U.S. Population Census statistics (taken every decade), combined with local area planning commission figures, provide a good starting point. The number of electric power meters and water taps give a solid indication of the number of families in a given area. Furthermore, the rate of increase or decrease is determinable from the number of new meters installed during a given period, less the number removed. The population of each neighborhood or subdivision in the trade area should be calculated, along with the estimated growth trend for each.

Income and Spending Patterns

Every decade the U.S. Population Census produces a set of figures on average income levels for each census district. Private market research organizations are constantly attempting to determine income levels in local neighborhoods. These figures are estimates at best, but they do provide a basis for analyzing the buying power of a given market or trade area.

How income is spent varies with the area in question. There are obvious differences in buying habits between rural communities and manufacturing centers, between commercial areas and service industry areas, between older people and younger ones, between upper-income and lower-income families, between two areas dominated by different nationalities, and many more. The Bureau of Labor Statistics (an arm of the U.S. Department of Labor) produces statistics on living costs in the different regions of the country, which provide a guide to how much is spent for basic necessities. Local research is needed to reveal the complete pattern of local spending.

The gross income of the entire trade area can be allocated among all the major categories of purchase. For example, food may take 12% of the income from the trade area; apparel, general merchandise, and appliances, 8%; drugs, 2%; and so on down the list of goods and services that are offered by the subject shopping center. The total buying power of the trade area in each category must then be reduced to that amount which can reasonably be attained by the subject center. Of the total amount represented by food purchases (12% of the gross income of the area), perhaps the subject center can attract only 65%. For general merchandise sold through department stores, competition is generally greater—

the subject location's market share could drop to, say, 40% of the trade area's total spending for this category.

With the market share calculated in dollar amounts for each category of goods and services, the shopping center investor can more readily compute the expected rentals from percentage leases. Furthermore, a carefully calculated market share for each category indicates the potential sales volume for each prospective tenant—an important figure for a merchant considering a new or additional outlet.

Shopping Center Leases

Chapter 15 discussed the subject of leases and rents for all income properties, but emphasized stores and shopping centers. The reason for this emphasis is that pre-leasing and quality of the lease are more important for shopping centers than for any other form of real property investment. The financing of a shopping center is uniquely dependent on its leasing program, and its overall success is heavily dependent on the quality of the tenants and the lease conditions. The lease restrictions peculiar to shopping center operations are considered next.

Exclusive Sales Covenants. All merchants love exclusive sales agreements. But for the shopping center owner-investor, these agreements are potential pitfalls. A major tenant, such as a supermarket or department store, may demand to be the *only* supermarket or department store in the shopping center. The owner may have to make this concession, but it may present problems downstream for two reasons: (1) the center may expand so that additional stores are needed to satisfy demand, and (2) the type of merchandise sold within a store tends to change as trade practices shift to meet competition. Motor oil is not a customary item in a grocery store, yet many supermarkets sell it. The variations in service and food offered under the name of "restaurant" are almost unlimited. Any covenant limiting the freedom of the tenant to offer specific products or services must be clearly worded, as conflicts can easily occur.

Lease Tie-Ins. A lease that is tied in to the continued occupancy of another merchant creates a potential loss of two tenants. A smaller merchant may count on the heavy traffic generated by a large department store outlet. But if the larger store develops internal problems unrelated to the center and withdraws to be replaced by another store, the smaller merchant under a tie-in would have the right to cancel the lease, compounding the center's problems.

Below-Cost Leases. In order to attract a major tenant to a new center, the owner is sometimes tempted to offer a less-than-cost lease arrangement under the expectation of recovering the cost from the smaller tenants that will follow. Major tenants are fully aware of their drawing power in the market, and they use it as an effective negotiating point. (The merchandising power of an organization like Sears, Roebuck is such that Sears seldom leases space anymore, choosing instead to buy land within a center to construct its own building.) However, any agreement by a shopping center owner to grant less-than-cost rental rates results in an extra burden for the rest of the tenants. The competitive disadvantage to the other tenants may preclude their successful operation—and shorten the economic life of the entire project.

Parking

Because they are the offspring of freeways and highways, shopping centers require more parking space than any other form of property investment. A rule-of-thumb has it that for every square foot of rentable shop space, there must be three square feet of parking area. The requirement varies a bit with the type of store—supermarkets have the greatest parking requirements, and service facilities the least.

The gradual increase in the number of smaller cars has changed parking lot design. Architects once assigned about 320 square feet to each car space, but today some have reduced this to 280 square feet. Some centers also provide remote parking lots for employees.

Management

In addition to the management requirements common to all forms of income property, shopping center owners must cooperate with tenants to promote the shopping center. Almost all percentage leases in shopping centers make the landlord a partner in the success of the tenant. Some managements participate passively, granting advertising allowances and special concessions for the tenants' promotional activities. Others take the lead in organizing and directing continuous advertising and promotional programs. The larger centers often provide entertainment or interesting displays in the public mall areas and feature the center's attractions in mass advertising programs.

The most common method of cooperation between landlord and tenants is some form of merchants' association. A requirement to join and contribute dues or assessments can be a part of lease requirements. In this manner, decisions on sales promotions are shared by all of those who can benefit from them.

Warehouses

Since the early 1960s, warehouses have increased in numbers, in the ways they are used, and in popularity as real estate investment. The older classification of a warehouse as one form of industrial property is no longer applicable. Warehouses have developed into service centers and retail outlets. "Mini-warehouses" have multiplied. Investor interest stems from several advantages: warehouses can be built on lower-cost land in outlying areas, they require minimal maintenance, and they require less management than the "people-oriented" operations of apartments and office buildings. The following section considers the three major classes of warehouses: (1) industrial-type storage, (2) office-warehouses, and (3) mini-warehouses.

Industrial-Type Storage Warehouses

Companies have traditionally used warehouses for part-time emergency or seasonal storage of goods and have preferred to rent warehouse space rather than build their own. Warehouse owners lease entire buildings or parts of buildings, or charge for storage based on the goods stored and the space and time used. Some warehouse companies operate public storage warehouses and provide transportation of goods as product distribution centers. This is a form of business property and not a subject of consideration in this section. It is the industrial warehouse, built for leasing to others, that can be classed as an investment property.

The special requirements of concern to the warehouse investor can be covered under accessibility, construction features, and management.

Accessibility. A warehouse does not require obvious visibility to the general public. It can be located on a back street or other out-of-the-way area, as long as large trucks can maneuver into a loading position. The availability of railroad siding promotes the usefulness of an industrial warehouse. Warehouses provide an excellent interchange point between rail and truck transportation. Dockside warehouses and the storage facilities at municipally owned airports are sometimes available for private investment.

Construction Features. Industrial warehouses can be built with floors either at ground level or at truck-loading height, although the latter is preferred. Warehouse floors must sustain heavy loads and should be constructed with 6″ concrete and reinforcing bars (compared with 4″ unreinforced concrete in a single-story shopping center).

Ceilings must accommodate high racking of stored goods and should be at least 14′ high. Ceiling panels are very seldom used in a warehouse, and the "height" is the clearance beneath the roof supports. The roof and walls should be as close to fireproof as practical, and in most areas the installation of a fire protection sprinkler system is an economical measure. Adequate fire protection can reduce the insurance cost for both the building and its contents and should allow a slightly higher rental structure.

In selecting a warehouse site, an investor must not only check the street sizes and patterns, but also research the water lines to make sure they will support a fire protection system. For the most part, warehouses are not air conditioned; when they are, adequate insulation is a necessity.

Industrial warehouses require little office space. Usually a shedlike structure inside the building—used for recordkeeping and security controls, and sometimes heated or air conditioned—will suffice.

Management. From the investor's point of view, an industrial warehouse leased to a stable tenant requires very little management. The building is constructed for minimal maintenance, the tenant requires few services, and the management consists mostly of keeping adequate accounting records of the lease operation.

Office-Warehouse

The expanding requirements of service industries, manufacturing plants in high-technology industry, and industrial supply outlets with storage requirements have spawned a new type of service-oriented sales center. These rows of single-story buildings with common wall dividers are 85% to 90% warehouse space and 10% to 15% office facility. Limited parking for employees and customers is usually available in front of the units while truck-loading accommodations are at the rear entryways.

Construction Features. The buildings are generally lightweight in that floors are not designed for heavy loads (usually being 4" concrete with a reinforcing mesh wire). Walls are block, brick, or tilt-wall concrete. Roofs are lightweight, with 12' to 14' clearance. Modules used in construction vary from 1,500 square feet to 3,000 square feet and can be leased singly or in multiples.

Office areas are generally well finished, with tile floors or carpeting. Heating and air conditioning units are furnished, but their operation is left to the tenants. The office area may be used for administrative work, clerical activity, or as a sales outlet with display racks and sales counters.

The exterior appearance is usually similar to an office park or modern industrial park, with modest landscaping and paved parking areas. Access need not be from highly visible freeways or thoroughfares, but many are so located because of the emphasis on sales outlets for possible tenants.

Rental Rates and Management. Office-warehouses are leased for rates that are generally higher than for industrial warehouses because of the office-warehouse's more accessible—and thus more costly—land. They offer a *combination* of office and warehouse space at somewhere in between the separate cost of each.

While office-warehouse space is usually offered for multi-tenant occupancy, the management responsibility does not approach the level required for either an office building or an apartment. Very few services are furnished to tenants. Interior maintenance, utilities, heating, and air conditioning are all responsibilities of the tenant. The management may have the chore of trash disposal and does maintain the exterior walls and roof. Parking lot and landscaping maintenance also fall to the management.

Mini-Warehouses

Another fairly recent development in warehousing is the "mini-warehouse." The demand for such space comes from the increasing number of apartment dwellers and others who have limited storage facilities and a growing amount of personal goods. Older apartment houses often furnish a small enclosure of space, usually in the basement, for the tenant to store out-of-season or surplus possessions. Modern apartments have done away with this feature, but not the need for the space. Thus, long rows of mini-warehouses have been built in most major cities.

Construction Features. Mini-warehouses are usually rows of single-story buildings with common walls separating the individual units, which are from 50 square feet to more than 400 square feet each. The construction is of fireproof block or brick, with a single large door to the front. There may or may not be a paved floor. Utilities may be limited to a single light, with no heating and no air conditioning. Usage is usually strictly limited to the storage of goods—no personal use may be made of the lease as a place to work or to offer anything for sale. (Where such rules have not been enforced, there have been cases where individual tenants converted mini-warehouse space into living quarters.)

Rental Structure. The big attraction for an investor is the high return provided from a relatively low-cost form of investment. The mini-warehouse requires little management other than policing the area. Costs and rents vary considerably, but one good rule-of-thumb has it that construction cost is approximately one-half of that for an apartment, while the rental rate per square foot is about the same as an apartment.

Location. Because the mini-warehouse caters to the general public, it is best located in an area that is easily accessible and generally visible from main thoroughfares. Since most customers come from apartments, it should be located near several apartment complexes.

Other Applications.   The concept of the mini-warehouse has much wider application than just storage space for apartment dwellers. It's said that the idea originated with an owner of enclosed boat stalls near a country lake. More and more, the owner found that his tenants were using the boat stalls not for boats and marine equipment, but for surplus furniture, clothes, and other personal equipment. The next step was to build "boat stalls" in the city! After all, the need was obvious. Many sports require special equipment which can be stored in protected cubicles while not in use. In some areas of the country, small tracts of farm land can be rented by city folks for "home gardening"—but special equipment needs to be stored. Families with vacation cabins in remote areas need protected space to secure furniture and other personal goods while they are away from the cabin. This story is a classic example of the free enterprise system—find a need, and then try to be the first to satisfy it.

Special Purpose Buildings

In a sense, all buildings are "special purpose" as their design restricts the use to a specific operation. However, in the jargon of real estate, *special purpose* has a more precise meaning. It is that category of building that offers a specific kind of service and is more difficult to convert to any other usage. Examples of special purpose buildings include fast food stores, bowling lanes, service stations, recreational structures, theaters, and automobile dealerships. Because of the close relationship between the building and its services, they are often owned by the business operators. But many are built for lease to professional operators and offer excellent investment opportunities.

Financing

As an investment property, special purpose buildings are seldom built without a lease in hand. Lenders are unlikely to advance money unless the usage is clearly spelled out in advance. The pre-leasing of a special purpose building might be handled by a major distributor or a franchise operation. Most service stations that are owned by individuals have been leased to a major oil company, who then sub-leases the premises to a qualified service station operator. A good lease from almost any major company is an attractive form of collateral for most lenders. Some companies in an effort to expand their outlets may offer to lease an acceptable building from an owner and then may add a partial guarantee to support a loan to build the building.

Some categories of special purpose buildings find financing support from product distributors. Such is the case with bowling lanes, some recreational facilities, some theaters, and auto dealerships. The tie, of course, is an assured outlet for the manufacturer or distributor of that product. Without such help, it is difficult to induce a lender to risk money for a building that is limited in its usage.

On a larger scale, most major hotels might be classed in the special purpose category. Principal hotel operators such as Hilton, Hyatt, and Marriott build a few of their properties, but many are investor owned. The hotel operator undertakes a management or a lease agreement with the hotel owner and grants the use of a valuable trade name. In this kind of transaction, the operator offers little or no financial support to the investor/owner. This kind of investment is made by large insurance companies, pension funds, and union trust funds, usually after a long-term management contract has been arranged with an operator.

Business Property Investment

This section focuses on an interpretation of a "business property" as one that comprises a business operation that uses land and buildings to create income. Professional real estate brokers have long been aware that a transaction involving a motel, hotel, a restaurant, or specialized recreational facility requires as much knowledge of the business operation as of the real estate involved. Brokers who trade in businesses sometimes list this type of property for sale as a business venture. But the disposition of a business property that involves real estate is a specialized field requiring brokers to be qualified both in real property transactions and in the management and operation of the business concerned.

While the concepts developed in this section center on a business operation, they have application in other areas of real estate investment. The thrust of this study is an evaluation of income and its effect on property value. The difference between business property and "income property" is that business property income is derived from services rendered *that are not always directly related to the property.* For example, a motel restaurant's success depends more on the quality of the food and service than on the quality of the building.

Projected Earnings Potential

The value of a business property is based on the *future* returns that may be realized over the remaining useful economic life of the property. The basis is approximately the same as for any income property, except that business property income derives from the sale of goods and services (in addition to property rentals) that add substantially to the overall value of the property. The following factors are considered in estimating potential income:

1. *The types of services offered.* For a motel, consider the number and size of rooms, plus the public facilities offered. For a restaurant, consider the kind of food offered. For a recreational facility, consider the activities that are provided.

2. *The style of services offered,* such as "luxury," "standard commercial," or "minimum utility."

3. *The proposed price* of the services.

4. *The available market.* How much demand is there for the services offered? Is there competition in the local area? Are there seasonal swings in activity? What is the statistical record for the proposed type of business in the local area? Are there any special events, sports activities, fiestas, rodeos, or other activities that stimulate the market?

5. *Normal operating ratios and cost ratios* for similar businesses in the area.

An estimate of potential earnings can be developed from the information assembled under these five headings. The statement of operations would contain the same basic information outlined in Chapter 11 for financial statements. The expenses of operation are deducted from the projected gross income, leaving the net operating income as a basis for property evaluation.

In an evaluation of business property income, the results from each department of activity (such as room rentals, restaurant sales, lounge and bar sales) should be assembled separately, as each involves separate projections. Multiple projections can be made for each department to reflect the highest and lowest estimates of business activity. This procedure is known as a *sensitivity analysis* and is described more fully in Chapter 14.

Relation Between Market Value and Earnings

To some degree, the market value of real estate used as a business operation is more sensitive to the business's earnings record than is an income property to its longer-term rentals. A well-managed motel in a prime location that produces high profits will reflect a value for the property far in excess of the cost of building it. While management is important to the operation of all income properties, it assumes dominant proportion when a complex business must be operated to produce an income from the property. The primary reason for a business property's greater sensitivity to its earnings record is the greater variety of income and expense components that affect the success of the entire operation.

There is no real difference in the ratio of market value to earnings for business real estate and income property. Both ultimately must reflect the capitalized value of the earnings, which can be either the past record of earnings or the projected figures. And the capitalization rate to be used is equally dependent on what the investor considers a fair return on his equity investment under prevailing market conditions. The market for business-type property is not so broad-based as for other income property, primarily because of the need for specialized management skills. As a result, the purchaser of a business property adds a premium for expertise and, thus, may demand a slightly larger return on the equity investment. This would, of course, result in a slightly lower price for a business property than for an income property with identical after-tax income.

Effect of Inflation on Price/Earnings Ratios

Since about the mid-1970s, inflation has been universally accepted as a major factor in investment analysis. Investors have begun to accept inflation as an element of value that can be projected into the analysis of future cash flows. As a result, some investors are ignoring the relation between market value and earnings, in favor of realizing an "ultimate" return when the property is sold at the end of the holding period. Thus, the value of earnings is capitalized at very low rates of return—like 2% or 3% or even at zero—thereby providing a substantial increase in the sales value of the property. When the investor adds back the anticipated gain upon final disposition, at an inflated value, the investment provides a reasonable return over the full holding period.

Keep in mind that the rate of capitalization is defined as *that rate necessary to attract capital.* And remember that the rapid growth in property values provides a viable addition to earnings, which increases the return on the equity investment—and this also attracts capital. So the effect of inflation, insofar as real property values are concerned, has been to *lower* the capitalization rates on *earnings* necessary to attract capital.

Conclusion

This book has "covered a lot of ground," all of it pertinent to an investment in real estate. Unfortunately, the field is so complex that the coverage of many subjects has been limited to an explanation or a suggestion that certain problems do exist. A full explanation of each facet of real estate investment would require a book so big that you couldn't lift it! It is hoped that the reader will explore the growing number of excellent books that examine the various subjects in depth. Many of these books are listed in the Bibliography.

It is not the purpose of this book to recommend one form of investment over another. Rather, the purpose is to point out the risks and the rewards that can be realized from the different forms of property investment. In the final analysis, only the investor can decide whether or not the risk is acceptable. More than the actual property is involved—the investor must consider personal goals; the area best suited to those goals; the type of property that he or she best understands; income and tax position, and how various investments will affect them; and yes, even such factors as his or her age and health.

Knowledge is successful investment's first essential ingredient. Use it well!

Bibliography

American Institute of Real Estate Appraisers. *The Appraisal of Real Estate*. 9th ed. Chicago, 1987.

Black, Henry Campbell. *Black's Law Dictionary*. 5th ed. St. Paul: West Publishing Co., 1979.

Blume, Marshall E., and Friedman, Jack P. *The Encyclopedia of Investments*. Boston: Warren, Gorham & Lamont, 1982.

Boykin, James H., and Ring, Alfred A. *The Valuation of Real Estate*. 3rd ed. Englewood Cliffs, NJ: Prentice-Hall, 1986.

Cooper, James R., and Pyhrr, Stephen A. *Real Estate Investment*. Boston: Warren, Gorham & Lamont, 1982.

Farrell, Michael D., and Greer, Gaylon E. *Investment Analysis for Real Estate Decisions*. 2nd ed. Chicago: Longman Group, 1988.

Friedman, Jack P., and Harris, Jack C. *Barron's Real Estate Handbook*. 2nd ed. Hauppauge, NY: Barron's Educational Services, Inc., 1988.

Friedman, Jack P., and Ordway, Nicholas. *Income Property Appraisal and Analysis*. 2nd ed. Englewood Cliffs, NJ: Prentice-Hall, 1987.

Hines, Mary A. *Real Estate Investment*. New York: Macmillan Publishing Co., Inc., 1980.

Jacobus, Charles, and Harwood, Bruce. *Texas Real Estate*. 4th ed. Englewood Cliffs, NJ: Prentice-Hall, 1987.

Jaffe, Austin J. *Analyzing Real Estate Decisions Using VisCalc*. Reston, VA: Reston Publishing Co., 1985.

Messner, Stephen D., Shreiber, Irving, Lyon, Victor, and Ward, Robert L. *Marketing Investment Real Estate*. Chicago: Realtors National Marketing Institute, 1982.

Nichols, Donald R. *Life Cycle Investing*. Homewood, IL: Dow Jones-Irwin, 1985.

Plattner, Robert H. *Real Estate Investment*. Columbus, OH: Merrill Publishing Company, 1988.

Reilly, John W. *The Language of Real Estate*. 2nd ed. Chicago: Real Estate Education Co., 1982.

Seldin, Maury, and Swesnik, Richard H. *Real Estate Investment Strategy*. 3rd ed. New York: Wiley Interscience, 1985.

Shenkel, William M. *Real Estate Finance and Analysis*. Plano, TX: Business Publications, Inc., 1988.

Sirota, David. *Essentials of Real Estate Investment*. 3rd ed. Chicago: Longman Group USA, 1987.

Unger, Maurice A., and Milicher, Ronald W. *Real Estate Finance*. Cincinnati: South-Western Publishing Co., 1978.

Wendt, Paul F., and Cerf, Alan R. *Real Estate Investment and Taxation*. 2nd ed. New York: McGraw-Hill, 1979.

Wiedemer, John P. *Real Estate Finance*. 5th ed. Englewood Cliffs, NJ: Prentice-Hall, 1987.

The Financial Desk Book. Consolidated Communications Group, Inc., 2000 Powell Street, Emeryville, CA 94608, 1985.

Your Federal Income Tax, Publication 17. Annual publication, Internal Revenue Service, Technical Publications Branch, 1111 Constitution Ave., NW., Washington DC 20224.

Glossary

Accelerated depreciation. (Tax term) Depreciation taken at any rate greater than provided by the straight-line method.

Accrual method. An accounting procedure that records income as it is earned and expenses as they are incurred, rather than as the cash is received and spent.

Active income. (Tax term) Income earned by one's labor compensated for in salary, wages, commissions, fees, or bonuses. Also called *earned income*.

Add-on interest. A method of computing interest for installment loans, whereby the amount of simple interest that would be due at maturity on the full amount of the loan is *added on* to the principal at the inception of the loan. The total is then divided by the number of installments in order to determine each payment amount.

Adjustable rate mortgage. A mortgage note that allows a lender to adjust the interest rate at periodic intervals. The rate change is most commonly limited to the movement of a regulator approved index.

Adjusted basis of value. (Tax term) The value of an asset as determined by tax procedures. It is the acquisition value, plus or minus subsequent permissible, or required, adjustments.

Alienation. A legal term meaning the transfer of rights to real property.

Alienation clause. An enlarged usage of the word "alienation" that has come to mean that clause in a mortgage that limits any transfer of interest with a loan assumption to those approved by the lender.

Amortization. The systematic and continuous payment of an obligation through installments until such time as that debt has been paid off in full.

Appraisal. An estimate of property value prepared by a qualified person.

Appreciation. An increase in the value of property due to factors inherent in the property or in the economy.

Assets. Something of value.

Assumption fee. The charge made by a lender for arranging the assumption of a loan by a new buyer. This fee is not permitted on FHA or VA loans.

At-risk rule. IRS rule that limits the amount of losses that may be deducted in any one year from certain business activities to the amount of cash and the adjusted basis of other property contributed by the taxpayer to the activity.

Audit. The examination of accounting records and the supporting evidence by a Certified Public Accountant to determine the adequacy and accuracy of the information.

Balance sheet. A statement in tabular form showing the assets, liabilities, and net worth of a person or business.

Balloon note. A promissory note that is only partially amortized over the term of the loan leaving a principal balance due at maturity.

Basis of value. (Tax term) The amount determined to be the taxpayer's investment in property, which is based on the method by which the property is acquired.

Basis point. A measure used in financial markets that amounts to one one-hundredth of a percent.

Blind pool. The sale of partial interests in property that has yet to be acquired.

Bond. An interest-bearing debt certificate that may be secured, such as a mortgage-bond—or unsecured, such as a debenture bond.

Boot. Used in property exchange transactions to identify *other unlike property* that is not cash or net mortgage loan relief.

Broker. A person or company who acts as an intermediary in a transaction between two other parties.

Building codes. An exercise of police powers of the state whereby standards are set for buildings to protect the health and safety of the general public.

Buy-down. A mortgage repayment design that offers lower initial monthly payments achieved through prepayment of a portion of the interest cost. The prepayment of interest is usually made by the seller to help attract buyers and to allow easier borrower qualification. It is a variation from the standard loan discount because it is limited to the first few years of repayment.

Capital gain. (Tax term) The profit realized from the disposition of an asset at a price higher than the seller's adjusted basis.

Capitalization. The process of converting future income from a property into a current value for the property.

Carrying charges. The costs incurred in holding land through the development phase or until disposition can be made. These costs include interest, taxes, maintenance charges, and any stand-by assessments that may apply.

Cash flow. A generalized term that means the amount of cash received over a period of time from a business operation.

Cash method. An accounting method of reporting income and expenses when actually or constructively received or paid out.

Casualty loss. As defined by the IRS, the destruction of property by fire, storm, accident, or other event of a sudden, unexpected, or unusual nature.

Certified Public Accountant. (CPA) A license granted by the various states to one who has met the requirements of experience, knowledge, and professional standards for accounting work.

Closing. The consummation of a real estate transaction whereby the seller delivers title to the property in exchange for the consideration.

Collateral. Something of value pledged as security for a debt.

Commercial loan. An imprecise term generally applied to an obligation collateralized by real property other than that used as a principal residence.

Commitment. A pledge or a promise to act: in finance, it constitutes the promise of a lender to make a loan at some future time.

Common areas. That part of a condominium property owned jointly by all unit owners.

Common stock. The evidence of an ownership interest in a corporation that carries the right to a share of the earnings, usually distributed in the form of a dividend.

Community property. Ownership as defined by state law, which considers each spouse to have an equal interest in property acquired by the efforts of either spouse during the marriage.

Component depreciation. A straight-line method of depreciation that assigns separate useful lives to each of the various parts of a building and then depreciates each part according to its own schedule. Its use was prohibited by the 1981 Tax Act.

Compound interest. The periodic reinvestment of interest earned, which is added to the principal to accumulate additional earned interest.

Condemnation. The process by which private property can be taken by a government for a public purpose without the owner's consent.

Condominium. An estate in real property defined by state law, that comprises an individual interest in a dwelling or commercial unit plus an undivided interest in the common areas associated with the property.

Consideration. Something of value given in exchange for property or services.

Construction loan. A type of mortgage loan to finance construction that is funded by the lender to the builder or developer at periodic intervals as the work progresses.

Conventional loan. An individual loan not underwritten by a government agency.

Cooperative. Corporate ownership of real estate wherein the stockholders are also the tenants through leasehold agreement.

Corporation. A form of business created under state chartering laws as an artificial person with limited rights and powers to transact business of a designated nature.

Cost approach. A method used by appraisers to determine property value, which calculates the replacement cost of a building, less depreciation, plus the value of the land.

Covenant. A written agreement between two or more parties that specifies certain uses, or nonuses of property.

Coverage ratio.   The margin between the debt service and the net operating income from a property usually expressed as a percentage of the debt service.

Credit report.   Information prepared from a credit bureau's files that reveals previous debt payment experience as well as other identifying data on an individual or company.

Creditor.   One who lends something of value to another.

Dealer.   (Tax term) One who owns and sells real estate parcels in the normal course of business.

Debt.   An obligation to be repaid by a borrower to a lender.

Debt service.   The amount of money necessary to meet the periodic payments of principal and interest. (Some lenders include the monthly payments for taxes and insurance as a part of their definition of debt service.)

Declining balance method.   A procedure used to calculate depreciation deductions at accelerated rates such as 175% or 200% times the straight-line rate. The accelerated rate is applied to the adjusted basis, meaning the tax basis after deduction of depreciation amounts claimed in prior years. Thus, the rate is applied to a reduced, or "declining," balance each year.

Deed.   A written instrument that conveys title to property from the grantor to the grantee.

Deed of Trust.   A form of mortgage wherein the borrower grants a conditional title as security to a Trustee who serves on behalf of the lender. This form is most commonly used in community property states.

Deed restrictions.   A restrictive covenant in a deed that limits the use of the property by the grantee.

Default.   Failure to comply with contract terms.

Delinquent payment.   Payment not made when required, incurring a late charge penalty.

Depreciation.   The loss in value to property due to wear and tear, obsolescence, and economic factors.

Devisee.   The recipient of property conveyed by will other than an heir.

Discount.   The difference in the face value of a note (or bond) and the cash amount paid for it. The purpose of discounting a note is to increase the yield to the lender.

Discounted cash flow.   Future returns from a property investment expressed as a value today.

Disintermediation.   The movement of funds out of savings institutions (the intermediary) into other forms of investment.

Disposition.   The right of a landowner to sell, lease, give away, or otherwise dispose of his land.

Distributive Share.   (Tax term) A partner's share of partnership earnings that encompasses the various forms of income and losses that can be taxed to the individual partner.

Dividend.   That portion of a corporation's earnings distributed to the stockholders.

Due-on-sale clause. A mortgage clause that calls for payoff of the loan in the event of a sale or conveyance of the collateral prior to maturity of the loan.

Earnest money contract. A sales agreement between a prospective buyer and seller that stipulates the conditions of the transaction and includes the deposit of cash by the buyer as evidence of firm intention.

Easement. A right to land limited to its use for a specific purpose.

Economic obsolescence. The loss (or gain) in value to property resulting from factors surrounding, but not a part of, the property itself.

Eminent domain. The right of a government to take private land for a necessary public use for the payment of a just compensation.

Encroachment. The unauthorized use as an intrusion on another's land.

Environmental impact statement. (EIS) A report that details the expected impact of a proposed development (or other specified activity) upon living conditions, including noise, air quality, health, vegetation, automobile traffic, energy consumption, as well as the need for sewer and water facilities.

Equity. The value of a property in excess of all indebtedness.

Escalation clause. A clause in a lease agreement that provides for an increase in rental payments in direct relation to an increase in the costs.

Escrow. The holding of money and/or documents by a disinterested third party pending satisfaction of the instructions that created the escrow arrangement.

Estate. The degree or quantity of interest that a person has in land, the nature of the right, its duration, and its relation to the rights of others.

Exclusive listing. A written agreement by which a landowner authorizes a single broker to sell the property limited to a specified time period.

Fair-market value. The highest monetary price available in a competitive market as determined by negotiation between an informed, willing, and capable buyer and an informed and willing seller.

Feasibility report. A study of a proposed or existing property to determine potential profitability based on a thorough analysis of the market.

Fee simple. An estate in land that entitles the owner to the entire property with an unrestricted power of disposition.

Finance fee. The charge made by a lender for preparing and processing a loan package, also called an origination fee.

Financial intermediary. A depository institution that accepts savings deposits and uses the money to make other investments.

Fixed expenses. Costs that continue whether or not the property is leased.

Fixing-up expense. (Tax term) Covers decorating and repair costs incurred solely to assist in the sale of an existing residence.

Flexible loan insurance plan. (FLIP) A graduated payment mortgage plan that requires an escrow deposit in lieu of down payment, with escrow funds used to supplement the buyer's monthly payments in the early years of the mortgage.

Foreclosure. Legal action to bar a mortgagor's claims to property after default has occurred.

Freehold estate. The right of title to land for an uncertain duration but at least for the life of the owner.

Functional obsolescence. The deterioration of property value resulting from design inadequacies.

Gap financing. A junior loan to bridge the gap created by a delay or hold-back of construction loan funding.

Grace period. Additional time allowed for payment without assessment of late charges.

Graduated payment mortgage. (GPM) An alternative mortgage design that allows lower initial monthly payments, computed on a partially amortized basis, rising in 5 or 6 years to a constant level payment that achieves full amortization. Purpose: easier qualification for the borrower.

Gross income. The total money received from an operating property over a given period of time.

Ground lease. A lease for land, also called a land lease.

Hard dollar. Payment made or received in cash rather than another form of consideration.

Heir. One who has the right to inherit property under statute of descent and distribution.

Highest and best use. The use of property that will produce the greatest return over a period of time.

Hold-back. A portion of a loan that is not released until certain conditions are met.

Homestead. An artificial estate in land devised to protect the possession and enjoyment of the owner against the claims of creditors.

Hypothecate. A pledge of property without delivering possession, such as in a mortgage.

Impound account. Money held for payment of an obligation due at a future time. Also known as an escrow account.

Imputed interest. (Tax term) Interest assessed by the IRS on a deferred payment transaction. Prior purpose was to distinguish ordinary income from capital gain. The requirement remains in effect to identify the kind of interest for determination of its deductibility against certain kinds of income.

Income. Money or other benefit received from the investment of labor or capital.

Income approach. A method used by appraisers to determine property value by the capitalization of an income stream.

Incumbrance. A claim against land such as a lien or easement.

Indicated gain. (Tax term) The gain in a property exchange transaction that would have been made if the property had been sold rather than exchanged. The term is synonymous with "realized gain" and is not the gain subject to tax: the "recognized gain" is subject to taxation.

Installment sale. The sale of an asset in a manner that allows payment over an extended period of time, and if handled in compliance with the tax code, permits the tax liability to be paid as the money is received.

Institutional investors.   Lenders entrusted with depositary funds owned by the general public, who are subject to regulation by a government authority.

Interest.   A charge for the use of another's money.

Interim loan.   A short-term loan made with the expectation of repayment from the proceeds of another loan; often used to describe a construction loan.

Internal rate of return.   The rate at which the present worth of future cash flows is exactly equal to the initial capital investment.

Investment income.   (Tax term) Term used in the tax law to distinguish property "held for investment" so as to limit the deduction of interest. Such investment is that producing income defined as interest, dividends, annuities, or royalties and any trade or business in which the taxpayer does not materially participate, as long as that activity is not treated as a passive activity. Investment interest expense is limited to net investment income (subject to phase-out in the 1986 Tax Act).

Involuntary conversion.   A change in the condition or ownership of property against the will of the owner, such as destruction by fire, or condemnation for public use.

Joint stock company.   A form of business ownership permitted in some states, which is a general partnership with some of the features of a corporation.

Joint tenancy.   The ownership by two or more persons of an undivided and equal interest in property acquired at the same time, which includes the right of survivorship.

Joint venture.   An association of companies and/or individuals organized for the purpose of undertaking a specific project.

Junior mortgage.   A mortgage of lower lien priority than that of another.

Land trust.   A form of ownership permitted in a few states that allows a landowner to convey title and the full power of management to a trustee and to designate a beneficiary.

Leasehold estate.   The right of a tenant to possession and use of land (but not the power of disposition) for a specified period of time.

Lessee.   The tenant.

Lessor.   The landlord.

Leverage.   Controlling a greater asset with less of the buyer's money, more of others'. The larger the percentage of borrowed funds, the greater the leverage.

Leveraged buy-out.   The acquisition of a company, financed primarily with borrowed money, using the acquired company's assets to collateralize the loans.

Liabilities.   Debts or obligations for which one is responsible.

Lien.   A claim on property for payment of a debt; an incumbrance.

Life estate.   The ownership of land with duration limited to the life of the party holding the land, or the life of some other person.

Like-kind property.   (Tax term) Property deemed under the tax code to be equal in quality or usage. Qualifying property may be exchanged in a tax-deferred transaction.

Limited partnership. A partnership consisting of one or more general partners who are liable for obligations and responsible for the management, and one or more special partners who contribute cash and are not liable for debts beyond the cash contributed.

Liquidity. The ability to convert other assets into cash.

Loan. A granting of the use of money in return for the payment of interest.

Loan constant. The debt service expressed as a percentage of the loan amount.

Lock-in clause. Prepayment of a debt is prohibited for a specified time period, unless interest is paid in full for the term required.

Long-term loan. As used in real estate finance, a loan with a term of 10 years or more.

Market approach. A method used by appraisers to determine property value by comparison of the subject property with sales prices of similar properties.

Maturity. The time at which the final payment is due on a loan.

Mortgage. A written pledge of property as collateral for a loan.

Mortgage-backed security. A type of security, a bond, or a certificate, that is collateralized by a large block, or pool, of mortgage loans and is sold to financial market investors. The cash flows generated by the underlying block of mortgages are passed through to the security holders in several different ways, depending on the nature of the security. Most of these securities are underwritten by an agency of the federal government (GNMA, FHLMC, or FNMA) and have become the major source of funding for residential mortgage loans.

Mortgage banker. A mortgage company with the capability of processing, funding, and servicing a loan.

Mortgagee. The lender.

Mortgagor. The borrower.

Multi-family. The term used by government agencies to designate a residential building with more than four dwelling units.

Negative amortization. An addition to the principal balance due on a mortgage loan, usually resulting from adding unpaid interest to the principal balance periodically.

Negative cash flow. An income stream insufficient to cover operating expenses and debt service.

Net lease. A property lease that requires the tenant to pay for maintenance, insurance, and taxes on the premises in addition to the rent.

Net operating income. (NOI) The operating profit defined as the gross income less all expenses (but before the deduction of debt service).

Net worth. Assets minus liabilities.

Note A unilateral instrument containing a promise to pay a sum of money at a specified time.

Open listing. An agreement with one or more brokers offering an owner's property for sale; the commission is paid to whichever agent makes the sale in accordance with the agreed-upon terms. A non-exclusive listing.

Operating expenses. The costs of operating an income property. More narrowly defined as those costs that fluctuate with the rate of occupancy.

Option. A right to buy property, that is granted by the owner for consideration, but without the obligation to purchase.

Ordinary income. (Tax term) Earnings subject to income taxation at tax table rates. Also identified as income other than capital gain.

Origination fee. The charge made by a lender for preparing and processing the initial loan package: also called a finance fee.

Participation loan. A loan in which the lender shares in the property income and/or acquires an ownership interest. In finance, a loan that is funded by more than one lender.

Partnership. An association of two or more persons to carry on a business as co-owners.

Passive activity income. (Tax term) A type of income first identified in the 1986 Tax Act as that resulting from a trade or business in which the taxpayer does not materially participate, or any engagement in rental activity. Losses incurred from such activities may only be offset by income from other passive activities.

Pass-through security. A bond, certificate, or other form of security that is collateralized by a block of mortgage loans, the income from which is distributed, or passed on, to the holders of the securities. Same as a mortgage-backed security.

Percentage lease. An agreement to rent space for a price based on a portion of the tenant's gross sales.

Permanent loan. A loan with a term extending over most of the economic life of a property.

Personal property. Those things that are movable and not a part of the real property.

Pledged account mortgage. A mortgage plan that requires the borrower to deposit a predetermined amount of cash in an interest-bearing savings account held by the lender. The lender has the right to make periodic withdrawals from this account to supplement the buyer's monthly payments in the early years of the mortgage term.

Point. One percent of a loan amount. As a unit of measure, the point is used to price loan fees and insurance costs, as well as the amount of a discount or premium on a loan.

Portfolio. A list of investments, often used to describe a lender's holdings.

Portfolio income. (Tax term) Identified in the 1986 Tax Act as interest, dividends, rents, royalties, and investment income that is not otherwise classified as passive activity income. It includes the gain or loss from the disposition of any property producing such income. Expenses (other than interest) that are clearly allocable to this kind of property must be applied to portfolio income.

Possession. The exercise of the right of use and enjoyment of property to the exclusion of all others.

Present value approach. A capitalization method of determining the worth of a property today by discounting future cash flows.

Present worth. The current value of money delivered at a future date. Also called present value.

Principal. The amount owed. Also identifies the party represented by an agent.

Principal residence. (Tax term) The place where the taxpayer lives, which can be only one place and cannot be assigned.

Private corporation. A company founded by and composed of private individuals for private purposes with no political or governmental franchises or duties.

Profit and loss statement. A financial report listing income and expenses with the difference between the two reported as profit or loss.

Pro forma statement. A statement that projects the impact of a financial transaction on future profitability.

Promissory note. A written promise to pay someone a specific amount of money at a specified time.

Property exchange. (Tax term) A trade of property in such a manner that all or part of the capital gain tax can be deferred.

Proportionate disallowance rule. (Tax term) A rule added in 1986 to the installment sale tax calculation that treats borrowed money the same as an installment payment received under certain conditions. If a taxpayer holds both an installment obligation and has debt outstanding at the same time, then a portion of the installment receivable is deemed paid at the end of the year. (Rule was abandoned in December 1987.)

Public corporation. An entity created by the state for political purposes to serve as an agency in the administration of civil government.

Purchase money mortgage. A mortgage loan wherein the proceeds are used to acquire the property offered as collateral. Also, the mortgage taken by an owner in a seller-financed transaction.

Rate of return. The earnings on invested funds expressed as an annual percentage.

Raw land. Unimproved and unproductive land.

Real estate. Land and the improvements attached thereto.

Real Estate Investment Trust (REIT). A form of trust authorized to sell shares and to invest the proceeds into real estate equities or into mortgage loans.

Realized gain. (Tax term) The amount of gain that would have been made had the property been sold instead of exchanged. (Synonomous with "indicated gain.") Realized gain is not the amount subject to taxation.

Recapture. (Tax term) The portion of a depreciation deduction, which has previously escaped taxation and is returned, or recaptured, to the category of ordinary income when the property is sold. The purpose became moot with the 1986 Tax Act, but remains in effect as applied to installment sales.

Recognized gain. (Tax term) That portion of a capital gain made in a property exchange that is subject to taxation.

Recording. The act of entering into the book of public records the written instruments affecting title to real property.

Redemption. The right of a borrower to recover property after default and foreclosure. The right varies with the different state laws.

Refinance. Paying off an existing loan with the proceeds of a new loan.

Remainder. An ownership interest (estate) in land that cannot take effect or be enjoyed until after another estate has been terminated.

Renewal fee. A charge sometimes made by a lender for agreement to renew a note.

Replacement residence. (Tax term) A house purchased when the principal residence is sold: designation is used in the qualifications for tax deferral of capital gain.

Repurchase option. The right of a leasehold tenant to purchase the premises.

Rescission. Annulling a contract and placing the parties to it in status quo.

Residential loan. As defined for savings associations, a loan for a building used as a dwelling. For government statistical purposes, a loan for a one- to four-unit dwelling (larger buildings are classed as apartments or multi-family structures).

Residential property. (Tax term) A building that derives at least 80% of its rental income from dwelling units.

Residual. The value of a property that remains at the end of an ownership term.

Return on investment. The total gain realized from an investment usually expressed as an annual percentage rate. Synonymous with yield.

Reverse cash flow. A loss.

Reversion. The right to future enjoyment of a property, at present in the possession of another.

Rule of 78. A mathematical procedure used to compute earned interest when an installment loan is prematurely paid off. Also may be used to calculate annual interest deductions for tax purposes on qualified installment loans of 5 years or less.

S corporation. A corporation that, for tax purposes, can qualify and elect to be treated similar to a partnership. Formerly known as "Subchapter S corporation."

Salvage value. (Tax term) The value that remains in depreciable property at the end of its useful life.

Scheduled gross income. The income that would be received if all units are rented at the scheduled rates.

Secondary financing. A loan of less than first mortgage priority. A junior mortgage.

Secondary market. The financial market that purchases and sells existing mortgage loans. Loan originators sell their loans in this market, to provide themselves with a source of funds.

Separate property. Property owned by a married person in his or her own right during the marriage.

Settlement procedure. The consummation of a real estate transaction as defined by the federal government.

Severalty ownership. The ownership of land by one person.

Short-term loan. A loan that matures in less than 3 years.

Simple interest. Interest computed on the principal alone.

Sole proprietorship. A business operated by a single owner.

Straight-line depreciation. Depreciation deductions computed at an equal annual rate that will fully depreciate the property over its useful life, or its cost recovery period.

Subdivision. A tract of land that is divided into two or more lots or units for the purpose of disposition.

Subordination. To place in a position of lower priority than that of another.

Syndicate. An association of individuals or companies, usually in the form of a limited partnership, organized to carry out a particular business activity.

Take-out loan. A type of loan commitment—a promise to make a loan at a future specified time. The term is often used to designate a higher-cost, shorter-term, backup commitment as support for construction financing until a suitable permanent loan can be secured.

Tax shelter. An investment that provides tax savings.

Tenancy by entirety. Property owned by a husband and wife, which cannot be disposed of during their lives without the consent of the other, and which passes to the surviving spouse upon the death of the other.

Tenants in common. Two or more persons holding undivided interests in land, each with a separate right of disposition and without the right of survivorship.

Term. That period of time over which a loan can be repaid.

Term lease. A lease for a short period of time with fixed rental payments, usually made monthly.

Title. The evidence of ownership in land.

Trade fixture. Articles placed in, or attached to, rented buildings by the tenant to carry on the trade or business and which remain the property of the tenant.

Trust. A fiduciary relationship whereby property is transferred to a trustee to be administered for the benefit of another.

Trustee. One who holds property in trust for another to secure performance of an obligation. The third party holding conditional title to property as collateral under a deed of trust.

Underwriting. In finance, the qualification of a loan applicant and the property offered as collateral.

Unstated interest. (Tax term) In an installment sales contract, interest that is not claimed by the seller on deferred payments. The IRS may assess an imputed interest rate to determine tax liability.

Use. The employment of property.

Useful life. (Tax term) That period of time during which a property can reasonably be expected to be useful in trade or business.

Usury.   The acceptance of a greater sum for the use of money than is permitted by state law.

Value gain.   That portion of an increase in property value resulting from the input of expertise by an owner or manager.

Variable rate mortgage.   (VRM) A mortgage loan with an interest rate that can be adjusted from time to time in accordance with a capital rate index.

Vendor's lien.   An implied lien in favor of the vendor for the unpaid purchase price of land where no other security exists beyond the personal obligation of the purchaser.

Warehouse fee.   A charge made by a mortgage lender, usually ¼ to ½ point, to cover the costs of holding the loan in a commercial bank when the bank's interest charge exceeds the rate on the mortgage loan.

Warehousing.   In finance, the holding of mortgage loans as collateral, usually by a commercial bank for the account of a mortgage company, until they can be sold.

Warranty deed.   An assignment of title to property with a guarantee of validity.

Wrap-around mortgage.   A new mortgage, subordinate to and encompassing an existing mortgage loan, that allows additional financing.

Yield.   The rate of return that the total income from an investment bears to the investment, taking into consideration the time period that the investment may be outstanding.

Zoning laws.   Regulations authorized under the police powers of a state that prescribe the use of land and the structural design and use for buildings within designated areas of a city.

Appendix

REMAINING BALANCE FACTORS

FOR 10% INTEREST RATE USING SELECTED TERMS

(TO COMPUTE: FACTOR TIMES ORIGINAL LOAN AMOUNT)

AGE OF LOAN	ORIGINAL TERM IN YEARS					
	2	3	5	8	10	12
1	.52488	.69926	.83773	.91404	.93866	.95454
2		.36702	.65847	.81908	.87089	.90433
3			.46044	.71418	.79603	.84886
4			.24167	.59829	.71333	.78757
5				.47027	.62197	.71988
6				.32884	.52105	.64509
7				.17260	.40955	.56247
8					.28638	.47120
9					.15031	.37037
10						.25898
11						.13593

ORIGINAL TERM IN YEARS

	14	15	20	25	30	40
2	.92731	.93619	.96517	.98007	.98830	.99582
4	.83859	.85832	.92267	.95574	.97402	.99071
6	.73032	.76329	.87080	.92606	.95660	.98449
8	.59819	.64731	.80750	.88983	.93533	.97689
10	.43654	.50577	.73024	.84561	.90938	.96761
12	.24016	.33303	.63596	.79166	.87771	.95629
15			.45419	.68762	.81665	.93446
20			.42768	.66407	.87992
25				.41303	.79019
30					.64256
35					.39965

PRESENT WORTH OF $1.00

YEARS	8%	9%	10%	11%	12%	13%	14%
1	.92593	.91743	.90909	.90090	.89286	.88496	.87719
2	.85734	.84168	.82645	.81162	.79719	.78315	.76947
3	.79383	.77218	.75131	.73119	.71178	.69305	.67497
4	.73503	.70842	.68301	.65873	.63552	.61332	.59208
5	.68058	.64993	.62092	.59345	.56743	.54276	.51937
6	.63017	.59627	.56447	.53464	.50663	.48032	.45559
7	.58349	.54703	.51316	.48166	.45234	.42506	.39964
8	.54027	.50187	.46651	.43393	.40388	.37616	.35056
9	.50025	.46043	.42410	.39092	.36061	.33289	.30751
10	.46319	.42241	.38554	.35218	.32197	.29459	.26975
11	.42888	.38753	.35049	.31728	.28748	.26070	.23662
12	.39711	.35553	.31863	.28584	.25667	.23071	.20756
13	.36770	.32618	.28966	.25751	.22917	.20417	.18207
14	.34046	.29925	.26333	.23199	.20462	.18068	.15971
15	.31524	.27454	.23939	.20900	.18270	.15989	.14010
16	.29189	.25187	.21763	.18829	.16312	.14150	.12289
17	.27027	.23107	.19784	.16963	.14564	.12522	.10780
18	.25025	.21199	.17986	.15282	.13004	.11081	.09456
19	.23171	.19449	.16351	.13768	.11611	.09806	.08295
20	.21455	.17843	.14864	.12403	.10367	.08678	.07276
21	.19866	.16370	.13513	.11174	.09256	.07680	.06383
22	.18394	.15018	.12285	.10067	.08264	.06796	.05599
23	.17031	.13778	.11168	.09069	.07379	.06015	.04911
24	.15770	.12640	.10153	.08170	.06588	.05323	.04308
25	.14602	.11597	.09230	.07361	.05882	.04710	.03779
26	.13520	.10639	.08390	.06631	.05252	.04168	.03315
27	.12519	.09761	.07628	.05974	.04689	.03689	.02908
28	.11591	.08955	.06934	.05382	.04187	.03264	.02551
29	.10733	.08215	.06304	.04849	.03738	.02889	.02237
30	.09938	.07537	.05731	.04368	.03338	.02557	.01963

CONSTANT ANNUAL PERCENT

COMPUTED AS THE SUM OF 12 EQUAL MONTHLY PAYMENTS

YEARS	8%	9%	10%	11%	12%	13%	14%
1	104.39	104.95	105.50	106.07	106.63	107.19	107.75
2	54.28	54.82	55.37	55.93	56.49	57.05	57.62
3	37.61	38.16	38.72	39.29	39.86	40.43	41.01
4	29.30	29.86	30.44	31.02	31.60	32.19	32.79
5	24.33	24.91	25.50	26.09	26.69	27.30	27.92
6	21.04	21.63	22.23	22.84	23.46	24.09	24.73
7	18.70	19.31	19.92	20.55	21.18	21.83	22.49
8	16.96	17.58	18.21	18.85	19.50	20.17	20.85
9	15.62	16.25	16.89	17.55	18.22	18.90	19.60
10	14.56	15.20	15.86	16.53	17.22	17.92	18.63
11	13.70	14.35	15.02	15.71	16.41	17.13	17.86
12	12.99	13.66	14.34	15.04	15.76	16.50	17.25
13	12.40	13.08	13.77	14.49	15.22	15.97	16.74
14	11.90	12.59	13.30	14.03	14.78	15.54	16.33
15	11.47	12.17	12.90	13.64	14.40	15.18	15.98
16	11.10	11.81	12.55	13.31	14.09	14.88	15.69
17	10.78	11.51	12.25	13.03	13.81	14.62	15.45
18	10.50	11.24	12.00	12.78	13.58	14.41	15.24
19	10.25	11.00	11.78	12.57	13.38	14.22	15.07
20	10.04	10.80	11.58	12.39	13.21	14.06	14.92
21	9.85	10.62	11.41	12.23	13.06	13.92	14.80
22	9.67	10.45	11.26	12.09	12.94	13.80	14.69
23	9.52	10.31	11.13	11.96	12.82	13.70	14.59
24	9.38	10.18	11.01	11.86	12.72	13.61	14.51
25	9.26	10.07	10.90	11.76	12.64	13.53	14.45
26	9.15	9.97	10.81	11.68	12.56	13.47	14.39
27	9.05	9.88	10.73	11.60	12.50	13.41	14.33
28	8.96	9.80	10.66	11.54	12.44	13.36	14.29
29	8.88	9.72	10.59	11.48	12.39	13.31	14.25
30	8.81	9.66	10.53	11.43	12.34	13.27	14.22

MONTHLY PAYMENT
TO AMORTIZE $1,000 LOAN

YEARS	8%	9%	10%	11%	12%	13%	14%
1	86.99	87.45	87.92	88.39	88.85	89.32	89.79
2	45.23	45.69	46.15	46.61	47.08	47.54	48.01
3	31.34	31.80	32.27	32.74	33.22	33.70	34.18
4	24.41	24.89	25.36	25.85	26.34	26.83	27.33
5	20.28	20.76	21.25	21.74	22.25	22.75	23.27
6	17.53	18.03	18.53	19.04	19.55	20.07	20.61
7	15.59	16.09	16.60	17.12	17.65	18.19	18.74
8	14.14	14.65	15.17	15.71	16.25	16.81	17.37
9	13.02	13.54	14.08	14.63	15.18	15.75	16.33
10	12.13	12.67	13.22	13.78	14.35	14.93	15.53
11	11.42	11.96	12.52	13.09	13.68	14.28	14.89
12	10.82	11.38	11.95	12.54	13.13	13.75	14.37
13	10.33	10.90	11.48	12.08	12.69	13.31	13.95
14	9.91	10.49	11.08	11.69	12.31	12.95	13.61
15	9.56	10.14	10.75	11.37	12.00	12.65	13.32
16	9.25	9.85	10.46	11.09	11.74	12.40	13.08
17	8.98	9.59	10.21	10.85	11.51	12.19	12.87
18	8.75	9.36	10.00	10.65	11.32	12.00	12.70
19	8.55	9.17	9.81	10.47	11.15	11.85	12.56
20	8.36	9.00	9.65	10.32	11.01	11.72	12.44
21	8.20	8.85	9.51	10.19	10.89	11.60	12.33
22	8.06	8.71	9.38	10.07	10.78	11.50	12.24
23	7.93	8.59	9.27	9.97	10.69	11.42	12.16
24	7.82	8.49	9.17	9.88	10.60	11.34	12.10
25	7.72	8.39	9.09	9.80	10.53	11.28	12.04
26	7.63	8.31	9.01	9.73	10.47	11.22	11.99
27	7.54	8.23	8.94	9.67	10.41	11.17	11.95
28	7.47	8.16	8.88	9.61	10.37	11.13	11.91
29	7.40	8.10	8.82	9.57	10.32	11.09	11.88
30	7.34	8.05	8.78	9.52	10.29	11.06	11.85

Index